Praise for *The L*

"*The Lost Hero of Cape Cod* is both a fascinating true-life history and a glimpse into the all-too-perilous world of the 1800's mariner. Meticulously pieced together from exhaustive research, Eldridge's story is a tale of war, peace, extra-ordinary heroism, and heartbreaking tragedy... Highly recommended..."

—*Midwest Book Review*

"...the author deftly creates a 'life and times' of Asa Eldridge that stands in requiem for not only Eldridge, but for a wider class of forgotten heroes..."

—*Sea History* magazine (National Maritime Historical Society)

"An old seafaring world comes to life in this examination of the coastal trade of the mid-1800s... Miles expertly describes the life of a sea captain in Eldridge's day... Readers already curious about the trans-Atlantic trade, the early days of steam shipping, and all that rigging and hauling should learn a lot from this deeply researched book. An absorbing and comprehensive study..."

—*Kirkus Reviews*

"...prose as lively and fast-paced as a clipper under full sail, and historical reconstruction as dependable as a copper-bottomed hull... Amid a broader sea-scape of shipwrecks, gold rushes, and frantic commercial competition, Miles paints a picture of the early days of Yarmouth and Cape Cod that will delight local history buffs."   —*The Register (Yarmouth)/WickedLocalCapeCod*

"...a great read for anyone who wants to immerse themselves in the peninsula's history and its impact on the nation."   —*Cape Cod Times*

"...collates vast amounts of references from shipping logs and newspaper articles to create a highly detailed account of Captain Asa Eldridge's life and accomplishments.... an intellectually stimulating read for any history buff, nautical adventure lover, and the casual reader... it should be included in every town library. Highly recommended."   —*The Portsmouth Review*

"This is a wonderful book! Focused on the life and career of Cape Codder Asa Eldridge, one of the ablest sea captains of his day, the book offers much more. Highly recommended!"

—*Norman C. Delaney. Ph. D., author,*
John McIntosh Kell of the Raider *Alabama*

The
Lost Hero
of Cape Cod

Captain Asa Eldridge

The
Lost Hero
of Cape Cod

CAPTAIN ASA ELDRIDGE AND THE
MARITIME TRADE THAT SHAPED AMERICA

Vincent Miles

Historical Society of Old Yarmouth
Yarmouth Port, Massachusetts

ISBN: 978-0-9625068-8-8 (paperback)
ISBN: 978-0-9625068-9-5 (electronic)

Published by the
Historical Society of Old Yarmouth
11 Strawberry Lane
P. O. Box 11
Yarmouth Port, MA 02675

Telephone: 508-362-3021
Website: www.hsoy.org

Printed in the United States of America

To Asa Eldridge and his fellow mariners,
forgotten heroes of American history

CONTENTS

Illustrations   ix
A Note on Terminology   xi

Prologue   1
1 Early Years on Cape Cod   3
2 Adventures in the Far East   17
3 To Liverpool by Sail   33
4 The Advent of Steam   53
5 Aspiring Tycoon   71
6 King of the Clippers   87
7 Mysterious End   107
8 Forgotten Heroes   127

Acknowledgments   137
Notes   139
Bibliography   151
Illustration Credits   157
Index   159

ILLUSTRATIONS

Asa Eldridge   *Frontispiece*
Schematic diagram of vessel types   xii

                                                              Facing page...
Schooner plaque on former home of Yarmouth sea captain   10
Plaque commemorating early local declaration of independence   10
Remnants of wharf in Yarmouth Port   10
Plan of Chatham saltworks   11
Photograph of same saltworks   11
Sail plan for full-rigged sailing ship   22
Map of Boston waterfront, 1814   22
Prime meridian at Royal Observatory in Greenwich   23
View of Boston, 1833   23
View of New York Quarantine, Staten Island, 1833   42
Canning Dock and Custom House, Liverpool, 1842   42
The *New York* (packet ship, Black Ball Line)   43
Classified ad for *Colombo* (ship), 1842   43
Classified ad for *Roscius* (packet ship, Dramatic Line), 1844   43
The *British Queen* (steamship, British & American Steam Navigation Co.) 64
Samuel Cunard and Edward K. Collins   64
The *Europa* (steamship, Cunard Line)   65
The *Atlantic* (steamship, Collins Line)   65
Classified ad for the Pioneer Line   80
View of San Francisco, 1850   80
Classified ad for travel to California via the *Illinois* and *Golden Gate* 80
The *North Star* (private steam-yacht, Cornelius Vanderbilt)   81
Cornelius Vanderbilt and Asa Eldridge   81

Donald McKay 94

The *Cutty Sark* (clipper ship) 94

The *Flying Cloud* (clipper ship) 95

The *Red Jacket* (clipper ship) 95

The *Washington* (steamship, Ocean Steam Navigation Co.) ... 116

The loss of the *Arctic* (steamship, Collins Line) 116

The *Pacific* (steamship, Collins Line) 117

The *Persia* (steamship, Cunard Line) 117

View of East River, New York, 1856 132

The *Adriatic* (steamship, Collins Line) 132

Obituary for Oliver Eldridge 133

The *Baltic* (steamship, Collins Line) 133

A Note on Terminology

SHIPS AREN'T what they used to be—not just physically, but linguistically. In modern usage, the word "ship" may signify almost any large vessel that travels on the open sea. But in the days when all seagoing vessels relied on the wind for propulsion, it was reserved for a specific type of vessel with a certain number of masts and arrangement of sails.

Nor is "ship" the only word whose usage during the age of sail may be unfamiliar to readers. While the use of maritime jargon—old or new—has been minimized in the narrative, several terms simply cannot be avoided and so will be explained here. All but one are words that distinguish between different types of vessel. The sole exception is the word "tons," as used to describe the size of a vessel.

Starting, then, with the various wind-powered vessels that were formerly common, six different types or classes are mentioned in the text: ships, barks (barques), brigs, schooners, ketches, and sloops. The key features that placed a vessel in a particular class were the number of masts it had and the main orientation of the sails on each one—which could be either "square" (perpendicular to the long axis of the vessel) or "fore and aft" (parallel to that axis, like the sails of a modern yacht). For the classes just listed, their configurations with respect to these key features are illustrated in the highly schematic diagram on the next page, and may be summarized as follows (where "SQ" denotes square-rigged and "FA" denotes fore-and-aft rigged):

- Ship: Three or more masts, all mainly SQ
- Bark: Three or more masts, rearmost FA, rest mainly SQ
- Brig: Two masts, both mainly SQ
- Ketch: Two masts, both FA, forward mast taller than mast behind it
- Schooner: Two or more masts, both/all FA, forward mast shorter
- Sloop: One mast, FA.

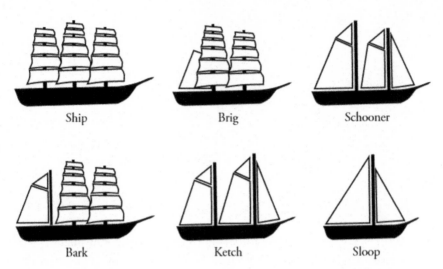

Schematic diagram of vessel types mentioned in the narrative.
Not all sails shown, and not to scale.

The use of the word "mainly" in connection with SQ masts is important; since square-rigged sails were mounted on the front of their masts, each mast had space for, and typically also carried, additional sails mounted fore-and-aft on its rear. One such sail, a rear "spanker," is shown in the diagram of the brig above.

All references to wind-powered vessels throughout this book conform with this classification scheme. Thus a vessel is only referred to as a "ship" if it had three masts (or in one case four), each of which was predominantly "square-rigged."

For steam-powered vessels the convention is different. Although early "steamers" were often equipped with a full set of masts and sails they relied primarily on their engines for propulsion, and so the old distinctions had no real meaning. All seagoing steamers were called "steamships" right from the start, and so were also referred to simply as "ships," as they are in later chapters of this book.

Whatever their form of propulsion, all vessels were also classified with respect to one other characteristic: their size. The unit of measure was a ton, which in this context referred not to a vessel's weight but to the volume of cargo it could carry. This figure was important because it was used to determine import duties and the fees charged by ports. It was estimated from the vessel's length, breadth and depth using a standard formula to correct for the non-rectangular shape of the hull. The same underlying principle is still in use today, although the method of calculation has evolved over time. In Asa Eldridge's day, the calculation was performed using what is known as the Old Custom House Formula, which required measurement only of the vessel's length (L) and breadth (B). The tonnage was then given by the formula $((L - 3/5\,B) \times B \times 1/2\,B)/95$. The two fractions of B in this formula were approximations that avoided the need for more intricate measurements: $3/5\,B$ was subtracted from the length to correct for unusable space at the ends of the vessel, while $1/2\,B$ was considered a reasonable surrogate for the depth of the vessel. The volume calculated by multiplying the corrected length, breadth, and estimated depth together was divided by 95 because that was the number of cubic feet defined as equivalent to one ton of cargo. The figure resulting from this division was the tonnage of the vessel, which was also commonly referred to as its "burthen" (an archaic form of "burden").

Prologue

JANUARY 23, 1854 was a cold and blustery day on the Liverpool waterfront, but that did not deter a large crowd from gathering. News had spread quickly that a fabled record was about to be broken. According to the crew of an American steamship that had just arrived, a Yankee clipper had stayed close behind them for much of the way from New York, and must therefore be on the verge of completing the fastest-ever crossing of the Atlantic by a sailing ship. This was too significant an event to be missed. The rivalries between the ships that regularly fought their way across the Atlantic were closely followed, with every departure and arrival faithfully reported in the newspapers; a record crossing would be big news, and the people rushing to the docks wanted to witness history being made.

Squinting into the strong westerly wind, they waited expectantly for the first sight of the clipper ship entering the mouth of the River Mersey. Soon enough, a magnificent vessel hove into view, slicing through the muddy brown waters at a remarkable speed. Initially, all that the watchers could discern was a huge cloud of sail, bulging above a hull that seemed too narrow to carry so much canvas. As the ship came closer more detail emerged: the strange carved figure above her bow—an Indian chief wearing the jacket of a British redcoat—and dozens of deckhands in the rigging, clambering to take up precarious positions along the spars that supported the numerous sails. To the puzzlement of the watching crowd, the clipper showed no sign of slowing down even as she neared the docks, quickly overtaking the tugboats that were vainly offering her towlines. Finally, at what seemed the last possible moment, the captain executed an astonishing maneuver, the like of which no one could recall ever having seen before. With a loudly barked command he ordered all of the sails released, and as

1

they crumpled in unison, he turned the wheel hard over and neatly guided the clipper in a precise rearward glide to her berth.

As the spectators roared their approval, the captain stepped to the rail of the quarterdeck and lifted his peaked cap in acknowledgment. Although middle-aged and somewhat portly, he still cut an impressive figure. Almost six feet tall, he retained a full head of brown hair, carefully combed from right to left over a face that was strong rather than handsome: blue eyes full of determination, with thick eyebrows above and noticeable bags underneath; a narrow but prominent nose; a thin upper over a fat lower lip; and a black beard with no mustache. His name was Asa Eldridge, and he had just sailed the *Red Jacket* from New York to Liverpool in a fraction over thirteen days—a time that has never been bettered by a sailing ship before or since.

Making this achievement even more remarkable, the *Red Jacket* was on her maiden voyage, manned by a ragtag assortment of sailors who had been hanging out on New York's South Street wharf hoping for work. Somehow, Captain Eldridge had managed to set the new record with no prior experience of either the ship he was sailing or the crew he was commanding. Clearly, this was no ordinary mariner.

Indeed, his new record confirmed Eldridge as the ablest member of an elite group who played a key role in American history: the nineteenth-century transatlantic shipmasters. Without their courage and skill in navigating the treacherous waters of the Atlantic, the boom in trade and immigration that shaped the country after its conflict with Britain was finally over would not have been possible. Much can therefore be learned from the careers of these men. And no man is a worthier example than Captain Asa Eldridge.

1

EARLY YEARS ON CAPE COD

CAPE COD. THE SEA. Since the last Ice Age they have always gone together, one sculpted by the other after the glaciers retreated until it resembles a giant arm bent upwards at the elbow—or in the words of Henry David Thoreau, "the bared and bended arm of Massachusetts."

Adorning the bicep of this metaphorical arm is the picturesque village of Yarmouth Port, with gray-shingled cottages and white-clapboard colonials lining its gently meandering main street. Founded in 1639, the village is one of the oldest in New England, and lies almost exactly at the midpoint of today's Old King's Highway Historic District. At thirty-two miles long this is the largest such district in the country.

Many of the houses in the village carry a distinctive oval plaque, with a schooner silhouetted in gold against a black background. The plaque identifies the former homes of sea captains, and is a particularly common sight along a section of Main Street known as the "Captains' Mile." With good reason: a recent survey of historical records confirmed that fifty-five houses in and around the village center once belonged to shipmasters.

One plaque-bearing house at the western end of the village is of special significance for this narrative. At the turn of the nineteenth century it was the home of a captain named John Eldridge and his wife, the former Betty Hallet. The Eldridges had many children, the first and the last of whom—John and Oliver—became well-known international seafarers. Neither, however, could match the fame of a third seafaring brother born almost halfway between them, eleven years younger than John, nine years older than Oliver. His name was Asa. And in the view of Cape historian Henry Kittredge, he became "the most distinguished shipmaster that the Cape ever produced... among the world's half-dozen greatest shipmasters."

A strong spirit of adventure clearly ran in the family, dating back to the earliest days of the village. Two of the first settlers in the 1600s were direct ancestors of Asa and his siblings who had made the grueling journey from England. The boys' fifth great grandfather on their mother's side, Andrew Hallet, first appeared in the village in March 1639, just a few months after it was established as an offshoot of the Plymouth Colony founded by the Pilgrims. On their father's side the first ancestor to arrive was William Eldridge, who was definitely a resident by 1645, and possibly before that.

For these early adventurers in the family, their one great move from England was enough. Once they had settled in Yarmouth they stayed there. So too did multiple generations thereafter, showing little inclination to wander. Indeed, when Betty Hallet married John Eldridge over a hundred and fifty years later they made their home in exactly the same neighborhood as the original settlers, less than a quarter mile from the site of the village's first dwelling.

That dwelling had been erected in 1638 by a man named Stephen Hopkins, one of the secular "Strangers" who had arrived with the Pilgrims on the *Mayflower*. He had since become so important to Plymouth Colony that its General Court would not allow him to move permanently to Cape Cod. The Court authorized him to build a house there only "provided it be not to withdraw him from the town of Plymouth." He thus became the first of a great many people to own a second home on the Cape.

The site Hopkins chose was on the raised bank of a sheltered tidal pond connected to Cape Cod Bay by a broad inlet. Easy access by sea was essential, since that was the only feasible means of travel to and from Plymouth, about thirty-five miles up the coast. Conveniently, the house he erected was also just off the main trail used by the local Wampanoag tribe to travel along the north side of the Cape. Over time, this trail evolved into the road now known as the Old King's Highway (or more prosaically as Route 6A).

Between Hopkins' arrival and Asa Eldridge's birth in 1809, the village had evolved in a manner typical of many coastal communities in New England. Thus the issues that shaped it were initially local—the basic need to subsist and establish a workable community—but gradually became broader as the regional economy developed and tensions with England grew. And throughout its development the waters off its shore played a key role, serving as the main highway for commerce and communication, and as a source of important products for the local economy.

The first generation of settlers—including the Hallets—were farmers, who prospered more quickly than the colonists they had left behind in Plymouth. They raised cattle, pigs, and sheep, grew corn and vegetables, and found abundant fish and game in the local waters and woods. In due course, their prosperity attracted a full range of craftsmen to service their needs: blacksmiths, carpenters, wheelwrights, coopers and cobblers, among others. By the late 1600s the new village—which had been named Yarmouth, after the port of Great Yarmouth on the east coast of England— had grown into a flourishing community of about a thousand people. The settlement also expanded southwards, so that it spanned the full five miles between Cape Cod Bay on the north and Nantucket Sound on the south. It also encompassed large areas that later became separate towns: Dennis, Harwich, Chatham, Brewster and the village of Cummaquid in Barnstable.

With two long borders consisting of coastline, the growing town inevitably conducted much of its business with the outside world by sea. Travel for any distance by land was simply too slow and difficult. Even to reach Plymouth, the main port of call in the settlement's early days, would have been a major trial for horse and man, requiring many long hours on rough trails through thick woods. And as new destinations beyond Plymouth gained importance, the advantages of maritime travel became even greater.

One new destination in particular stood out: Boston, the principal port and town of the Massachusetts Bay Colony. The latter had been founded in 1628 to the north of the Plymouth Colony, and soon surpassed it. By 1660 its population was already three to four times larger than the Plymouth Colony's, whose entire population of three thousand was matched by Boston alone.

Boston quickly became the busiest port not just in Massachusetts but in all of the American colonies, largely because it was the first town to build its economy around maritime trade rather than agriculture. Bostonians therefore had the most at stake when England first tried to prevent its colonies from trading directly with other countries in the latter half of the seventeenth century. Responding to increased commerce between the Americans and the Dutch, the English Parliament passed various Navigation Acts intended to secure a monopoly for England on trade with its American possessions. Under these Acts, almost all goods imported into the colonies had to be carried by English ships, and to pass through England on their way if they did not originate there. Similarly, most exports could only be made directly to England.

Given the importance of maritime trade to its economy, Massachusetts strongly resisted these restrictions. So too did other New England colonies. The King responded by revoking their charters and creating a single Dominion of New England under the control of an English governor. When it was formed in 1686, the Dominion incorporated the Colonies of Massachusetts Bay (which included present-day Maine), Plymouth, Connecticut and Rhode Island, together with the Province of New Hampshire. Later, it was extended to include all of the present-day coastal states from Maine to New Jersey, and Vermont as well.

For the colonists in these territories, the single most galling aspect of the new Dominion was that it took away all their rights to local self-government and regulation; all judicial and legislative powers were reserved to representatives of the King.

The Dominion lasted barely three years. In 1689, emboldened by the overthrow of King James II in the so-called "Glorious Revolution" in England, the colonists in Boston staged their own mini-revolution. They arrested the unpopular governor, Sir Edmund Ambros, and other officials of the Dominion, and sent them back to England for trial. The Dominion effectively dissolved, and for the next two years its various members resumed local self-regulation under the charters that had previously governed them.

By 1691, however, the usurper to the English throne, William of Orange, was secure enough in his position to turn his attention to the American colonies. He issued a new charter creating the Province of Massachusetts Bay, which differed from the former Massachusetts Bay Colony in two important respects. First, its governor would be appointed by the Crown rather than locally elected—an issue that would become increasingly contentious over the next eighty-five years. And second, it would now include what had formerly been the Plymouth Colony. Cape Cod thus became part of Massachusetts for the first time.

By the time of this reorganization, Boston had a population of around seven thousand and was on its way to becoming the third busiest port in the British empire, behind only London and Bristol. The town's rapid growth and international traffic had also made it an important hub for the colonists on Cape Cod: a market for the food they now produced in excess of their own needs, and the source of many goods they could not find locally. A thriving maritime trade had developed between Boston and the towns on the north side of the Cape, Yarmouth among them. The trade was conducted by a variety of small vessels—sloops, ketches and the like—that made their way regularly up and down the coast carrying passengers and cargo. More and more people on the Cape made their living on the water, and each coastal town could claim a number of sea captains among its residents. Like similar craft elsewhere, the vessels they operated were often referred to as "packets." The term had originally signified a vessel that carried packets of mail from one place to another, but gradually came to mean any boat or ship that operated to a regular schedule.

Also around this time, a development in the British Caribbean islands brought major economic benefits to the Cape and to Massachusetts more generally. Previously, their ability to capitalize on the huge stocks of fish in local waters had been constrained by the limited availability of salt, which was needed in large quantities if fish were to be preserved for later consumption or export. Salt for this purpose had generally been imported from Liverpool, where it was produced from local mines. Mediterranean salt was considered superior but was usually unavailable because of wars between England and France or Spain. But in the late 1600s, the process used in the Mediterranean—evaporation of salt water in shallow ponds under the fierce heat of the sun—was replicated in the British Caribbean islands, making high-quality salt available to New England and other British colonies. Salted fish became one of Boston's major exports, a good part of it produced by the fishermen of Cape Cod. Ships headed from Boston to the Caribbean full of timber and salted fish, and returned with cargoes of salt, rum and sugar.

As the next century progressed, maritime trade continued to dominate the economies of both Boston and Cape Cod. Accordingly, the increasing tensions between Massachusetts and England that ultimately detonated the American Revolution generally centered on matters of trade. "No taxation without representation" may have been the colonists' most famous mantra, but the taxation in question usually related to trade. The Molasses Act of 1733, the Sugar Act that replaced it in 1764, the Revenue Act of 1767 and the infamous Tea Act of 1773 all imposed duties on imported goods, and it was their economic impact as much as their constitutionality that outraged Bostonians. The so-called Intolerable Acts of 1774 again targeted trade. Enacted by the British Parliament in response to the Boston Tea Party, they closed the port of Boston indefinitely until reparation was paid to the East India Company for the tea that had been thrown into the harbor. The determination of the British to enforce the Tea and Intolerable Acts, and of the colonists to ignore them, led directly to the first clashes of the Revolutionary War in Concord and Lexington.

In Yarmouth, local opposition to the Tea Act had much less impact on the course of world history, but did lead to the first mention of an Eldridge in the historical record. Whereas the Hallets had been prominent figures in the village since its earliest days—so much so that the main street was named after them—the presence of the Eldridges had barely registered as they quietly progressed through several generations. But in 1774 Barnabas Eldridge, Asa's grandfather, was appointed to a committee "to see that no tea is consumed in Yarmouth."

The following year Barnabas became the first member of the family to enjoy the title of "Captain," though for an appointment on land rather than at sea. On September 29, 1775, he was given this rank in the First Barnstable County Regiment of the Massachusetts Militia. He may therefore have been among the men from Yarmouth who answered the call of General George Washington early in 1776 for "the militia of certain towns, contiguous to Dorchester and Roxbury, to repair to the line at those places with arms, ammunition and accoutrements." He certainly fought in the Revolutionary War after it started, because in 1778 he was one of a group of American prisoners released by the British in exchange for Royal Navy sailors captured off Falmouth.

Like Eldridge himself, his hometown of Yarmouth was a staunch supporter of the revolutionary cause. Two years earlier it had actually beaten the Continental Congress to the punch by declaring "a state of independence from the king of Great Britain" on June 20, 1776—but only "if in case the wisdom of Congress should see proper to do it."

For the next several years this show of bravado did the town little good, as the British warships patrolling the waters around the Cape prevented the coastal trade on which it depended. By the time the Treaty of Paris was signed in 1783, many of the boats that had been engaged in this trade before the War had rotted beyond repair.

As the Cape's economy slowly recovered after the War, salt again played a major role. Earlier in the century, the abundant new supply from the Caribbean had enabled local fishermen to preserve and export large quantities of salted fish. Now, thanks to the wartime activities of a local sea captain, salt itself became a key export.

Ironically, the catalyst for this beneficial development was the blockade that had crippled trade during the War. Imported salt was no longer available, leaving Cape Codders with no way of preserving fish. With time on his hands because of the blockade, Captain John Sears of Dennis began experimenting with the production of salt by evaporation from seawater. In addition to the usual expectations of profit, he presumably hoped to cash in on a recent decision by the Continental Congress. The fledgling country's new government was so concerned about the impact of a salt shortage that it offered a bounty of one-third of a dollar for every bushel of salt produced.

Sears' original evaporation process was simple but highly inefficient. He built a shallow wooden vat ten feet wide and a hundred feet long, hired laborers to fill it manually using buckets, and waited for the sun and the wind to do their work. His meager reward after a whole summer's effort was a mere eight bushels of salt. But through a combination of ingenuity and perseverance, Sears gradually developed a quite sophisticated process featuring windmills to pump water from the sea, inter-connected evaporation vats on three different levels, and movable covers to protect against rain. With favorable weather, a single set of three vats could produce a bushel of salt weighing about eighty pounds in three weeks. And Sears had access to plenty of land on which to build multiple sets.

Cape Cod was in fact an ideal place for the process he had developed, with an abundant supply of all the key requirements: sea water, sun, wind, and vast areas of relatively flat open shoreline to accommodate numerous large evaporation vats. The skepticism that had greeted Sears' original efforts gradually turned to envy, and many locals began to build their own saltworks modeled on his, particularly after the patent he had been granted was successfully challenged in court. By 1802 there were 136 saltworks on the Cape with over 1.2 million square feet of evaporation vats. When the industry reached its peak three decades later, the peninsula had over a hundred million square feet of evaporation vats in 881 saltworks producing over 20,000 tons of salt each year. Production had quickly exceeded the amount needed to preserve fish for local consumption, and salt had become one of the Cape's biggest exports.

A good part of that salt would have made its way to Boston, either for use locally or for further export. The salt would have been transported there by sea; although two centuries had now passed since the area had been colonized, the roads were still too crude for the carriage of goods in bulk. Even for places much closer than the Cape, transport and travel over water was preferred. The town of Hanover, for example, is only 25 miles from Boston by road, but according to the *Maritime History of Massachusetts,* "found it cheaper to send packet-sloops down the tortuous course of the North River and around the Cohasset reefs to Boston, than to use the road."

On the Cape itself, each town on the north side of the peninsula had its own fleet of small vessels that regularly sailed up the coast to Boston. In Yarmouth, the local fleet had long operated from an inlet known as Bass Hole on the eastern edge of the town's northern shore. That was about to change, however, as shifting sands made the inlet too shallow for all but the smallest boats. The focus of maritime activity gradually migrated two miles west to the mouth of present-day Mill Creek in Yarmouth Port (which at that time was still considered a separate community from Yarmouth). This was the very same opening to Cape Cod Bay that Stephen Hopkins had used almost two centuries earlier to access the pond-side area where he built his house. As traffic there increased, a wharf was built that could accommodate up to six vessels at a time. To this day, more than a hundred and fifty years after the area ceased to serve as a port, the street leading down to it is still known as Wharf Lane.

For one man of particular interest to this narrative, the shift to Mill Creek would have been highly convenient. Captain Ansel Hallet operated a sloop between Yarmouth Port and Boston, and lived only a few hundred yards from the new center of maritime activity. He was the first member of the Hallet family who is known for certain to have been a mariner. More pertinently, he was also Asa Eldridge's uncle, by virtue not only of his own marriage but also of his sister's. His wife Anna was the sister of Asa's father, John Eldridge, while his own sister Betty was Eldridge's wife—Asa's mother. And when Asa began his maritime career as a young boy, Ansel Hallet was almost certainly both his first employer and his chief mentor.

Betty Hallet was not John Eldridge's first wife, nor even his first from her family. In 1789 he had married Lucy Hallet, who was Betty's aunt but only eleven years her senior. Tragically, over the next five years Lucy produced two sons who both died at the age of fifteen months, and preceded the second of these sons to the grave herself. The dead boys' names, incidentally, were Asa and John, names their father would use again when he had another family. In an era when many children died young, it was not uncommon to name a newborn after an earlier child who had recently passed away.

In 1797, two-and-a-half years after Lucy died, Eldridge married Betty. Whereas his first bride had been close to his own age—twenty to his twenty-four—his second was much younger, seventeen to his thirty-four. Any gossip this age difference may have caused would have been forgotten the following year when the next union between the families occurred. John's sister Anna must have been visibly pregnant when she married Betty's

Schooner plaque on the former home of Captain Ansel Hallet.

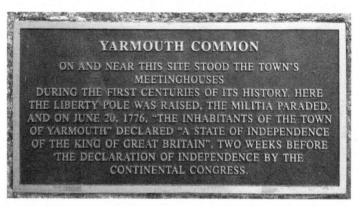

Plaque on Yarmouth Common commemorating the town's premature but prophetic declaration of independence.

Remnants of the once-busy wharf at the mouth of Mill Creek in Yarmouth Port.

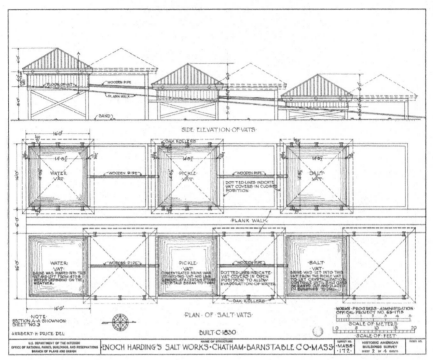

Plans for salt works in Chatham, based on the process developed by Captain Sears in nearby Dennis; created retrospectively by the Historic American Buildings Survey.

Photograph of same saltworks, probably taken in the 1860s, by which time these works were no longer in use and falling into disrepair.

brother Ansel, because three months later she gave birth to their first child, Edward. In an age when sex before marriage was completely taboo, this must have caused much tongue-wagging in the village.

Betty herself probably missed the "shotgun" wedding because her own first pregnancy was even more advanced; she gave birth to John Eldridge junior in April 1798, just a month after her brother's wedding to Anna.

John Jr. and Edward were the first of many cousins born to the two families. The Eldridges had ten children in all and the Hallets nine. Sadly, but typically for the era, many of these children did not reach adulthood. Each family lost two youngsters to early-childhood deaths, and the Eldridges lost three more in their teens. Asa Eldridge, the main subject of this narrative, was his parents' sixth child and second son, born in July 1809. His younger brother Oliver was the last to arrive, in September 1818.

The cousins must have played together often while they were growing up, since they were close to each other geographically as well as genealogically. The Eldridges lived on Yarmouth Port's main street (present-day Route 6A, but at that time still known as Hallet Street), and the Hallets down a lane just a few hundred yards away. Their house stood on the east side of Mill Pond, the tidal pond whose south bank had been the site of the village's first dwelling.

Like Ansel Hallet, John Eldridge senior enjoyed the title of captain, but in his case local records are less clear about the reason. None of these records link him directly to the command of a vessel, and he might conceivably have been a captain in the Barnstable county militia, as his father Barnabas had been.

There is, however, good evidence from a more distant source that his title was nautical rather than military. The source in question is the renowned maritime historian Carl Cutler, who co-founded the Mystic Seaport museum and produced two authoritative books on American sailing ships. These were based on years of research during which he examined over five thousand logbooks and compiled over thirty thousand index cards recording the departures and arrivals of vessels along the East Coast. In the second of his books, *Queens of the Western Ocean*, Cutler mentions a Boston shipowner called Eben Parsons and states that "John Eldridge from 'down on the Cape' commanded his schooner *Mary* in 1789." Guided by this statement, a search of historical newspapers reveals that a schooner of that name under the command of a Captain Eldridge arrived in Boston from Guadeloupe on October 4, 1789. John Eldridge would have been twenty-five at the time, a reasonable age for him to have become captain of his own vessel. Thus he does appear to have been a mariner—and indeed, a more ambitious one than his brother-in-law Ansel Hallet, sailing bigger vessels to more distant ports.

Beyond this, though, little can be said about his maritime career except that it was over by the time he reached his mid-forties. At that point he went into politics and took on responsibilities that would have required his presence on land rather than water, serving for a number of years as an elected official in both town and state governments.

This radical change of career appears to have started when Eldridge became involved in local opposition to an unpopular new law. The Embargo Act of 1807 had been passed by Congress at the express request of President Jefferson, who wanted to punish Britain, then at war with France, for repeatedly seizing American ships and forcing crewmembers into service in its own navy (a practice known as "impressment"). An Act passed in the previous year had blocked incoming trade by defining a list of goods from the United Kingdom that could no longer be imported; to stifle trade in the opposite direction, the Embargo Act now forbade any US ship to sail for a foreign port. How exactly this was supposed to hurt Britain was a mystery to New Englanders, who fiercely opposed (and often ignored) the embargo. What particularly galled them was that this blockade of their export business had been imposed not by some foreign power but by their own government. Their objections proved to be well founded, because the Act did far more damage to US producers and merchants than to anyone else. Its intended targets, the British, quickly found other trading partners, and also took advantage of the absence of American ships to move into markets previously dominated by the US.

Given its heavy dependence on the export of salted fish, Cape Cod was hit particularly hard by the ban on foreign trade. And in Yarmouth, John Eldridge was one of those chosen to voice the town's official opposition to the ban. At a Town Meeting on August 29, 1808, he and eight other men were appointed to draft a petition to President Jefferson to suspend the embargo. By itself the resulting document probably had little impact in Washington, but it formed part of a loud chorus of complaints that led to an early repeal of the Embargo Act. In March 1809, in one of his last acts as President, Jefferson signed the Non-Intercourse Act into law; this repealed the broad ban against US ships sailing to foreign ports, and replaced it with more limited restrictions directed specifically at Britain and France.

Although Yarmouth's petition may not have contributed much to this development, John Eldridge's role in drafting it seems to have launched his modest career in politics. In 1808, the year he worked on the petition, he was elected to the Board of Selectmen in Yarmouth, a position he held for the next eight years. And for six of those years he also represented the town in the Massachusetts legislature, to which he was elected in 1809.

Despite the offices he held, Eldridge was powerless to protect Yarmouth from another major hit to its economy a few years into his tenure. This new blow was caused largely by the same geopolitical issues as the previous one. American resentment towards Britain over trade-related matters and impressment still lingered, and were key factors in the decision by Congress to declare war on the United Kingdom in 1812. As they had during the Revolutionary War, the British imposed a blockade along the East Coast of the US, bringing most trade to a halt. Around Cape Cod, the Royal Navy went further than simply intercepting any vessels that tried to enter or leave the local seaways: it threatened Brewster and Orleans with the destruction of their saltworks unless each town paid a hefty ransom. Brewster capitulated and paid; Orleans refused, and then repelled the landing party that came ashore to set fire to the local saltworks.

In Yarmouth, John Eldridge found himself elected to another committee, this time to liaise with other towns on the Cape "to consult for the general good and safety." Local residents were no more enthusiastic about the War than they had been about the Embargo Act. Few agreed with the need for the conflict, whose purpose was far less clear than the adverse effect of the blockade on their incomes. The strength of local opposition to the War can be judged from the results of the Massachusetts gubernatorial election held in 1814. Given the choice between Caleb Strong, an anti-war Federal candidate, and Joseph B. Varnam, a pro-war Republican, 92 percent of Yarmouth's voters went for Strong.

A few months later, these electors got what they had voted for. The Treaty of Ghent brought the War to an end and ushered in a lasting peace with Britain. After almost four decades of intermittent but protracted stoppages stretching back to the Revolutionary War, the coastal trade entered a long period without interruption. In 1816, the year after the second war ended, Boston recorded the arrival of 1,684 "coasting vessels" (from all coastal locations, not just Cape Cod). By 1830 the corresponding figure was 2,938, and in 1851 it was 6,344, almost four times the number in 1816.

In Yarmouth, the end of the war allowed Ansel Hallet to resume his twice-weekly trips to Boston in the sloop *Betsey*. For his part, John Eldridge Sr. was reaching the end of his term as an elected official, and about to devote himself to farming; an entry in the oldest surviving "Cash Book" for the Town Dock at Bass Hole records his use of a cart and oxen for the transport of hay in September 1817. Sadly, however, he died less than a year after this transaction, at the age of only 54. His death was all the more tragic for the family because it meant that he never had the chance to see his son Oliver, who was born two months after he passed away.

By that time John Jr. had already been at sea for eight years, and in due course Asa and Oliver followed him too. All three made rapid progress in their careers, each rising to the command of a sizeable ocean-going ship in his early twenties. Little is known about the path they followed to ascend so quickly to such coveted positions. What can safely be said is that they started young. Thus one history of Yarmouth states that John "commenced his seafaring life at the age of 12 years," while another states that Asa "took early to the sea." A third is more specific about Asa's starting position, stating that he went to sea as a cook, and that this was a common practice for Yarmouth boys who eventually wanted to skipper their own ships. But how they climbed from the galley to the quarterdeck is not explained.

None of these accounts mentions the vessels or locations where John and Asa began their careers. One obvious possibility it that they worked on packet boats engaged in the coastal trade with Boston. This seems even more likely given the close relationship they would have enjoyed with their uncle, Ansel Hallet. He is known to have been highly active in the trade between Cape Cod and Boston, and after the death of the boys' father in 1818 probably became their chief mentor.

The brother who benefited most from their uncle's attention would have been Asa. At the time of their father's death John was already twenty and would have completed most of his training; Oliver had not yet been born, and would barely have started at sea before Ansel Hallet's own tragic death in 1832. (Hallet was killed when his latest sloop, the *Messenger*, rolled over on top of him as he was trying to dig her out after she ran aground.) Asa, in contrast, was almost nine when his father died, and twenty-three when his uncle was killed; it is tempting to think that he spent the early part of his career under Hallet's tutelage on a coastal sloop.

Even in that case, Asa's stay on his uncle's boat must have been relatively short, because he would otherwise have had difficulty gaining enough experience to become a deep-sea captain as quickly as he did. His likely path to that position will be discussed in the next chapter, but whatever time he did spend with his uncle in the coastal trade would have prepared him well. The waters off the Massachusetts coast offered many of the same challenges that might be encountered out on the ocean, but with a safe harbor never too far away if the weather turned rough. Crucially, the voyages were sufficiently long and unpredictable to allow Eldridge to learn the single most important skill for success as an international sea captain: how to convert wind from any direction into rapid forward motion. The longer the voyage, the more valuable this skill became. While saving an hour on an overnight journey between Boston and Cape Cod might not matter too much, shaving several days from a month-long westward crossing of the Atlantic most definitely would.

This is not to say that speed was not important to people engaged in the coastal trade. Customers may not have cared too much about an hour either way on the voyage time, but rival captains most certainly did—especially on those frequent occasions when they decided to turn the coastal run into a race. Many of these races were spontaneous, beginning when two packet boats happened to leave harbor at about the same time, provoking boastful banter between skippers and a wager over who was faster. Others were pre-arranged contests between boats from neighboring towns and villages, with significant amounts of money at stake—mostly in the form of wagers placed by residents of the competing communities, but sometimes in the form of prize money put up by local businessmen. These races would have given young Asa his first opportunity to learn the complex interplay between wind, sail, course and current that resulted in the fastest times.

Apparently, seamanship was not the only thing that Eldridge learned by sailing to Boston with his uncle. Ambition was another. While Ansel Hallet and his sloop were prominent in their hometown, the ships they encountered in Boston harbor would have made Asa realize there were much bigger opportunities to pursue—literally as well as metaphorically. Whereas coastal boats were typically about 60 feet long with one or two masts and a tonnage of between 50 and 100, an ocean-going ship might be 130 feet long with three tall masts and a tonnage of over 500. That ship would also be making much longer voyages—weeks or months instead of days—to much more exotic locations: England, India or China instead of Yarmouth Port, Dennis or Barnstable. As he dreamed of his future, it would have been natural for Eldridge to imagine himself in command of such a vessel. According to the historian Ralph D. Paine, "Any normal New York boy would sooner have been captain of a [transatlantic] packet than President of the United States." In this regard, Eldridge was presumably no different than his contemporaries from New York.

Unlike all but a few of them, however, Asa would ultimately turn this boyhood fantasy into reality. Doing so would place him at the very pinnacle of his profession. But first he needed to accumulate a vast store of knowledge and experience—and there could be no better way to learn than by sailing to those exotic locations he had heard about in Boston.

2

ADVENTURES IN THE FAR EAST

Be it Known, that on the day and date hereof, before me CLEMENT C. BIDDLE, ESQUIRE, Notary Public for the Commonwealth of Pennsylvania, residing in the City of Philadelphia, duly commissioned and sworn, and by law authorized to administer oaths and affirmations, personally appeared *Asa Eldridge* and made *oath* that he is a resident of *Yarmouth* in the State of *Massachusetts* and a CITIZEN of the United States of America, that he is aged *twenty-two* years, or thereabouts, of the height of *five* feet *eleven* inches, *fresh* complexion, *brown* hair, *blue* eyes, *and has a scar on his right shin from a cut.*

(Signature) *Asa Eldridge*

...

SWORN and SUBSCRIBED as above before me: and in Testimony whereof I have hereunto set my hand and affixed my Notarial Seal the *19th* day of *April* A.D. *1832* (Signature) Clement C. Biddle, Not. Pub.

SO READS the earliest document the author has found that can be linked with certainty to Asa Eldridge's maritime career. It is his application in 1832 for what was known as a "Seaman's Protection Certificate," a passport-like document mandated by Congress in 1796 to protect US sailors from being forced into service on British warships. Such "impressment" of Americans by the Royal Navy occurred routinely between the Revolutionary War and the War of 1812, and was a major cause of the latter. By affirming that the sailor who carried it was a US citizen, the certificate was supposed to protect him from this fate. Given that photography had not yet been invented, the certificate had to rely on descriptive details to identify the bearer: age, place of birth, height, complexion, hair color, eye color and distinguishing marks. To obtain a certificate, the seaman was obliged to submit an application providing these details and witnessed in the presence of a notary public by someone who knew him. The document cited above is a typical example, submitted by Asa Eldridge in 1832. By that time the risk of impressment had long since passed, but the certificates had turned out to be useful forms of identification and so the practice of issuing them continued.

More recently, these certificates have taken on new utility as valuable resources for genealogical research. In the present case there is a further utility; Asa Eldridge's application provides both a physical description of him and the only unambiguous documentation of a specific circumstance early in his career—namely that he was in Philadelphia in the spring of 1832.

The next circumstance for which equal clarity exists did not occur until 1842, a full ten years later. How Eldridge came to be in Philadelphia in 1832, and how he spent his time before that date or over the next decade, can only be inferred from snippets of evidence that are often ambiguous.

The most valuable sources of such evidence are online archives of old newspapers. On both sides of the Atlantic, databases have been developed that contain searchable digital scans of nineteenth-century newspapers. The information they contain about maritime activities falls into four main categories: the simple lists of vessels arriving and departing that were a standard feature in many newspapers; advertisements for forthcoming departures; articles about specific vessels or voyages that were newsworthy; and reports of recent events abroad that often stated which vessel had brought news of them.

Even with all this material and the ability to search it, information that relates unambiguously to Asa Eldridge can be difficult to find. Consider, for example, the daily listings of maritime traffic in newspapers, such as the "Marine List" in the New York *Evening Post*. Each entry usually gave the name of the vessel followed by the last name of the captain, but rarely indicated his first name or initial; and since a number of captains named Eldridge were active at the same time as Asa—including two of his own brothers—establishing that a particular reference was to him is often a challenge. Complicating matters further, some of the ships he commanded had very common names that were shared by multiple other vessels. Thus even when records are found that contain both his name and that of a ship he is known to have captained, they do not necessarily refer to him. To illustrate the point, the results of one particular search appear to identify him as the captain of a vessel operating out of Philadelphia for several years—which might seem like a promising lead, except that he was only seven years old at the time of this ship's first voyage under a Captain Eldridge.

In spite of these challenges, a combination of careful searching and plausible speculation allows a reasonable outline of Asa Eldridge's early career to be constructed. This goes as follows.

After starting out at around the age of twelve on the coastal sloop owned by his uncle, Ansel Hallet, Eldridge quickly transferred to a ship called *America* commanded by his older brother John. The *America* did not sail on a fixed route or schedule, but went wherever and whenever her owners could find cargo—sometimes on short runs between New York and Philadelphia, but occasionally all the way to India.

When Asa was in his mid-teens his older brother left the *America* to take command of the brig *Ranger*, which operated up and down the East Coast and also to Mexico and the Caribbean. Asa appears to have stayed where he was, however, and by 1829 had succeeded his brother as captain of the *America*. He was still only twenty at the time—young for a sea captain, but not impossibly so. Josiah Richardson, for example, an exact contemporary of Eldridge from Cape Cod, is known to have been master of a schooner by the age of twenty-one, and to have taken her to Russia within his first year in command.

Given the *America*'s roving pursuit of cargo-carrying opportunities, Asa quickly gained experience of sailing to a wide variety of destinations. Thus his first voyage as captain took him from New York to Savannah to Liverpool; his next ended in the same port but went via New Orleans; a third saw him sailing to and fro between Boston and Liverpool; and yet another was a roundtrip between Boston and Russia, returning via Denmark.

That long journey back from Russia was particularly harrowing, and probably explains why Eldridge was in Philadelphia in 1832 applying for a Seaman's Protection Certificate. It began quietly enough, with no incidents of note during the first two months after leaving Russia. The *America*'s starting point was Cronstadt, the island port on the Baltic Sea that serves St. Petersburg, which she left on October 6, 1831. After calling in at the Danish port of Helsingør (Elsinore), she headed for Boston towards the end of the month. By early December she was on the Atlantic, and that was where her troubles started. On December 6 she was hit by a storm that washed away both lifeboats and part of her bulwarks (the "walls" around the perimeter of the deck formed by the upper part of the ship's sides). This left her with little protection during a second storm twelve days later, when a big sea crashed over the exposed deck and swept away her foremast and bowsprit. At the time, the *America* was still almost six hundred miles away from Boston. She eventually limped into New York on January 9, 1832, over three weeks later—"in distress," as the *Evening Post* put it.

By then, this was probably also an apt description of her captain's Seaman's Protection Certificate. Eldridge had presumably obtained one some years earlier when he began to sail abroad, and would have been carrying it with him on the *America*. The seas that ravaged her on the way back from Russia may well have swept it away or ruined it, in which case the application notarized for Eldridge in April 1832 would have been for a replacement. It was in fact quite common for mariners to lose their certificates and be issued new ones. The reason Eldridge was in Philadelphia when he made his application may be that he had gone there to recuperate while his ship was being repaired; he would have been familiar with the city from his visits while serving on the *America* under his brother.

Eldridge apparently needed more time to recuperate than his ship. When the *America* next sailed in March 1832, a Captain Robinson was at the helm. Eldridge was still on sabbatical three months later when the *America* headed for Cronstadt again, this time under the command of a Captain Cloutman. Interestingly, when she arrived back in Boston in January 1833 her return journey had taken six days longer than Eldridge's a year earlier, even though it appears to have passed without serious incident. Eldridge had clearly made excellent progress before the storms arrived—hinting at what would happen next.

By March of 1833 Eldridge was ready for action again. This time his destination was not Russia but India. After sailing from Boston on March 27 the *America* reached Sand Heads, the anchorage for Calcutta, eighty-nine days later. No ship had ever made the same journey more quickly. Eldridge had set his first record, and an enduring one at that. Two decades would pass before it was beaten, and then only by one of the legendary clipper ships.

Within four years of taking over the *America*, Asa had therefore established himself as one of the most capable mariners on the high seas. Given the seafaring knowledge and leadership skills required, these accomplishments would have been noteworthy at any age; given that Eldridge was barely twenty when he assumed command of the *America*, they were truly remarkable.

A sense of the knowledge he must have acquired by this stage can be gained from a magnificent book entitled *The Young Sea Officer's Sheet Anchor, or a Key to the Leading of Rigging and to Practical Seamanship*. Published in 1808, this comprehensive work was written to assist young officers joining Britain's Royal Navy or East India Company. Its author was a man named Darcy Lever who worked for the latter, but not at sea. His motivation to write the book came from an experience he had while on his way to India to take up his position. Curious about the operation of the ship on which he was sailing, he had asked an officer a simple question about her rigging, and been taken aback by the terse reply he had received. Realizing that raw young recruits to the officer corps might experience similar treatment, Darcy set out to anticipate and answer the host of questions they must have.

His book therefore describes almost every aspect of the operation of a sailing ship in extraordinary detail. The first part, entitled "Rigging and Sails," is all about the "mechanics" of a typical ship and provides detailed instructions for a broad range of tasks, such as making ropes of various types; tying knots for different purposes; putting up masts, yards and booms; installing sails and rigging; setting and furling sails; and dropping and weighing anchor. The second part, "Seamanship," then explains how a vessel comprised of all the parts just described should actually be sailed. It begins with a brief theoretical discussion of the interplay between rudder, wind and sails, explaining (for example) how the influence of a sail on the speed and direction of a ship depends not just on the wind but also on the sail's position relative to the vessel's center of rotation. Building on this discussion, it goes on to describe which sails should be deployed, and how, under a variety of conditions: before a strong tailwind; against a headwind; in progressively heavier seas; in a fully-fledged gale; after suffering storm damage; and so on.

To make all of this information comprehensible, Lever included over six hundred beautifully executed diagrams. He took great care to arrange these next to the text that they illustrate; each two-page spread includes a whole page of diagrams directly opposite the instructions they help to explain.

What comes through most of all from this book is the sheer complexity of the vessels it describes. A nineteenth-century merchant sailing ship might have as many as thirty-six sails arrayed on three masts and its bowsprit. About two-thirds of these were "square-rigged," mounted perpendicular to the long axis of the ship, and the remainder were "fore-and-aft," mounted parallel to that axis.

Each mast carried between four and six square sails mounted vertically above one another on horizontal spars known as yards. Some of these yards could move vertically and others could not; the former were hoisted upwards to raise the sails attached to them, whereas the latter remained at a fixed height from which their sails could be dropped down. Whether at fixed or movable heights, all yards could be pivoted on their masts to present their sails to a wind that was not directly behind the ship.

The arrangement of the "fore and aft" sails was somewhat different. Most were mounted in the space between masts on "stays" (ropes that held the masts upright), and several more were located on the ship's bowsprit.

Controlling all of these sails were ropes, ropes and more ropes—literally miles of them. Some hauled sails up, others let them down. Some pivoted the yards to change the angle of their sails to the wind, others tautened or slackened corners to catch the wind more effectively. All were arranged in the same order on every ship, so that once a sailor "learned the ropes" he could move from one vessel to another with little retraining. Learning the ropes also meant mastering the dozens of different knots that were used to secure them for specific purposes.

Knowledge alone was not sufficient for effective use of the ropes. Strength and teamwork were also essential. In a brisk wind, more than a dozen men might be required to manage a single large sail—some hauling on the "braces" (the ropes at each end of the yard that pivoted the sail on the mast) and others on the "sheets" (the ropes at the lower corners of the sail that tautened or slackened it to change how much wind it caught).

At least this work could be done from the relatively safety of the ship's deck. Not so the most challenging task, which was tying or untying the square sails to their yards. Each sail had to be tied every time it was furled, so as to secure it from the tug of the wind. It then had to be untied again the next time it was deployed. Both operations were the stuff of pirate movies, performed from above by sailors spaced out every few feet along the yard. As many as eight men might be needed to secure or release one of the larger sails. To reach their positions they first had to climb up the rigging to one of several small platforms on the mast, then edge out sideways along the yard, shuffling along a horizontal footrope strung below it. A hundred feet or more above deck in a high wind and plunging sea, this was no task for the faint-hearted.

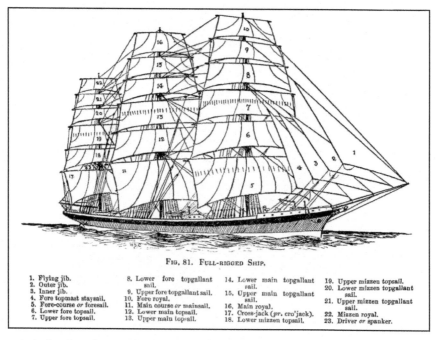

FIG. 81. FULL-RIGGED SHIP.

1. Flying jib.
2. Outer jib.
3. Inner jib.
4. Fore topmast staysail.
5. Fore-course *or* foresail.
6. Lower fore topsail.
7. Upper fore topsail.
8. Lower fore topgallant sail.
9. Upper fore topgallant sail.
10. Fore royal.
11. Main course *or* mainsail.
12. Lower main topsail.
13. Upper main topsail.
14. Lower main topgallant sail.
15. Upper main topgallant sail.
16. Main royal.
17. Cross-jack (*pr.* cro'jack).
18. Lower mizzen topsail.
19. Upper mizzen topsail.
20. Lower mizzen topgallant sail.
21. Upper mizzen topgallant sail.
22. Mizzen royal.
23. Driver *or* spanker.

Sail plan for a full-rigged sailing ship. This does not include any of the outboard "studding sails" that were often rigged on either side of the square sails.

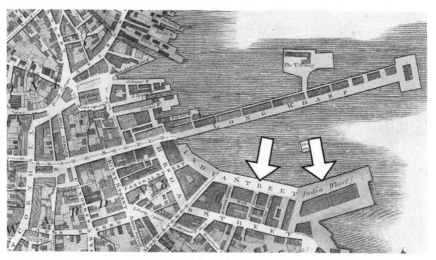

Map of Boston waterfront in 1814. Trade with India was already significant enough for a street and wharf to be named after the distant country (arrows).

The metal strip marking the prime meridian in the courtyard of the Royal
Observatory in Greenwich is a popular tourist attraction. The person straddling
the strip has one foot in the eastern hemisphere and the other in the western.

View of Boston from City Point near Sea Street, 1833.

Less perilous, but almost as daunting, was the responsibility for orchestrating all of this complexity—the captain's job. The first task he faced was to decide on the ship's course. To do so he needed to know his current position, which in the days before radio beacons and satellite navigation required significant skill to determine. Then as now, the two essential pieces of information for a captain were his current latitude (north-south position) and longitude (east-west position). To determine the former, Eldridge and his peers followed the long tradition of seafarers and looked to the sky, using a sextant to measure the angles between the horizon and various celestial bodies. The values recorded could then be looked up in the detailed tables of a nautical almanac to establish the ship's current latitude.

The determination of longitude had for centuries been a much tougher proposition. The basis for the determination had long been understood: that the local time at any given position depended on how far east or west the ship was, and so its distance from some reference point could be calculated from the difference in local times at the two locations. The local time at the ship's current position could be readily established from the height of the sun or a nighttime star in the sky; the challenge was to know what time it was at the reference point some distance away. For a vessel sailing between the US and England, the usual reference point was the Royal Observatory at Greenwich in London (which later became the reference point for the whole world). Although the time there could also be estimated using celestial objects, the procedure was complicated and prone to error. It depended on the movement of the Moon, whose position relative to other objects in the sky changes throughout each month in a manner that is predictable but depends on the location of the observer. As a result, the angles it forms with other celestial bodies at one location can be used to estimate the current time at another. The calculations involved were complex, but could be bypassed by referring to pre-calculated tables in a nautical almanac; after measuring various "lunar distances" (as the relevant angles were known) with his sextant, the captain could look up the time in Greenwich that corresponded to the values he had just determined. The difference between Greenwich time and the time at his current location could then be used to establish the ship's east-west position, with each hour of difference representing fifteen degrees of longitude.

The problem with this method was that it depended on highly accurate measurement of lunar distances, which was not always easy on a moving ship. Even small errors could be catastrophic: at the latitude of New York, for example, every minute's discrepancy between the estimated and actual times in Greenwich represents a distance of about fourteen miles, which might make the difference between avoiding an obstacle and sailing right into it. Moreover, the celestial objects on which the method depended were not always visible.

The obvious solution was for each ship to carry a clock permanently set to the time in Greenwich. The challenge was to develop a clock that would keep time precisely enough on a ship. Pendulum clocks were the most accurate timepieces then available, but only if kept completely stationary. Clocks of all types were also sensitive to changes in temperature. In the mid-1700s, however, a British carpenter named John Harrison decided to pursue a £20,000 prize his government was offering for a reliable method to determine longitude. His quest is described by Dava Sobel in her much-admired book, *Longitude*. After experimenting with three large clock-sized prototypes, Harrison realized that a smaller mechanism would keep time more accurately, and switched to a format resembling an oversized pocket watch. This incorporated two inventions that are still in wide use today: a bimetallic spring that automatically compensated for temperature changes, and caged ball-bearings to reduce friction. When it was tested against a reference clock his new chronometer was found to run a few seconds slow every day, but consistently, which meant that the correct time could easily be deduced if the number of days since the device's last reset was known. Crucially, the invention worked just as well out at sea. On its first trial crossing of the Atlantic in 1761, after correcting for the known daily loss, the chronometer was only five seconds off at the end of a voyage lasting more than eighty-one days. A timepiece good enough for navigational purposes had finally been developed.

But as recounted by Sobel, Harrison's efforts to claim the £20,000 prize were repeatedly thwarted by influential astronomers who were working on the lunar distance method and hoping to win the award themselves. They insisted on further tests of the new device and on various other onerous conditions that delayed official recognition of Harrison's achievement. Indeed, even after the intervention of King George III, he was never awarded the full prize money to which he should have been entitled.

Interfering astronomers were not the only obstacle facing the new chronometer. It was also hugely expensive. The first working copy was made by a London watchmaker, Larcum Kendall, after Harrison had been forced to disclose his design; the copy took two and a half years to build and cost £450—about thirty percent of the value of a ship at the time.

Expensive though it was, Kendall's copy amply demonstrated the real value of Harrison's invention. Its first trial could hardly have been sterner: Captain James Cook was charged with testing it during the second of his South Sea explorations. His reaction was all that Harrison could have hoped for. "[O]ur error [in longitude] can never be great," Cook wrote, "so long as we have as good a guide as [the] watch." Entries in his log refer to "our trusty friend the Watch" and "our never failing guide, the Watch." And at the end of the voyage, the world's most famous mariner reported that the chronometer had "exceeded the expectations of its most zealous advocate" and that, with occasional corrections based on lunar observations, "has been our faithful guide through all vicissitudes of climates."

Inspired by the performance of Harrison's "Watch," other inventors developed new and simpler designs that gradually reduced the cost of chronometers. By the 1780s, Sobel notes, a decent model could be procured for £65, and by 1815 about five thousand of the marine timekeepers were in use around the world.

Despite the widespread adoption of chronometers, many mariners would still have learned the lunar distance method, if only for occasional checks on the accuracy of their timepieces during long voyages. In all likelihood, therefore, Asa Eldridge would have been familiar with both the clock-based and celestial approaches for determining Greenwich time (and thus longitude), and would have used both on the *America*'s record-breaking voyage to Calcutta.

HAVING ESTABLISHED his ship's position and chosen its course, the captain could then focus on managing its progress. Even in benign conditions, he was often faced with complex decisions. Consider, for example, the situation with a brisk wind blowing in the direction the ship needed to travel. Few circumstances could be more favorable, but there was always a question about how much sail to carry. More was not necessarily better. A strong wind could place too much strain on the ship, tearing sails and even snapping masts. Given their height, the latter rarely consisted of a single continuous pole, but were made up of two or three sections held together by thick elmwood connectors and metal bolts; it was not uncommon for the top section to break off under too much canvas or too strong a wind, and sometimes the middle section as well. Ships carried spare mast sections, but installing and rigging them while out at sea was a major undertaking. Similarly, replacing a torn sail with a spare could also be time-consuming and dangerous. The captain was therefore faced with a continuing series of decisions about the balance between speed and safety.

Westward crossings usually presented the opposite problem: how to make progress against a prevailing headwind. The classic strategy known to all sailors is to zigzag back and forth across the opposing wind in a series of tacks, so that a decent area of sail can be presented at an angle to the wind for most of the time. This is relatively easy to accomplish in vessels that rely wholly or mostly on fore-and-aft sails, like the schooners of Eldridge's day and most modern sailboats; these sails are typically mounted on booms that can swing in a wide arc from one side of the vessel to the other, and so can be readily pivoted to catch wind from different directions. Square-rigged sails, however, could pivot only through a limited arc because of the fixed rigging around them, and so were significantly less effective at catching wind coming in from an angle. The whole process of tacking therefore required a carefully coordinated sequence of adjustments to the various sails on the several masts of the ship—a sequence that depended on the strength of the wind and the current, and which the captain would need to anticipate when setting his course.

And then there were storms, when all that mattered was survival. While carrying too much canvas during a storm could obviously be dangerous, so could carrying too little. Despite the high risk of damage from the wind, some minimum area of sail was needed to allow the vessel to be steered. Otherwise she would be more likely to be broached—hit from the side by large waves—and to sink as a result. The choice of sail was important, however. In very rough seas the lowest sails (known as courses) on the various masts might fill with water and split; the sails farther up the masts were safer in that respect, but required the crew to climb high up in the rigging in extremely dangerous conditions. And again, the captain was the person with ultimate responsibility for deciding between these options.

Clearly, then, the knowledge and expertise required to command an ocean-going vessel were immense. They could easily take decades to accrue. For a captain who started his career as a boy, which many did, a typical progression might be to start as a cabin boy running errands for the first mate; work for several years as a seaman to learn all about the ship's operation; move up to become "second mate"—in charge of the sails, rigging and masts, expected to enforce obedience, paid twice as much as the seamen, but in most other respects no better off than them; be promoted to first mate—responsible for implementing the captain's orders, deputizing for him when necessary, supervising the cargo and keeping the ship's log book; and then finally win an appointment as captain—lord, master, judge and jury over the entire enterprise. Having gone to sea around the age of twelve, most who followed this path did not become first mates until their late twenties or early thirties, and only a third of them ever made it to the highest position.

To be appointed captain of the *America* by the age of twenty, Asa Eldridge must have completed or bypassed most of these steps much more quickly than most of his peers. His rapid rise may have been due in part to the help and influence of his uncle and brother, but his voyage to Calcutta in 1833 showed that he also had extraordinary talent.

Nor was this talent limited purely to seamanship. To set a new record he must also have possessed the crucial ability to extract the absolute best from his crew. That ability could certainly not be taken for granted. The seamen who served on nineteenth-century sailing ships were renowned as some of the toughest characters on the planet. Their lives were in constant danger as they clambered around the rigging in high winds and heaving seas, adjusting sails to the captain's orders; many a seaman was lost overboard while attempting this task. Although the crew could never openly question an order from the captain, if they did not trust or respect him they might be less willing to push the limits of safety to squeeze that last extra ounce of speed from the wind. And over a long route, such unwillingness might add several days to the duration of the voyage, reducing the ship's competitiveness and profits. Owners were very much aware of this, and would only entrust command of a vessel to someone they thought was capable of cajoling the thuggish deckhands into giving of their best. Men in their early twenties did not usually qualify, but Asa Eldridge clearly did. And more than just qualify: as the *America*'s voyage to Calcutta clearly showed, he was able to inspire his men to become world-beaters.

The life of a common sailor during this period was certainly harsh. Two contemporary accounts describe it vividly. The more famous is *Two Years Before the Mast* by Richard Henry Dana, who worked as a seaman on a voyage from Boston to California in 1834, and then again on a return voyage to Boston in 1836. [The term "before the mast" refers to the location of the common sailors' quarters on a typical ship, in the fo'c's'le (forecastle) in front of the foremast.] At the time, Dana was taking a break from his studies at Harvard College because a case of measles had affected his eyesight. On his return to Boston he resumed his studies and became a prominent attorney and politician, but found time to write a detailed account of his experiences at sea.

Dana's account was much admired by the man who wrote the other contemporary description of life at sea, which was entitled *Redburn: His First Voyage*. Like *Two Years Before the Mast, Redburn* describes the experiences of a young man from a good family who chose to work as a "boy" (first-time sailor) on a long roundtrip ocean voyage, in his case from New York to Liverpool and back. The book was published as a work of fiction but is widely assumed to be autobiographical, since its author made the same voyage in the same capacity in 1839. This particular work quickly faded into obscurity—in sharp contrast to the author's next effort, which is arguably the most famous nautically-themed book ever written: *Moby-Dick*. *Redburn* was indeed the work of Herman Melville, and a valuable record of life at sea during the period when Asa Eldridge was first building his reputation as an outstanding captain.

Speaking of captains, a good sense of the very different relationships possible between them and their crew is provided by Dana. At the end of the first day of his voyage on the brig *Pilgrim*, the captain gave the following speech to the assembled crew:

> Now, my men, we have begun a long voyage. If we get along well together, we shall have a comfortable time; if we don't, we shall have hell afloat.— All you've got to do is to obey your orders and do your duty like men,— then you'll fare well enough;— if you don't, you'll fare hard enough,— I can tell you. If we pull together, you'll find me a clever fellow; if we don't, you'll find me a bloody rascal.— That's all I've got to say.— Go below, the larboard watch!

In the event, the captain proved to be more "bloody rascal" than "clever fellow." His actions during one particular incident had a profound effect on Dana. Having provoked an argument with a sailor, the captain proceeded to flog him and another man who tried to intercede on his behalf. Dana's horror at the brutality of the floggings, and dismay at being powerless to prevent them, turned him into a lifelong advocate for seamen's rights. In 1841, the year after he qualified as a lawyer, he published another book entitled *The Seaman's Friend*. In addition to detailed advice for sailors about the operation of ships—much like the advice Darcy Lever had provided for officers two decades earlier—Dana included an extensive review of the "laws relating to the practical duties of master and mariners." This quickly became the definitive text concerning the legal rights (and responsibilities) of seamen. Dana's commitment to the cause of sailors was not restricted to the theoretical, however. He frequently represented accused seamen in court, where they could land all too easily if they made any attempt to resist the cruel and arbitrary punishment that often came their way at sea.

Even when treated humanely, sailors hardly enjoyed the "comfortable time" suggested by the *Pilgrim*'s captain. Dana and Melville both describe an endless round of chores on their respective ships, broken only by the Sabbath. Manhandling the heavy sails was only one of a range of duties that fell to the crew. Maintenance of the vessel was a never-ending task. Ropes and rigging were constantly in need of attention to keep them taut, minimize chafing and replace worn sections. All of the materials for maintaining them were made onboard; sailors spent many hours "picking oakum"—teasing apart old ropes and cloth into individual fibers—and using a winch to spin these fibers into new threads and ropes for various purposes. Sails, spars and mast sections damaged in stormy weather needed to be repaired or replaced. Numerous parts of the ship required varnishing, painting, tarring, greasing or oiling. And every single day, the deck had to be washed down, scrubbed and swabbed. To quote Dana once again:

> In no state prison are the convicts more regularly set to work, and more closely watched. No conversation is allowed among the crew at their duty, and though they frequently do talk when aloft, or when near one another, yet they always stop when an officer is nigh.

So indeed, "comfortable" would not have been the adjective chosen by the crew to describe their time at sea.

Unlike the *Pilgrim*, the *America* had no scribe on board to record Asa Eldridge's behavior towards his crew, which can therefore only be a matter of conjecture. The very fact, though, that they set a new record together implies a good working relationship. Also worth noting are comments many years later in Eldridge's obituary, which noted "the universal regret expressed [at his passing] by all classes with whom he was brought into contact," and that "many tears will be shed for him by... mates, stewards and sailors"—all suggesting that he was considerate in his dealings with his men. So in spite of the hardships of their occupation, the *America*'s crew were hopefully on good enough terms with their captain to be excited about setting a new record with him.

This achievement would have been all the more satisfying because it came on a route that was well-traveled and highly competitive. Over the previous four decades, trade with India had become a major component of Boston's economy. Such trade was not allowed before independence, and was still limited for some time thereafter by a British prohibition against American vessels doing business with its ports in India. This prohibition was eventually removed by the Jay Treaty in 1794, and much of the trade that then developed was conducted from Boston and nearby Salem. Its historical importance to Boston is still evident today in the city's waterfront, which includes an India Wharf, East India Row and India Street.

The challenge for the merchants involved was that demand was initially one-sided: there were many more Indian goods that Americans wanted than *vice versa*. Most of America's exports at that time consisted of "products from nature" such as cotton, tobacco, furs, lumber and salted fish, together with sugar, coffee and rum imported from the West Indies. These had little appeal in India, either because they could be procured from other sources or did not fit local tastes; the most coveted imports were manufactured goods that were not yet available from the US. In the other direction, however, Indian materials such as cotton cloth, saltpeter, linseed, ginger, hemp, indigo and shellac were in high demand in the US. Sales of newly-imported "India goods" were widely advertised and highly popular.

To address this imbalance, vessels outbound from the US sometimes sailed to India via Europe, even though this made the overall voyage much longer. On the way to Europe they would carry their usual cargoes, the proceeds from which could then be used to buy manufactured goods for India.

In 1833, however, just a few weeks after Asa Eldridge sailed for Calcutta, so did the first shipment of an unlikely cargo that would transform the trade between Boston and India. The new cargo was another simple "product from nature": ice.

The man behind the shipment was a Boston entrepreneur named Frederic Tudor, who had been exporting New England ice to other warm climates for more than twenty-five years. When Tudor started this business in 1806 at the age of twenty-two he was regarded as crazy. Who in their right minds would spend time and money to cut ice from the surface of a lake, cart it to the waterfront, and load it on a ship, only to have most of it melt either in transit—filling the ship dangerously with water—or on arrival at its destination? The idea "excited the derision of the whole town as a mad project," Tudor later recalled. Even his father called it "wild and ruinous."

For the first couple of years all the naysayers seemed justified. Although losses during transit were not too severe, the ice melted too quickly at its destination for Tudor to make a profit. Then came the Embargo Act of 1807 and War of 1812, which brought his business to a halt and landed him in debtors' prison.

Over time, however, Tudor's determination, ingenuity and shrewd business sense overcame all major obstacles. By trial and error, he discovered that sawdust rather than hay was the best insulator for ice in transit, and that ice could serve as the ballast for a ship, allowing other cargoes to be carried on top of it. To extend the life of his product at its destination he built insulated icehouses, often with capital provided by local merchants in return for guaranteed low ice prices. He negotiated supply contracts with foreign governments that gave him monopolies in certain countries. To stimulate demand in new markets, he provided free ice to popular bars so that their customers could experience chilled drinks for the first time. And he substantially improved the process for harvesting ice from ponds and lakes around New England, greatly aided by one of his suppliers who invented a horse-drawn ice-cutter that produced uniform blocks of ice. These not only looked better but could be packed more tightly, which reduced melting in transit.

By the 1830s the Tudor Ice Company was a major enterprise selling ice in ports all around the southern US, the Gulf of Mexico and the Caribbean. In 1833 Tudor went into partnership with another Boston merchant to send his first shipment to India, which was much further away than any other country he had previously tackled; by the standard route around the southern tip of Africa, Calcutta was sixteen thousand miles from Boston. Unfazed by the distance involved, Tudor and his partner dispatched the brig *Tuscany* on that route with 180 tons of ice on board. The *Tuscany* left Boston just a few weeks after the *America* sailed for Calcutta under Asa Eldridge, and took considerably longer than his record 89 days to cover the same route; when the brig reached Calcutta on September 13 she had been at sea for 124 days. Nevertheless, a good portion of her precious cargo survived the voyage without melting: 100 of the original 180 tons. The ice caused a sensation, and not just among the locals who had never seen frozen water before. Even among those who had, few had seen ice of such clarity. Tudor had just opened up an enthusiastic new market, which over the next twenty years would become the most profitable of all those he served.

Back in Boston, news of Eldridge's record-breaking voyage would have arrived while Tudor was still anxiously waiting for confirmation that his ice had reached Calcutta safely. Keenly aware that faster voyages would preserve more of his unstable product for sale, Tudor must have been tempted to engage Eldridge immediately to transport ice on his behalf. If so, he would have had to be patient. Asa had another engagement in mind, of the kind that leads to a wedding. He appears to have stayed in the US throughout 1834, and in January 1835 he married Eliza Hallett, a distant cousin from the Boston suburb of Roxbury. (Her branch of the family chose to spell their last name with an extra 't,' but spellings in general were a lot less fixed in earlier centuries than they are today. Indeed, one of three official records relating to her marriage to Eldridge has her last name as Hallet. Similar inconsistencies can be found in records relating to Asa, whose last name was sometimes spelled Eldredge—for example in the US census of 1850.)

Having wooed and wed his bride, Eldridge quickly returned to sea. The summer after his wedding saw him sailing again from Boston to Calcutta, but not at the helm of the *America*; he was now commander of the *Steiglitz*. Perhaps he was carrying ice for Frederic Tudor on a vessel more suited for the purpose. The following year he had both a new ship and a new destination, guiding the *Humboldt* out of Boston in November 1836 bound for Manila. But by 1839 he was back on the Calcutta route in command of yet another vessel, the *Timore*.

As a married man, Asa presumably found the long voyages to and from Asia increasingly irksome. The four months taken by the *Tuscany* on the outbound leg was far more typical than the *America*'s three, and with the time required to find and load a cargo in Calcutta, the roundtrip could easily take the better part of a year. Spending that much time away from home must now have been less appealing.

The comforts of married life were not the only reason for Eldridge to seek shorter voyages. As an ambitious man turning thirty, he would have wanted to take the next major step in his career. The most prestigious routes for American ships all converged on one particular English port, and the captaincy of a ship that sailed there regularly would represent clear progression for Eldridge. He had already seen the port at first hand, having taken the *America* there several times before transferring to the India trade. But now he was determined to return on a regular basis. So it was that Asa Eldridge resumed his previously brief relationship with the port of Liverpool—a relationship that would dominate the rest of his career.

3

TO LIVERPOOL BY SAIL

TO MILLIONS OF PEOPLE around the world today, Liverpool is famous as the home of the Beatles. Back in Asa Eldridge's day the city was equally renowned but for a very different reason: as one of the world's greatest ports. Forty percent of the world's trade passed through its docks, and for a while the city was wealthier than London. "Sailors love this Liverpool; and upon long voyages to distant parts of the globe, will be continually dilating upon its charms and attractions, and extolling it above all other seaports in the world." So wrote Herman Melville in *Redburn,* based on his own experience as a Liverpool-bound sailor.

The port first rose to prominence in the eighteenth century on the back of history's most ignominious commerce: the Atlantic slave trade. Liverpool was a key apex of the infamous "golden triangle," the triangular trade between Europe, Africa and the New World that brought huge profits to those involved. In Liverpool's case, the triangle typically began with the shipping of textiles, ironware and guns to the west coast of Africa, where they were bartered for slaves. It continued with the transport of these slaves across the ocean to America or the West Indies, where they were auctioned in public markets. The profits from these odious transactions were then used to buy goods such as tobacco, sugar and cotton, which were shipped back to Liverpool to complete the triangle. By the late 1700s over one hundred slaving ships were leaving Liverpool each year, representing about three quarters of the entire European activity in slave trading. In all, Liverpool merchants were responsible for transporting around 1.5 million African slaves across the Atlantic.

By the time Asa Eldridge first crossed the same ocean, the vile trade on which Liverpool's prosperity was built had long since been abolished in

Britain. The Slave Trade Act of 1807 had made this business illegal throughout the British Empire, and the following year the Royal Navy—which largely controlled the world's oceans—established the West Africa Squadron to enforce it.

Fortunately for the merchants of Liverpool, a new form of trade was about to carry them to even greater levels of prosperity. By a happy accident of history, several of the key inventions that spawned the industrial revolution were made in nearby southern Lancashire, which became the first area anywhere in the world to industrialize. The spinning jenny and its successor, the spinning mule, were invented in Blackburn and Bolton, respectively forty-five and thirty-five miles from Liverpool. To exploit these inventions, enterprising local weavers created the world's first "manufactories"—a term quickly shortened to the more familiar "factories." The highest concentration of these new establishments was in Manchester, just over thirty miles inland from Liverpool. The formerly small town grew at an amazing rate to become the world's first industrial city, with so many cotton mills it was known as "Cottonopolis."

These developments created an almost insatiable demand for the import of raw cotton from America, and a reciprocal demand for the export of woven cloth from South Lancashire's textile mills. And connected as it was to the cotton towns by a network of canals, Liverpool was perfectly located to become the center of this trade. Its connections were further improved in 1830 with the inauguration of the Liverpool & Manchester Railway, the first inter-city railroad anywhere in the world. The cotton-related trade also drove commerce in many other items: eastbound, the tobacco, sugar, molasses and rum that had become staple cargoes during the slave trade; westbound, the manufactured goods now flowing from other new industrial towns in the north of England. By the middle of the nineteenth century Liverpool had the largest dock system in the world, covering two hundred acres. As many as three hundred ships might arrive on a single tide. Herman Melville was so taken with the docks he waxed lyrical about them:

> Previous to this, having only seen the miserable wooden wharves, and slip-shod, shambling piers of New York, the sight of these mighty docks filled my young mind with wonder and delight. In New York, to be sure, I could not but be struck with the long line of shipping, and tangled thicket of masts along the East River; yet, my admiration had been much abated by those irregular, unsightly wharves, which, I am sure, are a reproach and disgrace to the city that tolerates them.

> Whereas, in Liverpool, I beheld long China walls of masonry; vast piers of stone; and a succession of granite-rimmed docks, completely inclosed, and many of them communicating, which almost recalled to mind the great American chain of lakes: Ontario, Erie, St. Clair, Huron, Michigan, and Superior. The extent and solidity of these structures, seemed equal to what I had read of the old Pyramids of Egypt.
>
> …In magnitude, cost, and durability, the docks of Liverpool, even at the present day surpass all others in the world.

Melville's impressions of Liverpool were based on a visit he made as a cabin boy on the *St. Lawrence* in 1839. He turned twenty while onshore, which meant he was only a year younger than Asa Eldridge had been when he first arrived at the same destination almost a decade earlier. Their positions, however, could hardly have been more different: Eldridge had been making his inaugural voyage as captain of the *America*.

On that voyage, which spanned the end of 1829 and the beginning of 1830, the *America* had started in New York but did not proceed directly across the Atlantic. Instead, she sailed down to Savannah, Georgia—presumably to pick up a cargo of cotton—and from there to Liverpool. She was therefore following one of two routes that enabled Northern merchants and shipowners to profit handsomely from the export of Southern cotton to England, much to the chagrin of the South. Hers was the less common route, a triangle: down from a Northern port with manufactured goods, across the Atlantic carrying cotton, then back to the original port with more manufactured goods—at each port using the proceeds from the inbound cargo to purchase the outbound one.

The more common route was a dogleg rather than a triangle, involving two different sub-routes that intersected in a Northern port. The first sub-route was domestic, with vessels shuttling between New York or Boston and a Southern port (such as Savannah, Charleston or New Orleans), carrying manufactured goods on the southbound voyage and cotton on the way back. The second sub-route was transatlantic, with large packet ships transporting the cotton across the Atlantic to Liverpool, then returning with textiles, ironware and pottery from English factories.

For whatever reason, the Southern states never developed a robust maritime capability of their own, which meant that most of the export business for cotton was conducted by shipowners and merchants from the North. While these entrepreneurs did take on all of the financial risk associated with exporting cotton, they also kept a handsome share of the proceeds: forty cents out of every dollar paid by the eventual buyer. By the standards of the day, the amount of money made from this trade in New York was therefore huge. In 1822, cotton constituted 42 percent of the total value of the city's exports for the year: $3.9 million out of $9.3 million. This was more than five times higher than the value of any other export; northern flour and southern tobacco were the second and third most valuable commodities, at about three quarters of a million dollars each. And over succeeding decades the importance of the cotton trade only grew, as the demand from Lancashire's textile mills continued unabated. By the time Asa Eldridge sailed to Liverpool with cotton from Savannah in 1830, over half a million bales a year were being exported, three times the number in 1815. A decade later the number was over a million, and by 1859—just before the Civil War brought the trade to an abrupt halt—it was more than 3.5 million.

The cotton business was therefore an obvious setting for Asa Eldridge when he began sailing again to Liverpool after almost a decade in the Asia trade. The voyage he had made from Savannah to Liverpool in 1830 had been his debut as a transatlantic skipper, and his first run back in that role featured the same ports. Thus in April 1841 he sailed from Boston at the helm of his latest ship, the *Colombo*, stopped first in Savannah and then in Charleston, made his way across the Atlantic to Liverpool, and returned from there to Boston via the Welsh capital of Cardiff.

Although this particular itinerary was slightly unusual, the *Colombo* was clearly operating on the triangular route for the cotton trade. This continued to be the case for the next couple of years, but in mid-1844 she started making repeated roundtrips between Boston or New York and New Orleans—suggesting that she had been switched to the domestic branch of the "dogleg" route. Possibly disgruntled over this switch, Asa Eldridge left the *Colombo* soon afterwards. At the stage his career had now reached, he would in any case have been angling for a new appointment. While command of a vessel in the triangular trade had placed him in the upper echelons of his profession, there was still one final step to climb. The most prestigious position of all was the captaincy of a monster transatlantic packet ship on the New York-Liverpool route. Asa's older brother John had already reached that position, taking command of the 1,100-ton *Webster* at the end of 1842, and then of the 1,150-ton *Liverpool* a few months later. At the time, the *Liverpool* was the largest of the packet ships sailing to the port of the same name—and a sensation. The New York *Evening Post* reported that her "colossus-like dimensions have been the theme of every tongue, and the admiration of all skilled in ship building." Even if he had not already been ambitious, sibling rivalry would surely have provoked Asa into coveting a similar position.

And in late 1844 he landed one. On October 29, the *Evening Post* carried the first advertisement announcing that "The regular fast packet ship ROSCIUS, Capt. Asa Eldridge, of 1,100 tons" would sail to Liverpool on "her regular day" of November 26th. The *Roscius* was close to the *Liverpool* in size, and had in fact been the biggest American merchant ship ever built when she was launched in 1838.

The race to build ever-larger vessels was a sign of the robust competition in the transatlantic packet-ship industry, which had played a key role in the rapid expansion of trade after the War of 1812. The industry grew out of the frustration of five New York merchants with the wild unpredictability of cargoes' movements by sea. Part of this unpredictability was due to weather conditions and could not be avoided, but that was not the major source of the merchants' frustration. What irked them most were the long and indeterminate delays in departures from port. Traditionally, the normal practice almost everywhere was for vessels to wait until they had a full load before sailing, which made advertised departure times highly unreliable. A merchant or traveler who booked space early on a particular vessel might have to wait a long time for its cargo hold and passenger berths to fill, and even then face further delay if the captain deemed the weather unfavorable.

Seeing an opportunity in this situation, the five merchants decided to launch a line of vessels that would sail at fixed times on predetermined dates, come what may. They announced their intention with an advertisement in the New York *Evening Post* on October 27, 1817:

LINE OF AMERICAN PACKETS
BETWEEN N. YORK & LIVERPOOL

In order to furnish frequent and regular conveyances for GOODS and PASSENGERS, the subscribers have undertaken to establish a line of vessels between NEW-YORK and LIVERPOOL, to sail from each place on a certain day in every month throughout the year.

The following vessels, each about four hundred tons burthen, have been fitted out for this purpose:

Ship AMITY, John Stanton, master,

" COURIER, Wm. Browne, "

> "   PACIFIC, Jno. Williams,   "
> "   JAMES MONROE, –––   "

These ships… are known to be remarkably fast sailers, and their accommodations for passengers are uncommonly extensive and commodious…

… It is also thought, that the regularity of their times of sailing, and the excellent condition in which they deliver their cargoes, will make them very desirable opportunities for the conveyance of goods.

It is intended that this establishment shall commence by the departure of the JAMES MONROE from NEW-YORK on the 5th, and the COURIER from LIVERPOOL on the 1st, of First Month (January) next; and one of the vessels will sail at the same periods from each place in every succeeding month.

A similar advertisement appeared in Liverpool at the same time, with one further and crucial detail spelled out: that ships from the new line would "positively sail, full or not full."

The uncertainty associated with the traditional approach can be illustrated by considering another advertisement in the same issue of the *Evening Post*:

> For LIVERPOOL,
> The British brig ANN, Wm. Scott, master, burthen 190 tons; having the principal part of her cargo engaged, she will positively sail in the course of 10 days. For freight or passage, apply on board…

The same advertisement, with precisely the same wording, ran in every issue of the *Evening Post* until November 10, two weeks later. So much for the promise that the *Ann* would "positively sail" within ten days.

The owners of the new shipping line were much better at keeping their promises. They had advertised that the *James Monroe* would sail from New York on January 5, 1818, and sail on that day she did. No matter that she still had space for a thousand more barrels of cargo and twenty more passengers. No matter that a bitter north-easterly wind was plastering her with snow. The promise had been made and it was kept. At ten o'clock sharp the captain ordered her crew to cast off, and the *James Monroe* eased away from her berth on the South Street waterfront and into the East River, bound for Liverpool. As her fore topsail filled with wind a large black circle was revealed; a smaller version of the same shape decorated the red flag atop her mainmast. The "Black Ball Line" was now in business. In fact, its service had been inaugurated the previous day when the *Courier* had sailed out of Liverpool on the first westbound crossing. (This had originally been advertised as leaving on the first of the month, but by the time the service started, the regular day for the westbound crossings seems to have been changed to the fourth.)

One month later the Line's other pair of ships departed, the *Pacific* sailing from Liverpool on February 4 and the *Amity* from New York the following day. By then the *James Monroe* had already arrived in Liverpool, while the *Courier* was within two weeks of reaching New York on the westbound crossing—always much slower because it was against the prevailing wind and currents. Each was then in position at the beginning of March for her scheduled return to the port she had left two months earlier. As were the *Pacific* and *Amity* when April came around. And so it went on. The Black Ball Line was not only in business but delivering on its key promise: one scheduled sailing in each direction across the Atlantic every month.

Not everyone was convinced. The premise behind the new Line was widely regarded as foolhardy. Although fixed schedules had been successful on the heavily traveled Hudson River between New York and Albany, there was a huge difference between the calm waters of an inland artery and the churning seas of the Atlantic. To incur the cost and risk of a transatlantic voyage without the guaranteed return from a full load seemed like financial suicide.

But the skeptics were proved wrong. Customers loved the certainty of fixed departure times, which allowed them to avoid the cost and inconvenience of indeterminate delays. And they were willing to pay for this certainty. Indeed, to keep up with demand the Black Ball Line added four new and larger vessels to its fleet in 1822, which enabled it to add a second scheduled sailing in each direction every month. That same year also saw the arrival of competition, as other shipowners hoped to emulate the Line's success. The Red Star and Swallowtail Lines each had four ships and scheduled their sailings in the "off" weeks between those of the Black Ball Line. As a result there were now sixteen packet ships shuttling back and forth across the Atlantic on regular schedules, with a departure in each direction every week.

The growth did not stop there. By 1830, thirty-six packet ships were operating scheduled services between the US and Europe, with routes to London and Havre as well as Liverpool. A decade later, the corresponding number was forty-eight.

Beyond its obvious impact on the movement of passengers and cargo, the existence of this fleet also had a dramatic effect on communication between the Old and New Worlds. Until 1866, when the first durable transatlantic telegraph cable went into service, the only way that information could travel across the ocean was by ship. (An earlier cable had carried the first intercontinental telegraph message in 1858 but lasted barely a month before failing.) Newspapers and mail were the most eagerly anticipated items on any incoming vessel. News from the former was immediately reprinted by local newspapers at the ship's destination; news from the latter was vital for businesses and cherished by individuals. But before the advent of the packet lines that news was often very stale, dependent as it was on the sporadic departures of ships that were in no particular hurry. This was especially true in winter, when many vessels stayed in port to avoid the year's worst weather and the added complications of frozen sails and ice-coated rigging. Undaunted by such considerations, however, the packet lines operated year round. And given their regular scheduled departures and the competition between them to record fast crossings, the timeliness of transatlantic communications improved considerably.

The extent of the improvement can be gauged from the midwinter reporting of foreign news by the New York *Evening Post* before and after the packet lines were established. Each time a ship arrived from Europe, excerpts from the newspapers it brought would be printed in the *Evening Post*, often over a period of several days after the ship's arrival. In January 1817, the year before packet service began, such excerpts were scarce. The month began with news from papers dated November 16 that had arrived from Liverpool with the *Pacific* on December 28, forty-two days later. The next European news to reach New York also dated back to November 16 and arrived indirectly: information from French newspapers was reprinted in the *Charleston Courier* on January 1 and then reported in the *Evening Post* on January 9, at which point it was fifty-four days old. That still made it fresher than the only other news to arrive in New York during the entire rest of the month, which came from London papers dated November 19 that arrived on the brig *Traveller* on January 16, fifty-eight days later. On average, therefore, the European news printed in the *Evening Post* during January 1817 was 51.3 days old when it arrived in New York.

The statistics for one particular January could of course give a misleading impression of the midwinter news flow across the Atlantic, because the weather may just have been unusually bad during the month in question.

But the statistics for January 1818—the last month before Black Ball liners began arriving in New York from Liverpool—were not much better than those for the previous year. The *Evening Post* had only three direct arrivals in New York to draw upon for European news, all of them from Liverpool. The average age of their freshest news was 47.3 days. The paper also reprinted news originally received in other ports—from two arrivals in Philadelphia, one in Baltimore and one in Boston—whose average age by the time it appeared in New York was 49.8 days.

Contrast this with the flow of news in January 1830, by which time there were thirty-six packet ships operating between New York and the European ports of Liverpool, London and Havre. No fewer than eight vessels arrived in New York from these ports during the month—four from Liverpool and two each from London and Havre—and the average age of their freshest news was 33.6 days. So while communication was still painfully slow, the development of the packet lines had slashed a full two weeks off the time it took for information from Europe to reach the US.

AS THE TRANSATLANTIC packet business grew, so did the ships that conducted it. While the four original vessels in the Black Ball Line were each around four hundred tons, those added in 1822 were all almost a hundred tons larger. And with the inauguration of the Red Star and Swallowtail Lines that year, competition to claim the largest vessel in service became inevitable. The Black Ball Line was able to hang on to that claim throughout the 1820s, with the 586-ton *Pacific II* followed by the 647-ton *Caledonia*. The Swallowtail Line then surged ahead, its flagship the *Independence* being queen of the ocean in 1835 at 732 tons. As the decade came to an end the crown was held by a newcomer, the Dramatic Line, with the ship that would later become Asa Eldridge's first transatlantic packet, the 1,030-ton *Roscius* (in later years advertised as 1,100 tons). Not to be outdone, by 1845 the Swallowtail Line had reclaimed its bragging rights with the 1,207-ton *Henry Clay,* only to be overtaken by the Red Star Line, whose 1,560-ton *Constellation* was the largest of the packets in 1850. Although by then it was clear that steamships were taking over the major transatlantic routes, the packet Lines were not quite done yet; by 1855 their largest vessel was a massive 1,771 tons, the *Amazon* on the Black X Line's New York-London route. Less than four decades after the Black Ball Line had pioneered packet services across the Atlantic, the vessels operating those services were more than four times larger than the original ships.

Size was not the only attribute of packet ships that increased during this period. Quality and comfort did as well. Asa Eldridge's *Roscius* perfectly illustrates the point. When she was launched in 1838 she prompted the following panegyric in a New York paper—which is quoted extensively because of the valuable detail it also provides about her capacity, layout and amenities:

> It was with more than ordinary feelings of national pride that we yester-day went through and examined this superior specimen of American naval architecture. The Roscius was built by E. K. Collins, and is... by far the largest merchant vessel ever built in this country... She is built entirely of live oak and locust, and put together in a manner calculated to bid defiance to the elements, and outstrip in fleetness the fastest ship that navigates the ocean. Her model combines the principles of strength and beauty in a superlative degree, and her hull is moulded with such consummate skill in its proportions, as to give to the enormous mass of timber the symmetry and grace of a vessel of half her tonnage.... The length of her keel is equal to that of the Constitution frigate, and she is calculated to carry under her decks 3200 bales of cotton. Her cabins are situated upon the main deck, constructed with a regard to comfort and luxury in a most gorgeous style, infinitely superior to those of the Great Western, or indeed any other craft that ever floated. The main cabin is composed of a spacious saloon, extending from the mainmast to the stern, with a range of state rooms on each side, that may be thrown open or enclosed at pleasure. Each state room is provided with two comforta-ble sleeping berths, being ventilated and lighted by a side window to each berth, that may be opened and closed at will, and also lighted from above by two deck lights placed over each state room. These rooms are also furnished with a complete toilet, washstand, closets for clothing, &c. The ladies' saloon or cabin, with its ranges of state rooms, is situated amid ships, and finished in a style of workmanship that may challenge the competition of the world. The state rooms throughout are orna-mented as follows:—Satin wood stiles and pannels [*sic*]—rosewood binding—zebra moulding—blinds to each state room of satin wood, with rose-wood forming—imitation porcelain pilasters between the state rooms, superbly gilded, and polished to a surface like ivory—splendid imitations of inlaid ebony and gold; the whole interior presenting a scene, even in its present unfinished state, of unparalleled magnificence. The furniture and fixtures of the cabins, it is said, will be of the most costly description, and will correspond with the beautiful vessel they are intended to adorn. The Roscius is to sail for Liverpool on the 25th of

View of the New York Quarantine, Staten Island, 1833.

Canning Dock and Custom House, Liverpool, 1842.

The packet ship *New York* of the Black Ball Line.

Classified ad from *Liverpool Mercury*, March 1842.

Classified ad from New York *Evening Post* for Asa Eldridge's first voyage
in command of the *Roscius*, November 1844.

November—a memorable day in the history of New York—and is calculated to accommodate forty passengers. Her officers and crew are to consist of Captain Collins [Asa Eldridge's predecessor] and three mates, thirty seamen before the mast, nine stewards and cooks, and two boys—making, all told, 45 in number.

The references in the opening sentence of this excerpt to "national pride" and "superior specimen of American naval architecture" are telling. To the delight of many Americans, their upstart nation completely dominated the transatlantic trade with Britain, which in most other respects was the world's greatest maritime power. Virtually all of the ships active in this trade were owned and operated by Americans; vessels from other countries simply could not compete.

The article's passing and unfavorable comment on a British ship called the *Great Western* is also significant. This might simply reflect the author's obvious wish to trumpet the superiority of American shipbuilding, but may also indicate his anxiety about a feature of the *Great Western* that was far more important than her country of origin: she was powered by steam, the very first steamship to enter regular transatlantic service. She had completed her maiden voyage to New York just a few months earlier, in a fast time that boded poorly for the future of sailing packets. Her arrival on the Atlantic signaled the start of a battle between sail and steam that would last for several decades—and which would have major implications for both Asa Eldridge and the owner of the *Roscius*.

For the moment, though, American sailing packets reigned supreme, a fact that was of considerable concern to the British government. In its 1844 report to Parliament, the Select Committee on Merchant Shipping identified a variety of factors that contributed to this dominance. These included the superior design and construction of American ships, better adherence to published schedules, skilled captains capable of driving their vessels hard, and thorough maintenance. With these advantages, the Yankee sailing packets could complete voyages more quickly and deliver cargoes in better condition—and so command higher freight rates, with fatter profits for their owners.

The most famous of those owners was the man who had built the *Roscius*, Edward Knight Collins. The *Roscius* was the flagship of his Dramatic Line, so called because all of its vessels were named after famous theatrical figures. Collins had founded the Line in 1836 when he was thirty-four. This was not his first venture into the packet trade, although the first spanning the

Atlantic. As a partner in the family shipping business established by his father, he had extensive experience from two prior Lines: one between New York and Mexico that he and his father had started, and another between New York and Louisiana that he had taken over. Having grown up on Cape Cod (although in Truro rather than Yarmouth) he may have known the Eldridge family, and certainly showed a repeated willingness to hire the seafaring brothers. At various times, all three of them worked as captains for him.

"Dramatic" was the perfect adjective not just for his transatlantic shipping line but also for E.K. Collins himself. He was a short man who wore tall hats to try and disguise the fact, and was known for his loud mouth and showmanship. His approach to business was equally brash; he might almost have invented the mantra "bigger, better, faster," so enthusiastically did he embrace it. Having started the Dramatic Line in 1836 with the relatively modest *Shakespeare*, a mere 142 feet long and 747 tons, he then added three identical ships that were considerably larger, the *Garrick, Sheridan* and *Siddons*—each 158 feet and 895 tons. Finally came the *Roscius*, the 168-foot 1,030-ton monster that was described in detail above and emphatically demonstrated Collins' commitment to "bigger and better."

When it came to "faster," Collins had his own counter-intuitive approach that turned out to be a winner. Against the advice of his shipbuilders, Collins ignored the conventional wisdom that a V-shaped bottom was required for a ship to move quickly through the water, and built his vessels with relatively flat-bottomed hulls instead. His insistence on this feature came from his experience with the Louisiana Line, whose ships all had flat bottoms so that they could negotiate the shallow bar at the mouth of the Mississippi. Surprisingly, they also proved quick and stable on the open sea between New Orleans and New York. Those same qualities were retained in the much larger vessels Collins now built, with the added benefit that the flat-bottomed hull could accommodate significantly more cargo. The Dramatic liners also carried huge areas of sail on extremely tall masts. The width and height of the sails on the *Roscius*, for example, were comparable to those of the famous clipper ship *Flying Cloud*, which was built over a decade later with an obsessive emphasis on speed—her mission being to shorten the voyage to California during the Gold Rush.

As Collins expected, his approach did result in "faster." In 1839, the first full year of service for the *Roscius*, the Dramatic Line's average voyage times across the Atlantic were significantly better than those of the nearest competing Line: two days shorter in the eastbound direction (20.12 *vs.* 22.12 days), and three in the slower westbound direction against the prevailing winds and currents (30.12 *vs.* 33.17 days). The superiority of the Dramatic liners was acknowledged by no less an authority than Commodore Hull, widely revered for guiding the USS *Constitution* to several victories over the Royal Navy during the War of 1812. Having seen the *Siddons* and *Roscius* in action, he declared them capable of out-sailing any ship in the US Navy.

Size, luxury and speed did not come cheaply. The *Roscius* cost $100,000 to build, $40,000 more than any other packet ship before her. This typified Collins' investment style: he was willing to make much bolder bets than anyone else in the shipping industry. And in the case of the Dramatic Line this paid off; as they made their faster voyages across the Atlantic, his ships were able to carry more cargo than their competitors because of their flat-bottomed design, and to attract more high-paying passengers with their luxurious accommodation.

One other ingredient was crucial for Collins' success: the quality of the Dramatic Line's captains. Here again, Collins' philosophy paid dividends. In any industry the best talent usually migrates towards the highest-paying jobs, and the compensation structure for transatlantic shipmasters would have made the Dramatic Line a particularly attractive employer. Packet captains were already very well paid as it was, typically earning about $5,000 a year at a time when the average annual *per capita* income in the US was around $110. Much of their compensation came from performance-related payments. Their basic salary was only around $40 a month, but on top of this they usually kept all of the fees for carrying mail, and received about 5 per cent of the revenue from cargoes and 25 per cent of the fares paid by passengers. For captains in Collins' employ, these last two items would have been especially significant; the larger carrying capacity of the Dramatic liners and the appeal of their luxurious quarters to passengers would have translated into significantly greater income for their skippers.

Collins was careful in the men he chose to enjoy such rewards. In the case of the *Roscius*, the largest ship with the highest earning potential, he initially kept the rewards within his own family. For her first six years in the fleet she was under the command of Edward's uncle, Captain John Collins.

On one of her very first voyages, Captain Collins distinguished himself in a manner that must have greatly enhanced the reputation of the Dramatic Line. On December 5, 1839, during typically atrocious weather on an eastward passage to Liverpool, he came across another vessel in severe distress. The *Scotia* was carrying timber from Québec to Glasgow but had been wrecked by the storm; her masts were broken and she had seventeen feet of water in the hold. Observing her plight, Collins tried to approach close enough to rescue the crew, but was forced to take evasive action when the crippled vessel lurched out of control towards the *Roscius* in the heavy seas. With night falling, he hove to about a mile away from the *Scotia* and signaled with a lantern to her crew, who then took to the churning seas in two small boats and rowed towards the *Roscius*. As each one came alongside, Collins somehow managed to synchronize the pitching of his vessel with the wallowing of the boat long enough to rescue its desperate occupants. Barely had they scrambled on board when a violent nor'easter blew up that would have made the rescue impossible. All twenty-four members of the *Scotia*'s crew were saved, and would surely have perished otherwise.

The goodwill generated by this rescue was amplified by the publicity it received when the *Roscius* arrived at her destination. One of her passengers, a Dr. Madden, provided a detailed account to the *Liverpool Mercury*. In addition to reciting the facts of the rescue, he commended Captain Collins in the strongest terms for putting humanitarian above commercial considerations. From the phrasing of his commendation, Dr. Madden was clearly very much aware of the emerging threat to the future of the packet-ship industry from the recent arrival of steamships on the transatlantic route. The newly built steamer *British Queen*, the largest ship in the world, had been scheduled to leave New York less than a week after the *Roscius*, and Captain Collins was understandably eager to arrive in Liverpool before her. But to quote Dr. Madden's account in the *Liverpool Mercury*:

> It is impossible sufficiently to commend the conduct of Captain Collins: his anxiety to reach Liverpool before the steamer, which was to have sailed six days after us, made every moment of importance; we had, moreover, seventy steerage passengers and twenty-one in the cabin; and to forgo taking advantage of a fair wind, and to lay to for a night in a heavy sea, with every appearance of an approaching gale, was a determination which, I greatly fear, many a master of a ship would have found great difficulty coming to. Captain Collins, however, made this resolution prompt, and without any expression of impatience at the detention it occurred.

These comments must have done wonders for the image of the Dramatic Line, not just its captain. So too must the renewed publicity Collins received a month later. The Underwriters' Association awarded him the freedom of their rooms in Liverpool, apparently such an honor that the Association's citation was printed in full in the *Liverpool Mercury*. And a few weeks later, his receipt of a gold medal from the Humane Society was covered by newspapers as far away as London and Kent.

Dr. Madden's comments were revealing not just about the character of Captain Collins, but also about the pressures under which he and his fellow shipmasters operated. The never-ending drive to push complex sailing ships to the limit of their performance under all manner of conditions placed captains under enormous strain. The average tenure of a packet-ship commander was only about five years. Some were replaced because of declining performance due to burnout, while others made their fortunes and then opted for an easier life, often in the form of a desk job on shore.

Whether for one of these reasons or because his nephew really did need help, in 1844 Captain Collins agreed to Edward's request and took up a managerial position in the Dramatic Line's New York office. The *Roscius* needed a new skipper. Collins had already shown his faith in two of the Eldridge brothers in his Louisiana Line, having entrusted the *Huntsville* and *Yazoo* to John and the *Gaston* to Oliver. Neither of these brothers was available, however. John had recently joined the rival Blue Swallowtail Line as master of the *Liverpool* on the transatlantic route, while Oliver had just accepted command of the *Coquette* in the China trade after briefly serving as John's first mate on the *Liverpool*.

But then there was Asa, who by now had over a dozen years' experience in international trade, including one record voyage to India and several years plying back and forth between US ports and Liverpool. An approach was made, negotiations were initiated, a deal was struck, and Asa Eldridge became the new skipper of the *Roscius*. So began a working relationship that would ultimately have enormous consequences for both men.

THE *ROSCIUS* first sailed out of New York under Asa Eldridge's command in November 1844. Over the next four years she made a total of twelve roundtrips across the Atlantic with him at the helm. The Dramatic Line offered one departure in each direction across the Atlantic every month, one ship leaving Liverpool on the 11th and another sailing from New York on the 26th. Each vessel operated on a four-month cycle, with just over six weeks between the date it left New York and the date of its return sailing from Liverpool, and close to eleven weeks between the latter date and the next departure from New York. Having initiated his command of the *Roscius* by sailing out of New York on November 26, 1844, Eldridge therefore began his first return voyage from Liverpool on January 11, 1845, and his second eastbound passage on March 26 of that year. And so on.

While these transatlantic crossings may have been repetitive, they were never routine. Westbound voyages almost always involved a battle against headwinds, making them ten or eleven days longer on average than crossings in the opposite direction. And whichever direction a ship was headed, the notoriously stormy North Atlantic was quite capable of conjuring up extreme peril at short notice.

Like Captain Collins before him, Asa Eldridge saw his fair share of that peril. 1846 was a particularly bad year in this regard. After leaving Liverpool on January 13 for her first westbound crossing of the year, the *Roscius* was hit by four separate violent storms and bitterly cold conditions. At various points in the crossing, heavy seas smashed in the bulwarks, the cabin windows and the main hatches, letting in large quantities of water. Canvas and rigging froze solid, making it impossible to perform the normal and necessary furling of sails as winds grew stronger. As a result, the top sections of all three masts were blown down, whereupon they were (to quote an excerpt of the ship's log in the *New York Herald)* "thumping to and fro, cutting and chafing the spars and rigging, and all the sails blowing from the gaskets to atoms, making, upon the whole, a dismal scene." During a period of over five weeks between January 20th and March 1st the *Roscius* made almost no progress westward, and was forced to go south so as to thaw the ice on the rigging and sails. She eventually arrived in New York on March 7th, almost two months after leaving Liverpool. Three other packet ships that arrived on the same day reported very similar experiences. All four vessels had been feared lost. So too were the dozen or more packet ships that were still out on the Atlantic beyond the time they would normally have arrived. One of the ships still out there was John Eldridge's *Liverpool.* Fortunately she made it to New York a few days later, as did all of the others.

Seven months later, on her third and final westbound passage of the year, the *Roscius* ran into a severe gale that lasted for sixty hours. She had 450 people on board at the time. By keeping just one closely reefed sail aloft Eldridge was able to ride out the storm, but then encountered another ship in great distress. The *Cromwell,* sailing from Québec to Liverpool with a heavy load of timber, was waterlogged beyond recovery. Under Eldridge's direction a lifeboat from the *Roscius* made four trips to the doomed ship and was able to rescue all but one of the thirty crewmembers—the exception being an officer who had been grievously injured by a log during the storm. Like Captain Collins before him on the *Roscius*, Asa Eldridge had added to his own and the Dramatic Line's reputation with a skillful act of mercy.

THE STRENGTH of that reputation must have been reassuring for the owner as he made a move worthy of the Line's name. On Monday April 5, 1847, the following advertisement appeared in the New York *Evening Post*:

> FOR SALE—The Liverpool Line of Packets, consisting of the ships SIDDONS, SHERIDAN, GARRICK and ROSCIUS. They have all been newly coppered, new rigged, and put in perfect order within the last twelve months. The great superiority of these ships is to [sic] well known to need description. Apply to EDWD. K. COLLINS, 56 South st [sic].

Dramatic this move may have been, but hasty it was not. Collins had been working for more than six years to start a new steamship line, and the sale of the Dramatic Line was a necessary step in that process. As far back as 1838, even before the *Roscius* was launched, the maiden voyage of the *Great Western* had signaled that steam would one day replace sail on the Atlantic. For various reasons this took longer to happen than some observers had originally imagined; as will be discussed in the next chapter, the impact of steamers on the most important transatlantic route, between New York and Liverpool, was relatively modest for most of the next decade. The far-sighted Collins, however, was quick to recognize that steam power would eventually take over. In 1840 he confided to a friend that "I will build steamers that shall make the passage from New York to Europe in ten days or less"—an ambitious vision when the average crossing by a sailing packet still took twenty-two days.

As Collins considered how to start his own steamship line, he was attracted by the business strategy adopted by one of the existing companies, which had secured a lucrative contract from the British Admiralty to carry mail across the Atlantic. This was effectively a substantial government subsidy that gave the company a significant advantage over its competitors.

Anxious to compete on an equal footing, Collins quickly set out to win a similar subsidy from the US government for the steamship line he was planning. He first proposed such a subsidy to Congress in 1841, taking a leaf out of his British rival's playbook by offering to build steamers that could serve as warships if necessary. Congress was not impressed, however, by the hectoring tone of his proposal, and rejected it.

Six years later, though, the story was different. The subsidized British line was now the clear leader in transatlantic steam, and a major threat to the long-established American dominance of the cargo and passenger trade across the Atlantic. Moreover, Collins had emerged as much the most likely contender to repel this threat. When Congress finally awarded him a mail contract in early 1847, he needed to raise additional capital to build the steamships he had promised. And so, as noted above, he put the Dramatic Line up for sale.

The sale did not go smoothly. Impatient to move on to his next venture, Collins scheduled an auction for July 20, 1847, little more than three months after first advertising his intention to sell. Somewhat caustically, the *Baltimore Sun* commented that Collins "abandons the business with a fortune, to make another and larger one out of the contracts he has with the government." Two days after the auction, the *Sun* reported that a firm called H. & D. Cotheal had purchased the Dramatic Line for $174,000 "for the whole." The transaction must not have proceeded as planned, however, because in August 1848—more than a full year later—Collins placed another ad offering "his interest" in the Line for sale.

This time matters did proceed smoothly. Within three weeks of the new ad appearing, the *New York Shipping List* reported that Collins had disposed of the aforementioned interest for "a round sum" to Spofford, Tileston & Co., who were "well known in this community as the agents of the Charleston line of steamers." The new owners were to assume control of the *Sheridan* in New York immediately, and of the other three ships as they arrived back from Liverpool. At the same time, Collins had also sold his New Orleans line of packets to another buyer. The *Shipping List* was enthusiastic about the completion of these transactions, noting that "Mr. Collins... will now devote his untrammeled energies to the successful establishment of his line of steamships between this port and Liverpool; he will, we are sure, meet with success in this important undertaking—at any rate, we know he will deserve it."

The sale of the Dramatic Line was a turning point not just for Collins but also for Asa Eldridge. At the time of the sale in early September he was in Liverpool preparing the *Roscius* for the return leg of her regular summer voyage, which proved to be his last as her commander. She arrived back in

New York on October 13, and within weeks the new owners were advertising a different captain for her next departure: Asa's older brother, John. The owners were perhaps confused, however, about which Eldridge was which, because John was still master of the *Liverpool* for a rival line. The brother they had actually hired was Oliver, the youngest of the three, and he it was who took command of the *Roscius* when she sailed out of New York on November 26.

Subsequent events suggest that Asa left the *Roscius* voluntarily to pursue a major new venture of his own. Had he been fired, he would hardly have chosen the partners he did for this venture: Spofford and Tileston, the new owners of the Dramatic Line. Nor would he have agreed to come back and captain the *Garrick*, which he did for two voyages in 1849 and one in 1850—presumably because the new venture was taking longer to organize than he had anticipated. The third of these voyages was not completed until April 12, 1850, when the last of many entries documenting his movements for the Dramatic Line appeared in the New York *Evening Post*: "*ARRIVED THIS FORENOON*. Packet ship GARRICK, Eldridge, for [*sic*] Liverpool. March 14th." (A separate notice in the same issue about passengers arriving on the *Garrick* makes it clear that the voyage was "from" rather than "for" Liverpool.)

Although Asa's association with the Dramatic Line was then over, the Eldridge family's continued for a while longer. Oliver remained with the Line until 1852, mostly on the *Roscius* but occasionally on the *Garrick*. The oldest brother, John, also served the Line briefly. His nine-year tenure on the Blue Swallowtail Line's *Liverpool* came to an end in 1851, and he took command of the *Roscius* on her first voyage of the following year. She thus enjoyed the rare distinction of having been captained by all three of the Eldridge brothers.

The *Roscius* had in fact achieved that distinction several years earlier, thanks indirectly to an event greatly feared by all seafarers—an outbreak of cholera. The outbreak occurred on the *Liverpool* as John Eldridge was bringing her home to New York in March 1849. In the confined space of a ship, cholera was particularly deadly. Forty of the *Liverpool*'s passengers died and many more became severely ill. When the ship reached New York she was immediately placed in quarantine. While the passengers and crew would have been released fairly quickly after new cases stopped appearing, the ship herself appears to have been out of commission for several months. So when

Oliver Eldridge needed a deputy to take the *Roscius* on her summer voyage to Liverpool, John was able and willing to step in for him.

That voyage and the one he made early in 1852 were John's only turns at the helm of Asa's former command. He completed the second of these on May 24, 1852, and when Oliver arrived back in New York on the *Garrick* a few weeks later the long involvement of the Eldridges with the Dramatic Line came to an end. Shortly thereafter, so too did the long history of Collins' original ships with the Line. In 1853 Spofford & Tileston decided that they needed even larger vessels to remain competitive, and sold the original Dramatic liners to James Foster Jr., who had been a part-owner during the Collins era.

One sad footnote to the history of these liners is that the *Roscius* was lost at sea in 1860. Almost within reach of New York on a return crossing from Liverpool, she was hit by an enormous sea that stove in her bulwarks, shifted her cargo, and caused her to spring a major leak. So began two terrifying days with the crew manning the pumps continuously in a losing battle against the inrushing water. Just as they reached the point of exhaustion, a passing ship arrived in response to the distress rockets they had fired, and all on board were rescued. A few hours later, the *Roscius* slipped under the surface and was gone forever. Fittingly, given her history with the family, her last voyage was presided over by a close relative of the Eldridge brothers: Captain Charles Hallet, grandson of Captain Ansel Hallet, the uncle who had (very likely) been Asa's first mentor at sea.

The *Roscius*' load for that final voyage showed how far she had fallen. Her cargo was coal, one of the least profitable of all commodities, and she had no passengers except the wives of two crew members. The fine goods and first-class clientele that had once generated handsome profits for the sailing packets had long since migrated to steamships. That E.K. Collins played a prominent role in this transition is well known; almost any history of steam power on the Atlantic will include an account of the "Collins Line" he established. That another alumnus of the Dramatic Line tried to compete directly with him has been almost completely overlooked—an omission that will shortly be redressed. But to set the context, a brief history is in order of the transatlantic steam industry and of Collins' own efforts to join it.

4

THE ADVENT OF STEAM

TIMING IS EVERYTHING, so the saying goes.

At first blush, the timing of Edward Collins' move into steamships might seem poor. By the time he sold his sailing packets in 1848 steamers had been crossing the Atlantic regularly for more than a decade. When they first began doing so he had not even finished building the Dramatic Line; recall from the previous chapter that a steamer called the *Great Western* had beaten the *Roscius* into regular service by several months. And now, ten years later, he was just beginning to build his first steamships? A little late, it might seem.

Actually not. Although they had been around since 1838, transatlantic steamers were only now becoming a serious threat to the sailing packets. As yet there was just one firmly established operator, and no American presence on the world's busiest maritime route between New York and Liverpool. The market was therefore ripe for new entrants. An account of its early years will explain why.

The first serious advocate for steam power on the Atlantic was a London-based American called Junius Smith. Appalled by the fifty-four days it had taken him to reach New York on a sailing packet in 1832, he began seeking support on both sides of the ocean for a transatlantic steamship company. His original plan was to install British-built steam engines into American-built ships, neatly combining the different technological superiorities of the two countries. But unable to secure the necessary cooperation across the Atlantic, he settled for a purely British enterprise. The only trace this bore of his original ambition was its name: the British & American Steam Navigation Company (henceforth called the "B&A" for convenience). There was no trace of bilateralism, however, in the name chosen for the company's first vessel. She was to be called the *Royal Victoria*, in homage to the British crown princess.

Despite the difficulties Smith had experienced in winning support for his ideas, the B&A soon faced competition. This originated from an unlikely source: a railway company. The Great Western Railway had been founded in 1833 to build a rail link between London and the port of Bristol on the west coast of England. Bristol had long been the main hub for England's trade with North America, but was rapidly losing business to Liverpool. The rail link with London was seen as a way to restore Bristol's pre-eminent position in transatlantic trade. This goal appears to have been the inspiration for a jocular suggestion made by the company's young chief engineer at a Board meeting in 1835. During a lively discussion about the length and cost of the new railway, the engineer suddenly asked a seemingly outrageous question. Instead of terminating the line at Bristol, why not extend it all the way across the Atlantic with a steamboat sailing to New York?

At least one Board member took the idea seriously, and began exploring it further with the engineer. Since neither knew much about ships they consulted a former naval officer, who then involved a shipbuilder. Together the four men formed the Great Western Steam Ship Company ("GWS"), and drew up plans for a steamer that would be capable of crossing the Atlantic. Like the company, the ship was to be called the *Great Western*. And though his main contribution to her design was the engine, the man who originally proposed building her is often given credit for the entire ship. This overly generous attribution presumably reflects his later fame as one of the greatest engineers in history. For the man in question was Isambard Kingdom Brunel.

The B&A and GWS were now locked in a race to be first onto the Atlantic. Initially the B&A seemed to have the advantage, placing their order for the *Royal Victoria* with shipbuilders ahead of the corresponding move by the GWS. But their decision to take the lower of two bids for the ship's engines proved unwise, as their chosen provider went bankrupt. The delays caused by switching to the more expensive bidder—who presumably was less committed to an aggressive schedule than he would have been as the B&A's first choice—allowed the GWS to surge ahead. Meanwhile, the death of King William IV had elevated Britain's crown princess to the throne, causing the *Royal Victoria* to be renamed the *British Queen*.

Delayed but not defeated, the B&A found another way to compete. When it became clear that the *Great Western* would be ready long before their own flagship, they chartered a steamer called the *Sirius* that had recently been built for the route between London and Cork. Loaded to the gunwales with coal, she steamed out of the Irish port for New York four days before the *Great Western* left from Avonmouth (Bristol). Even with this early lead, victory for the *Sirius* was far from assured. Despite sailing from a port 250 miles more distant, the bigger and more powerful *Great Western* almost caught up with her. The crew of the *Sirius* had to resort to desperate measures to stay ahead, burning furniture, spars and a mast after the supply of coal ran out. But their efforts paid off. When the *Sirius* reached New York on the morning of April 23, 1838, she was still a few hours ahead of the *Great Western*. She and the B&A could claim victory.

The *Great Western* could of course claim to have made the faster crossing, and indeed the shortest-ever westward passage across the Atlantic. No sailing packet had ever reached New York from Europe in less than seventeen days; she had needed only fifteen. Even the nineteen days taken by the supposedly short-haul *Sirius* had rarely been bettered. One of the few sailing packets with a faster time on record was the Dramatic Line's *Garrick*, which had reached New York from Liverpool in eighteen days on her maiden voyage in 1836. As it happened, the *Garrick* was also the first Dramatic liner to sail westward after the race between the *Sirius* and *Great Western*; on that occasion her crossing took twenty-one days, still fast for a sailing packet but slower than both of the steamers.

Unfortunately for the B&A, the ruse that had enabled them to claim victory in the race against the GWS was not sustainable. Whereas the *Great Western* was able to continue immediately with regular ocean crossings, the *Sirius* was too small and too expensive to charter beyond her first two roundtrips across the Atlantic. The B&A then had to wait another year before the *British Queen* was ready for service. By that time a third English company had swooped in ahead of them. Copying the B&A's example, the Transatlantic Steamship Company had jumpstarted their service with a chartered coastal steamer, the *Royal William II*, which sailed from Liverpool to New York in July 1838. Unlike the B&A, the Transatlantic did not have to wait long for their own purpose-built steamer to be completed; within three months the aptly named *Liverpool* took over from the *Royal William II*. So when the *British Queen* finally entered service in July 1839, the B&A had to settle for third place in the race to establish regular steamer service across the Atlantic.

On her maiden voyage the *British Queen* reached New York in sixteen days from England, which was longer than the *Great Western* had taken the previous year, but respectable in view of the strong headwinds she faced for most of the voyage. The slowing effect of those winds can be gauged from that month's scheduled crossing by the Dramatic Line, whose *Sheridan* sailed a few days after the *British Queen* and needed thirty-three days to reach New York.

A year after the *British Queen*'s debut, in July 1840, yet another British steamship company joined the transatlantic club. This one was different in several important respects. The first was its route, linking Liverpool and Boston via Halifax, Nova Scotia. The second was the contract it had secured from the British government to carry mail between these ports, which was the reason for Halifax being on the route—as will shortly be explained. And the third was the fleet it had built: not just a single ship but four, of nearly identical design. The need and a good part of the money for these ships came from the mail contract, which required two crossings a month in each direction for most of the year and one a month during winter. The name of the new enterprise reflected this commitment: the British and North American Royal Mail Steamship Company. But it quickly became known by the name of its Canadian founder, Samuel Cunard. The legendary Cunard Line had been born.

The fact that the first four transatlantic steamship companies were all British was no accident. The British had been leaders in steam-engine technology ever since the start of the industrial revolution, and now saw their strength in this area as a way to break the near-monopoly of transatlantic trade by American sailing ships. Britannia may have "ruled the waves" for a good part of the country's history, but had been unable to match the upstart shipbuilders and shipmasters across the Atlantic. Steam power offered the opportunity to reclaim the ocean and a bigger share of the trade it conveyed.

Pride and profit were not the only issues at stake. The American dominance was also considered a potential threat to national security. Mail was the only means of communication across the Atlantic, and most of it was being carried by American ships—a situation that might place British interests at risk if relations with the US were ever to break down again. And although the British government did operate a monthly mail service between Falmouth and North America, the armed sailing brigs on this service could not compete with the speed or frequency of the packet ships. Recognizing this situation, in 1836 a parliamentary committee decided that the service should be contracted out to a private company—which would of course enjoy an advantage over its competitors because of the funding it received under the contract.

The responsibility for implementing this decision rested with the Admiralty, which already had significant experience with steamships in the Royal Navy. And by the time the agency was ready to solicit bids from the private sector in late 1838, the *Great Western* had proved that British steamers could outperform American sailing packets on the Atlantic. So when the "DEPARTMENT of the COMPTROLLER for VICTUALLING and TRANSPORT SERVICES" issued a notice on behalf of "The Commissioners for executing the office of Lord High Admiral" on November 7, 1838, its preference for steam was unambiguous:

> STEAM VESSELS required for CONVEYING Her MAJESTY'S MAILS and DESPATCHES between ENGLAND and HALIFAX (NOVA SCOTIA), and also between England and Halifax and New York.

The "STEAM VESSELS" in question would be required to transport mail across the Atlantic once a month in each direction, and were to be "of not less than 300 horses [*sic*] power each." Tenders were to be submitted by Saturday, the 15th of December, barely more than six weeks later. The notice stated clearly that "No tender will be received after 2 o'clock on the day of treaty," and that every submission "must also express when and where the vessels will be ready for survey, and when they will be completely ready for sea."

Halifax might seem a strange choice as the first destination for the government's privatized mail service, but was home to both a major Royal Navy base and a large population of families so loyal to the Crown that they had moved north from the US after independence. Both seemed especially important after two recent rebellions in other parts of Canada.

As it happened, Halifax was also the home of Samuel Cunard, who grew up in one of those loyalist families. Cunard had been dreaming for some time of establishing a transatlantic steamship company, but did not learn of the Admiralty's solicitation until news of it arrived from England in January 1839— several weeks after the deadline for submission of tenders. Regardless, he took the next ship to England to see what he could do.

Once there he discovered that the Admiralty had already rejected the two tenders it had received. The two unsuccessful bidders were the GWS and the St. George Steam Packet Company, the latter being the owners of the steamship *Sirius*, the vessel that had raced the *Great Western* across the Atlantic under charter to the B&A. Both companies had offered to provide monthly mail service between Halifax and their home ports (Bristol and Cork respectively) for £45,000 a year, but neither could do so soon enough for the Admiralty's liking. In each case the issue was the time required to build ships for the new service. The GWS, for example, had projected that the three new steamers it proposed to build might take two years to complete.

So even though the tender process was supposedly over, Cunard was able to use his excellent connections in London to submit a late bid of his own. His experience certainly qualified him to do so. He had been in the shipping business all of his working life, spanning more than thirty years, and had operated the British mail service between Boston, Halifax and Newfoundland for over two decades. Since 1825 he had been the Halifax agent of the world-renowned East India Company. And in 1830 he had played a prominent role in forming the Halifax and Québec Steam Boat Company, and then in commissioning its first and only steamship, the *Royal William*. Although this venture was unsuccessful, the *Royal William* became one of the first steamships ever to cross the Atlantic, making a one-off voyage to England in 1833 to be sold there as a coastal steamer.

Cunard's original vision for the mail service was much more ambitious than either of the competing bids—and indeed than the Admiralty's expectations. To steal the business from the sailing packets he wanted to offer the same weekly service that they did, not the monthly service for which the Admiralty had requested tenders. When it became clear, however, that this would cost more than the government was willing to pay, he scaled back his ambition and submitted a proposal for twice-monthly service. To shave time and cost off the US leg of the service, he would operate it to and from Boston rather than New York. And crucially, he would do all of this for £55,000 a year and begin service within twelve months. Compared with the GWS and the St. George, he was thus offering to provide twice the service in half the lead-time, and asking only £10,000 more in annual compensation. Not surprisingly the Admiralty accepted his proposal, over the strenuous protests of the GWS.

Now began a frantic few months for Cunard: dealing with shipbuilders and engineers in Glasgow, Scotland, to design and negotiate prices for four steamers and their engines, then raising much of the capital to construct these ships from the same people and their networks. Finally in June he was ready to sign the contact with the Admiralty, which specified that service would begin in May of the following year.

In the event he missed that deadline, but not by much. Barely five weeks after the end of the promised month, his first ship steamed out of Liverpool. By a strange coincidence her departure provided patriotic symbolism on both sides of the Atlantic: her name was *Britannia,* and she sailed on July 4, 1840. But symbolism aside, her maiden voyage was much more favorable for her namesake country than its independent offspring. Britain now had four transatlantic steamship companies, America none.

The one-sidedness of this scorecard was not due solely to Britain's lead in steam-engine technology. American complacency also played a major part. After two decades of bossing the Atlantic with their large fleet of superior sailing packets, most US shipowners found it hard to imagine that a handful of smelly and smoky steamers could be much of a threat. Dismissively, they referred to the new competition as "tea kettles."

And for a while their complacency seemed justified. For several years, the British steamship companies had relatively little impact on transatlantic trade. Two of the three that sailed to New York went out of business quickly, and the third had just a single ship in service for most of its limited existence. By the end of 1846 the Cunard Line was the only one of the original four still operating—but with its American base in Boston, it had little effect on the flow of passengers and cargo between Liverpool and New York.

This was in spite of the clear performance advantage of steamships. The fast times recorded by the *Great Western* and *Sirius* in their initial race across the Atlantic proved to be no fluke. In 1839, the first full year of steamship service, the three companies operating to New York cut the crossing time from England by half. On average, the *Great Western, Liverpool* and *British Queen* completed the crossing in a mere 17 days, compared with the 34.12 days taken by their wind-powered competitors. Even on the easier eastbound crossing the steamers saved a full week, averaging 15.42 days from New York to England rather than 22.1.

While clearly faster, however, the early steamships still had many limitations. These were not the sleek ocean liners of later decades; they bore about as much resemblance to those highly evolved forms of transport as the original horseless carriage did to the modern car. Indeed, like the horseless carriage these vehicles were essentially modified versions of their immediate predecessors, with only modest changes to accommodate their new drivetrains. Thus they had wooden hulls and an almost full complement of masts and sails, with room made below deck to accommodate a steam engine coupled to paddle wheels on either side of the midship area. Further large areas below deck were devoted to the coal and freshwater supplies needed for the engine. And therein lay the major weakness of these vessels: their propulsive machinery was not only expensive to build and to operate, but also consumed much of the space that on a sailing ship could be devoted to income-generating cargo. So although their speed allowed owners to charge higher prices and make more frequent crossings, the early steamships were not particularly profitable—as the Transatlantic Steamship Company quickly discovered, surviving for only eighteen months before suspending operations at the end of 1839.

Nor were these vessels any less vulnerable to accidents at sea, which hastened the demise of the other two companies operating steamers to New York. First to go was the B&A, which folded in 1841 after its second steamer, the *President*, was lost at sea with 136 people on board. The GWS lasted another five years, relocating the *Great Western* from Bristol to Liverpool so she could compete more effectively with the sailing packets, and then making a reasonable profit from her operations. What killed the company was its second steamer, the *Great Britain*. This leviathan creation of Brunel was the first-ever propeller-driven ship with an iron hull, and was by far the largest vessel on the ocean when she was completed in 1845. But she had taken six years to build instead of the twelve months originally projected, at a cost massively greater than Brunel had estimated. The expense continued during her first year of service, during which she required multiple repairs and modifications because of design flaws. So when she ran aground off the coast of Ireland in September 1846—just fifteen months after her maiden voyage— the GWS simply had no money left to deal with the loss of revenue and the cost of re-floating her. Another company took on that task a year later, by which time the GWS was defunct. Ironically, after two major refits the *Great Britain* became a stalwart on the England-Australia route, and despite a checkered history thereafter, survives to this day as a museum ship in Bristol.

The *Great Western* continued to operate for a couple of months after the *Great Britain* ran aground, but left New York for the very last time on

November 26, 1846. Presumably because this was Thanksgiving Day, an American ship that would normally have left on that date pushed back its departure until early the following week: the *Roscius*, with Asa Eldridge at the helm. While the *Great Western* easily beat him to Liverpool, she never again made the same crossing. So by the time the *Roscius* arrived some days later, Eldridge and his fellow packet captains had the all-important "Atlantic railroad" between New York and Liverpool to themselves once again. For the first time in eight years, there was no steamship operating to a regular schedule on this route.

Even as their renewed monopoly began, however, the packet skippers knew it would not last for long. Three of the original steamship companies may now have foundered, but the Cunard Line was still very much alive. And not just alive, but preparing to challenge the packets directly by offering service between Liverpool and New York.

In its early years the Line had struggled financially, as Cunard discovered that his operating costs were much higher than the payments he had negotiated from the British government. But after sharing his figures with the Admiralty and pleading hardship, he had twice won increases in those payments. And while his steam-based competitors stumbled and the sailing packets engaged in a price war, he did neither. Rather, he established a reputation for speed, safety and dependability that allowed him to maintain high prices and attract more cargo business, eventually reaching profitability.

Between 1840 and 1845 his ships made a total of 110 trips across the Atlantic in an average time of 14.8 days. Even the New York press was forced to admire the Line's "regularity almost unexpected and wholly unsurpassed." This was achieved without a single loss of life among passengers or crewmembers—a vital statistic at a time of great public concern over the safety of steamships, following the loss of the *President* and explosions on various coastal steamers. (Not that the Line's safety record was perfect. One ship had sunk after hitting a reef in dense fog, but was close enough to land that all on board were rescued. And eight crewmembers on smaller vessels had died in collisions with "Cunarders.")

By 1845 Cunard was importing over a million dollars' worth of freight into Boston, up from a mere three thousand dollars' worth in the second half of 1840. And his fare for the Atlantic crossing was $120, only $5 less than it had been when he started out; the comparable fare for "cabin" (first class) accommodation on the *Roscius* had fallen from $140 in 1840 to $75 in 1843 because of a price war between the packet lines. Although it then recovered to $100 for a couple of years, by 1847 this fare was back down to $75 on the packets, whereas Cunard was still able to charge $120.

In sharp contrast to most owners of the American sailing packets, Cunard did not allow success to make him complacent. He was well aware of the efforts by E. K. Collins (the one packet owner who was clearly *not* complacent) to copy his own example by securing a mail contract from the US government that would subsidize a new line of steamships. And as he confided to one of his partners, he was convinced that once the Americans got involved they would "introduce all of our improvements, together with their own" and "be alive to every thing."

His anxiety could therefore only have grown when politicians in the US finally began to show interest in subsidizing a line of ocean-going steamers. Their interest was based on military concerns. Cunard's mail contract stipulated that his vessels must be built so as to be readily convertible into warships, which could be commandeered by the British government in time of war. Similar contracts had also been awarded to companies operating to the East and West Indies. In addition to the steamships it had built for the Royal Navy, Britain therefore had an extensive fleet of steam-powered "auxiliary warships" at its disposal. The US, in contrast, had no ocean-going steamers suitable for military use—neither purpose-built warships nor convertible commercial vessels. Given the clear superiority of steam over sail, this could leave the country vulnerable to naval attack. Recognizing that the cost of building a fleet of steam warships would be very high, Congressional proponents for an expanded navy latched on to the model that had been established in Britain with the Cunard Line. Relatively modest subsidies to operators of commercial ships that were built with private capital but adaptable for naval purposes would be a much cheaper way to provide the navy with steamers.

Advocates for this approach finally achieved a breakthrough in March 1845, with a bill signed into law by President John Tyler on his last full day in office. The new law authorized the Postmaster General to contract with American-owned shipping companies for the transport of mail to foreign countries, with preference to be given to companies using steamships. Later that year the new Postmaster General appointed by President James Polk, Cave Johnson, solicited bids for the transport of mail on a variety of ocean routes. After careful scrutiny of all the applications he awarded the first contract in January 1846. His choice of recipient was a surprise. Rather than an established shipowner on a crucial route, Johnson selected a neophyte operator on a route of minor importance. For $400,000 a year, the newly formed Ocean Steam Navigation Company ("OSNC") was to transport the US mail between New York and Bremen in Germany, calling along the way at Cowes (for Southampton) on England's south coast.

Perhaps acknowledging the strangeness of this decision, when he submitted the contract to Congress for ratification and funding Johnson also included a proposal from E.K. Collins for service between New York and Liverpool. This was rejected, though, as a result of opposition from inland States. Their representatives were highly skeptical about what they saw as unnecessary subsidies for Eastern commercial interests; only by deleting the Collins proposal were proponents of the bill able to secure a narrow majority for approval of the original OSNC contract.

That contract took direct aim at Cunard, specifying that the OSNC's steamers must be at least as fast as his. In practice, however, its effect was to help Cunard and to harm the American interests it was meant to promote. Although the OSNC and its new route were unlikely to have much impact on Cunard's business, by portraying them as a threat to British interests he was able to secure an expansion of his mail contract with the Admiralty. And the expansion he secured would ultimately do far more damage to the US shipping industry than his successful service between Liverpool and Boston had ever done. In May 1846, just two months after the OSNC's contract was ratified by Congress, the British government approved a new contract with Cunard to establish service on the most important of all routes: between Liverpool and New York. Four new ships were to be built to operate this service, with departures to New York and Boston on an alternating basis, weekly for most of the year and fortnightly during winter. In addition to the £85,000 ($413,000) he was already receiving from the British government, Cunard would earn an extra £60,000 ($292,000) each year for the new service.

This was bad news for American shipping—and not just for the embryonic OSNC. To this point the long-dominant sailing packets had largely been immune to the threat from British steamship companies, mainly because none of the latter had been able to put enough ships on the ocean to match the packet Lines' schedules to and from New York. Now, however, Cunard would be coming close, and would take many of the high-value cargoes away from the packets.

Cunard's new contract did at least lead to one positive development for the American shipping industry. E. K. Collins finally got the mail contract he had been seeking. The key breakthrough came in March 1847. Thanks to some deft procedural maneuvering by one of Collins' supporters, Congress passed a bill with a last-minute amendment authorizing the Secretary of the Navy "immediately to accept the proposals of E. K. Collins & Co.... for the transportation of the United States mail between New York and Liverpool." For this service Collins was to receive $385,000 a year—slightly less than the OSNC, and an amount that would later become a major issue. His ships were to be built under the watchful eye of the Navy Department, in such a way that they could be converted "at the least possible cost, into war steamers of the first class." Just as it had for Cunard, the notional ability of his steamers to serve as warships had helped Collins win financial support from his government.

The year 1847 was therefore a major turning point for the sailing packets. With their most important route now certain to see competition from two strong and subsidized steamship companies, their future was bleak. Ironically, as previously explained, the year itself was the first for some time in which they faced no real competition from steamers on that route. The *Great Western* had made her last voyage the previous December, and although the OSNC began service from New York in June, this went to Southampton and Bremen rather than Liverpool. The new company was also plagued by mechanical problems with its first steamer and construction delays with its second. The only other "steamer" to run between Liverpool and New York that year was a new British vessel called the *Sarah Sands*, but she was primarily a sailing ship that used steam for auxiliary power, and in any case did not operate to a regular schedule.

The reprieve for the sailing packets was brief. New Year's Day, 1848, marked the beginning of the end for them. The Cunard Line chose that day to inaugurate its new service, dispatching two steamships in opposite directions across the Atlantic: the *Cambria* from Liverpool and the *Hibernia* from New York. Henceforth, Cunard's steamers would churn their way between these two ports with the same regularity they had established between Liverpool and Boston. And in parallel, the importance of the sailing packets would gradually but irrevocably decline.

For the next two years Cunard faced no competing steamers on the premium transatlantic route. Although Collins now had his mail contract he still had his interest in the Dramatic Line to sell, and as noted in the previous chapter, the original sale fell through. Not until September 1848 was Collins finally able to conclude a sale to Spofford, Tileston & Co., selling

The *British Queen*, the first-ever steamer commissioned for transatlantic travel, and clearly conceived as a sailing ship with an engine and paddle wheels added.

Samuel Cunard (left) and Edward K. Collins.

The *Europa*, one of a new class of larger steamships introduced by the Cunard Line in 1848 in response to emerging competition from the US.

The *Atlantic*, which inaugurated the Collins Line's transatlantic service in 1850.

his Louisiana Line sailing packets at the same time to another operator in the coastal trade.

But from that point forward his efforts quickly gathered momentum. Just a month later he announced the names of the five steamers he intended to build, this time inspired by the world's oceans rather than the stage: the *Atlantic, Pacific, Arctic, Baltic* and *Adriatic*. By February 1849 the first two of these had been launched—although like most new ships, at the time of launch they were still just empty hulls with their decks installed. By August they were receiving their engines, and by early 1850 undergoing final fitting. Appropriately given the ocean they would be crossing, the *Atlantic* was then chosen to inaugurate the Collins Line's service. In mid-April she underwent both an official inspection for the Navy and her sea trial, coming through each of these tests successfully. And then, at last, came a day of huge significance for the American shipping industry. On April 27, 1850, the *Atlantic* steamed out of New York for her maiden voyage. One month later the *Pacific* entered service, and was followed in October and November by the *Arctic* and the *Baltic*. The Cunard Line finally had an American competitor.

Even as he achieved these milestones, Collins was experiencing his first taste of the governmental oversight that would become a major issue in years to come. With public funding came public scrutiny. In spite of his rapid progress since selling the Dramatic Line, he had missed two deadlines set by the Secretary of the Navy for the start of his mail service; the Senate's Post Office Committee wanted to know why. Collins may have chafed at their scrutiny, but at least in this instance the outcome was positive. The Committee concluded that the delays were due to his laudable decision to build larger and more powerful ships than were required by his mail contract; they recommended no change to the contract, except that it should be supervised by the Post Office Department rather than the Secretary of the Navy.

Out on the ocean, meanwhile, Collins was demonstrating that he could compete very effectively with Cunard. This was true even during his first six months in operation, when the Collins Line had only two ships in service compared with the nine advertised by its competitor. The most important component of the schedule was the frequency of departures from New York, and though the Cunard Line offered an eastbound crossing every week, its sailings alternated between Boston and New York. Departures from the latter therefore came around only once a fortnight—a frequency that Collins could just about match when he had only the *Atlantic* and *Pacific* in service, and could manage comfortably once they were joined by the *Arctic* and *Baltic*.

Moreover, Collins' new steamers offered much more than just a competitive schedule. True to form, he had spared no expense in their construction. The "bigger, better, faster" philosophy he had shown when building his Dramatic liners was even more apparent. Whereas the new ships Cunard had built for the New York route were 30 percent bigger than his most recent Boston steamers, Collins' liners were over 20 percent bigger again. They averaged over 2,800 tons, larger than any other steamer ever built except Brunel's (in)famous *Great Britain*. And while Cunard's new ships were finished in his usual "plain and comfortable" style, with "not the least unnecessary expense for show," the Collins' liners were downright luxurious. The list of amenities included steam heat in the passenger areas; deep carpets and fine furniture; paintings, mirrors and elaborate decorations on the walls; an expansive menu prepared by a French chef; and even a barber's shop.

Most important of all, Collins' ships were fast. This became apparent from the very first westbound crossing of the *Atlantic*, completed in a record time of eleven days and two hours. On her next voyage she broke the record for the eastbound crossing too, then bettered her own time for the return leg. And so it continued. In 1851 the *Pacific* became the first ship ever to cross from New York to Liverpool in less than ten days, and the *Baltic* the first to do so in the opposite direction. For the year as a whole—its first full year of operation—the Collins Line bettered Cunard's crossing times by an average of seven hours heading east and twenty-two heading west.

As in the case of the Dramatic Line, Collins had had to spend lavishly to get the ships that he wanted. Between them his four steamers cost almost three million dollars to build, 50 percent more than he had projected. One third of this sum came from the sale of shares in the company, and a further $317,500 in the form of advances from the Navy Department; the rest had to be borrowed. His running expenses were also inordinately high, those speedy crossings coming at the cost of heavy coal consumption and frequent mechanical repairs. The subsidy from the government for carrying mail was nowhere near sufficient to cover these expenses. So even as his steamers were setting new records, a typical roundtrip across the Atlantic was costing Collins almost $17,000 more than he was taking in. And as a later chapter will recount, his response to this situation only increased the pressure for faster (and thus more expensive) crossings.

But in the meantime, he and Cunard were stealing away all of the most valuable business from the sailing packets. Historically, the packets had derived their income from three main sources: cargoes, passengers and mail. The last of these was the first to be taken over by the steamers, which were paid by their governments to carry it. This transition had little effect on the packet owners but a major impact on the captains, who had previously kept all of the income from carrying mail as a private service. The owners' turn came soon enough, however, as the steamers also took over the best cargoes and passengers. This particularly hit revenues from westbound crossings, where the advantage of steam over sail was greatest. The cargoes that packed the highest values into the smallest space—textiles and manufactured goods from England's factories—now went by steamer, leaving the sailing packets to fight over heavy bulk commodities they had scorned for decades, such as coal and iron. Similarly, the wealthy passengers who paid high prices for cabin accommodation now traveled by steamship, leaving the packets to take on the less affluent customers they had also once scorned—emigrants who could only afford shared accommodation in "steerage," the cramped and airless space between decks that was typically used for cargo on the eastbound passage.

Because of an ongoing tragedy, the sailing packets were protected for some time from the full impact of these changes. That tragedy was the Great Famine in Ireland, which brought increased business in both directions across the Atlantic. Heading westbound, the packets saw a massive increase in the number of steerage passengers as Irish families fled to the US to escape the famine. And heading eastbound they now carried flour, wheat and grains, which had ceased to be subject to prohibitive import duties after Britain repealed its Corn Laws in response to the famine.

Statistics cited by historian Robert Albion in his excellent book, *Square Riggers on Schedule*, reveal the magnitude of the shift in the passenger trade. In the whole of 1826, the sixteen Liverpool packets then in operation transported a total of 749 people to New York, 454 in cabins and a mere 295 in steerage. In 1852, which was the peak year for emigration on the Liverpool packets, the Swallowtail Line alone carried a total of 5,793 passengers on its three ships, all but twenty of whom traveled in steerage. Similar changes in the number and nature of passengers were also seen at other packet lines.

The vastly increased number of people traveling in steerage helped to keep the packet industry in business. These passengers could be packed in at high density and also at very little cost; apart from a modest ration of bread and potatoes mandated by law, they were required to bring all of their own food. Most of the twenty dollars that each emigrant paid for passage was therefore pure profit for the shipowner.

Encouraged by that profit, many packet lines took a somewhat paradoxical step. In spite of clear evidence that the age of sail was coming to an end, they built new and bigger ships—primarily to increase capacity for, and profits from, steerage passengers. When the Great Famine began in 1845 the largest of the sailing packets was the 1,207-ton *Henry Clay*. At that time the steamships had not yet captured any real business on the New York route, but when they started to do so a few years later, the enthusiasm for investing in new sailing ships might have been expected to falter. Instead, the opposite happened. During the late 1840s and early 1850s a whole series of new packets bigger than the *Henry Clay* were built. Between them, the four packet lines operating between New York and Liverpool added fifteen new vessels, with an average size of 1,409 tons. Every single one was bigger than the *Roscius*, which as recently as 1840 had been the largest of all packets. The new owners of the Dramatic Line were in fact the most aggressive of all during this construction boom. They sold off the liners they had bought from Collins and replaced them with four new ships averaging 1,666 tons; the largest of these vessels, the *Calhoun*, was a huge 1,749 tons.

Unfortunately for the packet lines there was one fatal flaw in their logic: the assumption that, like themselves in former times, the steamer companies would not actively pursue steerage passengers. But in the early 1850s two new steamship lines did precisely that, and in due course their competitors followed suit. The packets then simply became freighters, transporting the low-value commodities that were of no interest to the steamship operators. Six of the original lines were still in business in the late 1860s, but by 1880 they were all gone. Their real importance, however, had ended three decades earlier, when Cunard and Collins had transformed the ocean crossing between New York and Liverpool with their steamers.

As the outstanding American contributor to that transformation, Edward Collins had shown himself a true visionary. He had been astute enough to recognize immediately that steamers would make sailing ships obsolete, and bold enough to sell his highly successful packet line in order to act on that vision.

One man in particular had been deeply affected by that sale. As captain of the line's flagship, Asa Eldridge had been faced with a big decision—whether to stay on with the new owners or look for another position. In the event he did neither. Perhaps inspired by Collins' example, he decided to become an entrepreneur. And his new venture was a steamship line.

5

ASPIRING TYCOON

BY MOST ACCOUNTS, Edward Collins was not a reticent man. During four years as captain of the *Roscius*, Asa Eldridge must therefore have heard Collins hold forth on many occasions about the future of transatlantic shipping. Steam was going to rule the ocean. Period! Eldridge would also have witnessed at first hand his employer's determination to be a key player when that happened. For much of those four years Collins had been lobbying Congress to subsidize his proposed steamship line, and then pushing to get rid of the Dramatic Line. The sale of the Line in September 1848 would therefore not have been a surprise to Eldridge.

His thoughts at this time can only be imagined. He was now thirty-nine years old and had spent most of his life working towards a position that until recently had been regarded as one of the most prestigious on the planet: the captaincy of a New York-based packet ship sailing to Liverpool. But even as he reached what he had thought was the pinnacle of his profession, the skills that had taken him there appeared to be on the brink of obsolescence. His employer clearly believed that the age of sail was coming to an end—which for Eldridge would mean that his singular ability to conquer and harness the wind would no longer distinguish him. And if he doubted Collins' view of the impact of transatlantic steam, he had only to look at what was happening on his own ship. The manifest for his penultimate westbound crossing on the *Roscius* in June 1848 listed 381 passengers, who to judge from their occupations would almost all have been in steerage; 266 were from Ireland. The few who could have afforded a cabin would have paid $75 in first class or $25 in the newly introduced second class—mere fractions of the $120 the Cunard Line was charging its cabin passengers that summer. If Eldridge wanted to maintain his status as one of the most important captains on the Atlantic, he clearly needed to switch to steam.

The simplest way to achieve this would presumably have been to stay with Collins and take command of one of his new steamers when they were ready. This may not have been an option, however. When selling the Dramatic Line, Collins may have been required to agree not to hire any of its key employees for a certain period of time—captains in particular. Similar commitments are common today when a company is sold, and it is note-worthy that Collins did not hire Eldridge or any of his other captains from the Dramatic Line for his new steamers.

And as it turns out, Asa Eldridge had plans of his own for transitioning to steam. He teamed up with the new owners of the Dramatic Line, Paul Spofford and Thomas Tileston, to start a steamship venture with a partially philanthropic purpose: to provide European emigrants with a safer and more comfortable passage to the New World.

The need for such an initiative was great. As may be imagined from the brief description provided in the previous chapter, the conditions under which most emigrants traveled—as steerage passengers on sailing packets—were appalling. To quote from *Merchant Sail*, the six-volume encyclopedic work by historian William Fairburn, these emigrants were effectively treated as "paying human freight." Typically, they were crammed into any available space in the low-ceilinged area between the cargo hold and the weather deck, with little privacy or ventilation. No meals were provided; to eat, they had to cook for themselves on coal fires burning in stone grates on the upper deck. These fires were often extinguished by flying spray, and even when alight, were difficult to access because of the crowds jostling to use them. And if bad weather intervened, as it often did, the steerage passengers had to stay below deck with the hatches battened down and no means of cooking at all. Since they also had no access to fresh air or sanitary facilities, con-ditions quickly became almost intolerable. As Fairburn recounts, "Men, women, and children screamed all night in terror." And as a cabin passenger noted in 1845, whenever a skylight was opened to allow some air into the steerage area "the effluvia was such as to compel me in all weathers to go on deck."

Not surprisingly, contagious diseases spread rapidly under these con-ditions, and mortality among steerage passengers was high. The outbreak of cholera on John Eldridge's *Liverpool* noted in an earlier chapter was not an isolated incident. According to an article in the *New York Herald* in 1853, the overall mortality rate on sixteen ships that arrived from Europe between September 9 and October 21 of that year was more than 5 percent. Between them, the sixteen ships had boarded a total of 6,318 passengers, of whom 330 died at sea. On three of these ships the mortality rate was more than 15 percent, meaning that about one in six of the original passengers had died.

Having transported his fair share of emigrants on the *Roscius* and then on the *Garrick*, Asa Eldridge would have been all too aware of the conditions in which they traveled and the risk of death they faced. And after Spofford and Tileston took over the Dramatic Line, he began working with them on a new steamship designed specifically to serve the emigrant trade—partly (one would assume) because of the business opportunity this represented, but partly too out of a humanitarian interest in improving the lot of those emigrants who could only afford passage in the steerage.

This new venture seems to have had a long gestation period. Word of it first emerged in the fall of 1850, two years after Eldridge had left the *Roscius* following the sale of the Dramatic Line to his new partners. The original stories in the New York papers are now difficult to find, but were well reported on the other side of the Atlantic by the *Liverpool Mercury*. As will be apparent, they described a very different approach to poor emigrants by the new enterprise, and also expressed a high regard for Asa Eldridge:

> OCEAN SCREW STEAMERS.—The New York papers announce that a series of emigrant screw steamers are about to be built in that port, by Messrs. Spoffred [*sic*] and Tileston. They have determined to adopt an entirely new arrangement with regard to the steerage passengers. Instead of allowing the steerage passengers, as is now the custom in every emigrant ship, to supply their own food, they intend to furnish them from the ship's stores, with good and wholesome provisions during the voyage. The first vessel will be named the Pioneer. She will rate 2000 tons... and will be commanded by Captain Eldridge, late of the packet-ship Roscius, a gentleman intimately known to be a thorough commander by all in the habit of voyaging between Liverpool and the United States...

Also notable in this excerpt is the high level of interest in the *Pioneer*'s drive system, with references to "screw steamers" in both the title and the first sentence of the article. This term was used to describe steamships that were driven by a rear-mounted underwater propeller rather than the traditional side-mounted paddle wheels. Although this mode of propulsion allowed more of the available space to be devoted to passengers and cargo, its adoption on the Atlantic had been slow; until recently, the only steamer to use it had been Brunel's *Great Britain*, whose troubled history was no great advertisement for the technology. Earlier in 1850, however, a propeller-driven steamer called the *City of Glasgow* had entered transatlantic service from that city, and a few months later Samuel Cunard had declared his intention to build a whole new line of screw steamers. With Edward Collins having committed all of his capital to paddle steamers, the prospect of an American response to Cunard seemed slim, which is why the choice of screw propulsion for the *Pioneer* was of such interest.

In February 1851 the new steamer was reported to be under construction at a shipyard in New York. Spofford & Tileston were described as "agents and part owners," although the identities of the other owners were not disclosed. Interestingly, the same shipyard was also building a new schooner called the *Asa Eldridge*, further illustrating the general high regard for the *Pioneer*'s new skipper. It was an honor indeed to have a ship named after you while still alive!

The owners' original goal was to have the *Pioneer* ready to convey passengers to London for the "Great Exhibition" (or "World's Fair") taking place that summer at the Crystal Palace. This proved too optimistic, however, and the ship was not finally completed until October.

In the meantime, Thomas Tileston had provided more detail about his altruistic motives for building the *Pioneer*. During the trial run of a coastal steamer for another venture he operated with Spofford, he explained to the press that his goal was "to bring over the starved and oppressed of Europe… in good steamships, feed them well on the passage, and take care of their health and lives, so that they would not be dying off in scores on the passage, and find a grave in the bosom of the stormy Atlantic."

This noble ambition was also evident in the advertisements he placed for the *Pioneer*'s maiden voyage:

> The steerage passengers will be served regularly with their meals, cooked by experienced and popular persons employed expressly for this department, and by this means they will be relieved from the trouble and annoyance of laying in their own provisions, and from the injurious effects consequent upon being compelled to eat improperly cooked provisions.

Moreover, the ads promised, the "rates of passage are such as cannot fail to be satisfactory."

Sadly, Tileston's fine words proved to be just that. After one disappointing roundtrip to Liverpool, the *Pioneer* was diverted to an enterprise that promised far greater profits: transporting would-be participants in the Gold Rush to California.

First, though, that disappointing trip to Liverpool. The *Pioneer* finally steamed out of New York for her maiden voyage on October 18, 1851, three days later than first advertised. The original newspaper stories about her had stated that "Her owners feel assured of her making the passage between Liverpool and New York easily in sixteen days." But in the easier opposite direction, she now took almost nineteen days to cross the Atlantic. Given that steamers often experienced mechanical problems on their first voyages, this might have been considered acceptable—if only the competition had not been so much faster. Earlier that year, Edward Collins' *Pacific* had recorded the first-ever passage to Liverpool in under ten days, almost twice as fast. And on the day the *Pioneer* arrived in Liverpool so did the *Atlantic*—the crucial difference being that she had left New York a week later. Nor were the mighty Collins liners the only ships with markedly superior performance. The new Havre Line's *Humboldt* left New York on the same day as the *Pioneer* but needed seven days fewer to reach England.

The return journey was no better. As on the outbound leg, the *Pioneer* took nineteen days for the crossing. And also as on that leg, this was almost twice as long as a new benchmark recently set by the Collins Line, whose *Baltic* had reached New York in less than ten days just a few months earlier. Further echoing the outbound run, another steamer on the ocean at the same time completed the crossing much more quickly: the Cunard Line's *America* left Liverpool a few minutes after the *Pioneer* but reached New York a full week earlier.

Asa Eldridge's pride must have been hurt. The contrast between the slowness of his own voyage and the speed of Collins' new liners was painful. The men commanding those liners were all former packet captains he had regularly matched on the *Roscius*; now they were setting record after record and he was lagging way behind. The *Pioneer*'s performance might improve as its machinery bedded in and he became more familiar with the ship, but was unlikely ever to approach that of the Collins liners. The one small consolation he could claim was that he had been at the helm for the first roundtrip across the Atlantic by an American screw steamer. But her sluggish performance suggested that propellers were not yet ready to displace paddle wheels as the preferred drivetrain for steamships.

Eldridge never got the chance to improve the *Pioneer*'s performance. Her first voyage across the Atlantic was her last. Despite their avowed intention to save the poor of Europe, her owners opted instead to pursue the riches of California—or to be more precise, the rich opportunities for shipowners created by the Gold Rush. They switched the *Pioneer* to a popular route that offered a faster passage to San Francisco than the long and perilous voyage around the tip of South America. This faster alternative involved crossing Panama more or less along the same path now followed by the Canal. Migrants traveled by ship to Chagres on the Caribbean coast of Panama, took a boat up the Chagres River to its head about halfway across the isthmus, completed the second half of the crossing on land, and finally sailed from the town of Panama to San Francisco on a second ship. The *Pioneer*'s new assignment was to operate on the first leg of this route, shuttling back and forth between New York and Chagres.

The demand for passage on her initial run to Chagres must have delighted her owners. When she steamed out of New York on January 25, 1852 she was carrying 500 passengers. Despite one report to the contrary, Asa Eldridge does not appear to have been at the helm. That report came in the "Marine Intelligence" column of the *New York Daily Times* on the day after the *Pioneer*'s departure, which listed him as captain. But three days previously the same paper had said that her skipper for the voyage would be a man called Kittredge, and his was the name it reported when she arrived back on February 21 (although now spelling the name "Kitleridge"; it was in fact Kittridge, so the paper got it wrong twice).

Whether Asa had chosen to leave the *Pioneer* or been relieved of his command can only be a matter of conjecture. It seems unlikely, however, that such an experienced mariner would have been fired after just a single voyage, particularly since new steamships were often temperamental on their early runs.

Any discussion of his position may have been complicated by another issue that is also unclear: whether he owned some share of the steamer. On the *Pioneer*'s first two departures from New York the daily shipping reports cited Spofford, Tileston & Co. as the owner, but as noted above, a newspaper article in February 1851 described them as "agents and *part* owners." That article did not name any co-owners, but when the *Pioneer* arrived in Liverpool the London *Standard* stated that "She belongs to Messrs. Bird and Gillinan." A firm of that name operated as merchants in Liverpool and importers in New York.

According to a more recent publication, however, there was a third co-owner of much greater interest to this narrative. The *Pioneer* was one of the ships listed in Volume 1 of *Early American Steamers*, published by historian Erik Heyl in 1953. Heyl states that from 1851-52 she was owned by "Asa Eldredge" (a common misspelling of his name), who sold her to Spofford, Tileston & Co. in 1852 after one roundtrip to Liverpool and another to Europe. While some aspects of this account are obviously not consistent with contemporary records such as the newspaper stories cited above, it does suggest that Eldridge had a significant ownership position in the *Pioneer*. His fractional share (rather than the entire ownership) may then be what he sold in 1852. One plausible scenario is that he did not agree with the decision to switch the steamer to the Chagres route, and so resigned his command and asked his co-owners to buy him out.

The success of the *Pioneer*'s first voyage to Chagres only whetted the appetite of Spofford and Tileston for transporting gold-seekers to California. For the ship's next voyage they decided to go all the way, sending her on the traditional route around Cape Horn to San Francisco with Captain Kittridge at the helm and another full complement of passengers. But while she was at sea her fortunes changed yet again, as she became part of a new enterprise belonging to America's greatest tycoon, Cornelius Vanderbilt.

Long before he built his railroad empire Vanderbilt was a shipping magnate, with such a large and successful fleet he became known by the unofficial title of "Commodore." When the Gold Rush began he was among the first to offer passage to San Francisco via Panama, but was convinced he could develop an even faster route via Nicaragua. The ocean voyages on either side of North America would be significantly shorter, he reasoned, and although the crossing between the Caribbean and Pacific coasts would be longer, much of it could be accomplished by boat on the Rio San Juan and Lake Nicaragua. So after negotiating exclusive rights from the Nicaraguan government to transport passengers and freight between the country's coasts, he inaugurated his new service in July 1851. As he had predicted, it was faster than the alternative via Panama, saving about a week—which for people desperate to get to California was a major selling point. By 1852 he needed extra capacity for the Pacific leg of the route, and since the *Pioneer* was already on her way to that side of the Americas, he added her to his fleet.

Vanderbilt would soon have cause to regret that decision. The *Pioneer* seemed to be jinxed. While she was anchored off the coast of Chile taking on coal, a sudden gale blew her onto a reef. Although the captain managed to free her she was now leaking badly, requiring continuous operation of her pumps all the way to Panama. Even while she was at anchor there, her engines had to be kept running to power the pumps. But there was no time to stop for the repairs that were urgently necessary. When the *Pioneer* arrived in Panama, Captain Kittridge would have learned that he was now working for Vanderbilt and was already several weeks late for his first assignment: the Commodore had advertised that the *Pioneer* would pick up passengers at San Juan del Sur on the Nicaraguan coast at the end of June, and it was now mid-July. And even without those extra customers, the ship already had hundreds of people on board who were anxious to reach San Francisco and frustrated by her slow progress.

Not all of these passengers were willing to risk their lives for gold; a number were so afraid of her condition that they decided to stay behind when she left Panama. But the space they vacated was quickly re-occupied when she called into San Juan, and she headed for San Francisco with a full load. And the further she went, the more desperate her situation became. By the time she reached southern California she was out of coal and missing two of the original three blades from her propeller. Then came the final blow. During another storm she was slammed repeatedly by heavy seas, making her leaks even worse. To save her from sinking Captain Kittridge coaxed her into the shelter of St. Simeon's Bay and ran her aground, close to where Hearst Castle now stands, about two hundred miles south of San Francisco. Fortunately, a passing coastal steamer called the *Sea Bird* was able to rescue all those on board with no loss of life. Twenty had died during the voyage, but none did so during the shipwreck itself.

Remarkably, Asa Eldridge arrived in San Francisco via a different route just as these events were unfolding, and actually became involved in the rescue. He reached San Francisco on August 18, 1852 on the US Mail steamer *Golden Gate* from Panama, having presumably traveled from New York via the "short" route across the Panamanian isthmus. Two days later the *Sea Bird* arrived with 224 passengers rescued from the *Pioneer*. This was as many as she could carry, but represented only about half of the people who had been aboard the stricken steamship. So after quickly unloading, the *Sea Bird* turned right around and headed back to the wreck to pick up the rest. And for the second leg of her rescue mission, her captain was joined by three other experienced mariners: two sent by the *Pioneer's* insurers to assess the damage she had suffered, and the third someone with deep knowledge of the steamer that might be helpful—Asa Eldridge.

After all of the effort he had put into building the *Pioneer*, Eldridge must have been devastated by the condition in which he found her. But at least he was able to help in a rescue that ensured no lives were lost. The remaining 148 passengers and 70 crew members arrived safely in San Francisco on August 23, six days after Captain Kittridge had run the ship aground.

The insurance assessors who had traveled with Eldridge to the wreck declared the *Pioneer* a total loss. This was not as great a concern for Vanderbilt as might have been imagined. When details of the *Pioneer*'s insurance coverage surfaced in October, the newspapers reported that "She was owned by Messrs. Spofford, Tileston & Co., of New York, and was at the time of the disaster running in the Nicaragua line to San Francisco." Vanderbilt must therefore have leased rather than acquired the *Pioneer* from her New York owners. Indeed, he seems to have courted their active involvement in his new venture; in July he engineered a place for Thomas Tileston on the board of the Nicaragua Transit Company, which operated the link between San Juan del Norte on the Caribbean coast and San Juan del Sur on the Pacific.

As an aside, one of the insurance assessors was a highly renowned mariner who had recently fallen from grace. Captain Robert Waterman had set several records on voyages between China and New York, first on a cotton freighter called the *Natchez*, and then on a clipper ship he made famous, the *Sea Witch*. But he was also known for being tough on his crew, and in 1851 this trait landed him in big trouble. He and his first mate were put on trial for their alleged violence against various seamen during the voyage of a new clipper ship, the *Challenge*, from New York to San Francisco. He was found guilty of assault, and the first mate of murder. Waterman escaped without a sentence, but never again sought command of a ship. He did, however, still recognize a good opportunity to profit from one. When the wreck of the *Pioneer* was put up for auction in March 1853—presumably by the insurance company—Waterman purchased it for $1,500. He then pumped out the hull, patched the leaks, and chartered a steam tug to tow the *Pioneer* back to San Francisco. In May of that year, just nine months after she was deemed a total loss, her value was estimated to be $100,000.

THE PRECEDING ACCOUNT of the *Pioneer*'s demise leaves one major question unanswered: why did Asa Eldridge arrive in San Francisco just as his former ship was in need of rescue? This was too much of a coincidence to have been one. And in fact, a careful reconstruction of his movements and those of the *Pioneer* strongly suggests it was not.

Details of Eldridge's journey to San Francisco can be deduced from an article in the local newspaper the day after he arrived on the *Golden Gate*. In its issue dated August 19, 1852, the *Daily Alta California* devoted significant space to accounts of the steamer's arrival the previous day, and of the news she had brought in papers from New York. From these accounts it is clear that many of her passengers had started their journey on a steamer called the *Illinois* that had left New York for the Panamanian port of Aspinwall (present-day Colón) on July 20. Indeed, according to newspaper advertisements earlier in 1852, the schedules of the *Illinois* and the *Golden Gate* were deliberately coordinated to ensure the fastest possible passage from New York to San Francisco. Thus Asa Eldridge may safely be assumed to have taken advantage of this coordination, and to have set out from New York on the *Illinois* on July 20.

By that time Cornelius Vanderbilt would have been desperate to know the whereabouts of the steamer he had recently leased from Spofford & Tileston. Having left New York on March 17, the *Pioneer* would have been expected to arrive in Panama around the middle of June, and news of that event should have reached New York about a fortnight later, by the end of the month. But nearly three weeks into July, Vanderbilt had still heard nothing. This was particularly worrying because he had been counting heavily on her timely arrival in Panama. The loss of another steamer off the coast of Mexico in February had left him short of capacity on the Pacific leg of his San Francisco route, and newspaper reports had started to appear about disgruntled customers facing long waits for connections in Nicaragua. He had already advertised that the *Pioneer* would be there to pick up passengers who had left New York on June 5; to do so she would have needed to reach Panama by June 26 or 27, but had clearly not.

Vanderbilt really needed to understand why that was. So as the date approached for the departure of the *Illinois* from New York for Aspinwall, he decided to send someone to Panama to investigate. His emissary might need to mount a search and deal with the authorities in a foreign port, and so could not be a mere messenger; only a highly experienced captain would do. And who better than Asa Eldridge, who had all the necessary qualities *and* deep first-hand knowledge of the missing ship? For his part, Eldridge would have been just as concerned as Vanderbilt about the *Pioneer* once

Classified ad for the Pioneer Line, October 1851.

San Francisco, 1850, with a harbor full of ships.

Ad showing coordinated schedules of steamers *Illinois* and *Golden Gate*, April 1852.

The *North Star*.

Photographs of Cornelius Vanderbilt (left) and Asa Eldridge, from
Rev. Choules' account of the *North Star*'s European cruise.

he learned that she was missing, and would have readily agreed to the Commodore's request that he investigate.

The first news he discovered would have been both reassuring and concerning. When he reached the Pacific port of Panama around the end of July he would have learned that the *Pioneer* had arrived there on July 12, and had since departed for Nicaragua and San Francisco. So at least she was safe. (Ironically, news of her arrival in Panama had reached New York on July 23, just three days after Eldridge had left.) But he would also have heard about her battered condition, and so been anxious to confirm that she had made it all the way to her final destination. Fortunately, the coordination of the schedules of the *Illinois* and *Golden Gate* meant that the latter was just about to depart for San Francisco, so Eldridge was able to resume his pursuit of the *Pioneer* with little interruption. The *Golden Gate* was known for her fast passages, and reached San Francisco on August 18 in just under twelve days, after what the *Daily Alta California* described as "one of her extraordinarily quick trips."

Since Panama is about 3,300 miles from San Francisco, the *Golden Gate* must have traveled about 275 miles each day, which means that she would have passed St. Simeon's Bay sometime on August 17—the very day that Captain Kittridge deliberately ran the *Pioneer* aground there. In the shelter of the bay, the struggling steamer must not have been visible to the *Golden Gate*, which would surely have stopped had her captain been aware of a ship in distress. Asa Eldridge must therefore have been stunned when he arrived in San Francisco only to discover that the *Pioneer* had not yet done so. The arrival of the *Sea Bird* two days later with the first load of passengers from the *Pioneer* would have come as an enormous relief, and Eldridge would have been only too glad to take part in the second phase of the rescue.

Having done what he could to protect Vanderbilt's interests in the aftermath of the wreck, Eldridge would then have headed back to New York to report to the Commodore.

WHILE MUCH of this account is supposition, its accuracy seems to be confirmed by subsequent events. These relate to the unusual project on which Vanderbilt now embarked. Earlier in 1852 he had commissioned two new steamers for his Nicaraguan venture, but then decided to use one of them, the *North Star*, for an enterprise he had never previously attempted: a vacation. In a career spanning more than forty years he had never allowed himself that luxury. And although his lifestyle was surprisingly modest in general, on this occasion he was willing to spend lavishly. He fitted out the *North Star* as a luxurious private yacht the size of an ocean liner, and invited a small group of his family and closest friends to accompany him on a four-month cruise around Europe—all at his expense. Newspapers speculated that his costs would be between $250,000 and $500,000, which in those days were astronomical sums.

As he drew up his plans in detail, Vanderbilt faced a decision that would be crucial for the success of the enterprise. Whom should he appoint as captain of the yacht? Having parlayed his own start as a ferry-master into a vast shipping empire, he knew exactly what qualities he wanted in his captain—and how difficult it would be to find them all in a single individual. Consummate skill as a mariner was only the starting point. In addition to navigating the treacherous waters of the Atlantic, the captain would be expected to charm Vanderbilt's distinguished guests on a daily basis in a wide variety of social situations, and to act as his ambassador in the many foreign ports he intended to visit. But above all, he would be responsible for the safety of all the people the Commodore cared about most in his life.

For that reason, Vanderbilt would only have chosen someone he had seen in action and trusted completely. And the man he chose was Asa Eldridge—a selection that validates the account given above of Eldridge's role in the final days of the *Pioneer*, which would have been his sole previous opportunity to make such a favorable impression on the Commodore.

Regardless of the precise circumstances that led to it, Eldridge's appointment to the *North Star* was just the fillip he needed after the disappointment of the *Pioneer*. While he may indeed have distinguished himself in her final hours, her sluggish debut on the Atlantic must have raised questions about his ability to make a successful transition to steam.

Those questions may have returned briefly when the *North Star* first tried to leave New York on May 19, 1853. As she eased her way along the East River she hit a rock and damaged her keel, raising fears that she would capsize. The explanation given for the accident was that she had not built up a full head of steam, a mistake for which Eldridge must surely have been responsible. The damage proved relatively minor, however, and the *North Star* was able to leave without incident the following evening. From that point forward the cruise was a great success.

The *North Star*'s first stop was in Southampton, which she reached in a perfectly respectable twelve days. The British were agog at the sight of her.

Their reaction was nicely captured by the Paris correspondent of the New Orleans *Daily Picayune*, who made a detour to see the *North Star* on his way back from a trip to London; Vanderbilt had agreed to throw the yacht open for public viewing while he and his party were visiting the English capital. Over five thousand people attended the all-ticket event, and although Vanderbilt himself was away, "... he left a fitting representative behind, in the person of Capt. Asa Eldridge, and under his polite guidance we went entirely over the noble steamer..." The general reaction was awe:

> There were lords on board, and admirals, and all kinds of high notabilities, and one and all fairly acknowledged that they must knock under, and that Queen Victoria's favorite steam yacht was but a floating scow by comparison.

The dignitaries' admiration was "not doled out reluctantly or stintedly, but frankly and honestly expressed." One issue did, however, baffle the British:

> What seemed to puzzle all was the fact that a private individual, of a nation dating but from yesterday, should conceive and have the means of carrying out the idea of constructing such a magnificent floating palace, and for the express purpose of giving his family an opportunity of seeing the world comfortably and safely: this not one of the visitors could understand.

The correspondent also found space in his report for a handsome compliment to Asa Eldridge:

> Even in selecting a captain her owner has carried out his plan of having everything of the best on board; for Eldridge will pass for as fine a specimen of the stalwart Yankee skipper as ever paced a quarter deck.

And as he demonstrated at his next public engagement, Eldridge could also pass for a fine specimen of a Yankee diplomat. The occasion was a banquet thrown for the Vanderbilt party by Southampton's mayor. Speeches and toasts flew back and forth between the hosts and their guests, and towards the end of the proceedings it fell to Eldridge to reply to a toast. Like the rest of the speeches his response was recounted at length by the local newspaper, whose report is one of the very few first-hand accounts now available of any verbal communication by Eldridge. For this reason it is reproduced in full below. While his remarks consisted mostly of standard pleasantries, he clearly knew how to choose the right words to please his audience:

> Capt. Eldridge said he was much obliged to them for the honor they had done to the toast, especially for the way in which it had been received. It went down as though it was good. (Laughter and cheers.) It was always gratifying to a man, and especially on such an occasion, to have his health drank so unanimously, with such kind feeling. He was glad to say that he felt no embarrassment—he felt quite at home. (Hear, hear.) The reception they had experienced was a source of gratitude to himself, and his officers and crew, most of whom, he was proud to say, were the sons of gentlemen. (Hear, and cheers.) This was the first time he had visited Southampton; and he was much pleased with the port, the entrance of the docks, and the excellent accommodation afforded (loud cheers), at the courtesy they had experienced, and the police and all other regulations appertaining to the docks. (Hear.) The visit of the North Star had created some interest, and he thought it was justly due. It was a noble and glorious enterprise, and he felt proud of the ship and the position he held in her. The commodore had conferred an honor upon him in giving him the command, and he thanked him for it. He was proud of him as a man, and also of his sons and daughters, he loved them all. Every captain was proud of his own ship, and he had no wish to be particular in this respect. (Laughter and cheers.) He thanked Mr. Andrews for the courtesy, kindness and hospitality, he had received at his house; and he thanked them all for the honor that had been conferred on the gallant commodore and his party. The North Star was opened to the public last week, and he then hoisted the English flag by the side of the American, and so he hoped the two flags would long continue. (Loud cheers.) England and America, if separated, may get into difficulties, but, united together, they will whip the world. (Loud cheering.)

From Southampton the *North Star* proceeded to St. Petersburg, the first of many destinations on an itinerary that took her through the English Channel, the North and Baltic Seas, and then back again to Normandy; along the Atlantic coasts of France, Spain and Portugal; into and around the Mediterranean; and finally out past Morocco and Madeira towards home.

The entire voyage was documented in great detail in a book published the following year by the ship's chaplain, Reverend J. C. Choules, who had been invited to join the party at the request of Vanderbilt's pious daughters—the Commodore himself having little time for religion. Rev.

Choules' account ran to 353 pages, with a title clearly indicating the extensiveness of the tour: *The Cruise of the Steam Yacht North Star; a Narrative of the Excursion of Mr. Vanderbilt's Party to England, Russia, Denmark, France, Spain, Italy, Malta, Turkey, Madeira, etc.*.

Included in Choules' account are several observations about Asa Eldridge, which have particular value because they are almost the only available assessments of his character and abilities based on direct interactions with him.

On one occasion, for example, the chaplain spent most of the short midsummer night off Denmark "in agreeable chat with Captain Eldridge, whose fund of knowledge, acquired by extensive travel and nautical experience, combined with great shrewdness of observation, always afforded us entertainment."

On another, he noted that bad weather in the English Channel…

> …had little effect in delaying the voyage, or hindering our exact course, and the abilities of our accomplished commander were only made more apparent. I shall not soon forget the satisfaction with which he made the light-ship on the Godwin Sands, after the thickest fog, coming down directly upon her, according to his prediction. I have never felt such abiding confidence in any man's judgment as in that of Captain Eldridge. All his movements are in exact unison with his statements made beforehand, and he exhibits that perfect acquaintedness with his profession which inspires confidence in the breast of every person around.

And finally, as the great adventure came to an end:

> Every one on board the yacht felt the amount of indebtedness under which he labored to Captain Eldridge, whose nautical skill is only equalled by his cheerful-hearted every-day kindness. I do not exaggerate his merits when I say that those who have seen him navigate the Mediterranean, where he had never been, and enter ports without a pilot, are quite satisfied that an abler seaman never trod a quarter-deck. Long may he live, an honor to his profession, and the object of regard to his friends!

Rev. Choules' account also includes one small bonus for the present narrative: a brief tribute to Asa Eldridge's wife, who accompanied him on the voyage as a guest of the Vanderbilts. Although short and somewhat generic, this provides the only information available about her other than the usual basic facts in public records: "Mrs. Eldridge, I will simply remark, will have through our lives our highest respect, to which her admirable good sense and virtues entitle her."

THE *NORTH STAR* arrived back in New York on September 23, 1853, completing her westbound crossing from Madeira in less than ten days. During the four months she had been away she had covered over 15,000 miles. For most of that distance Eldridge had fired up only two of her four boilers, but still cruised along at thirteen knots—faster than the *Baltic* during her record-breaking run between Liverpool and New York in 1851. With all four boilers in operation he had recorded a speed of eighteen knots, previously inconceivable for a vessel the size of the *North Star*. There could no longer be any doubt about his ability to handle a steamer; the sluggish performance of the *Pioneer* had clearly been due to the ship, not its commander.

On the back of this success, Eldridge could presumably have had his pick of almost any steamer on the ocean for his next command. Indeed, in November 1853 newspapers on both sides of the Atlantic reported that the record-setting captain of the *Baltic* was leaving the Collins Line and that Asa Eldridge would succeed him.

The rumor was unfounded. Eldridge had some unfinished business to complete. In the years since his decision to abandon sail for steam, one particular class of sailing ship had enjoyed an enormous boom. The boom was driven by a greatly increased need for fast passages on certain routes, which led to the construction of numerous ships built primarily for speed. These ships needed captains of extraordinary skill to sail them, and Asa Eldridge was itching to prove once again that he belonged in that category. So before he committed himself unreservedly to steamers, he simply could not resist the lure of one last voyage under sail. Otherwise, he would never know what he might have achieved on a ship in that most fabled of all classes: the clipper.

6

KING OF THE CLIPPERS

IF THE HALLMARK of the packet ships was their regularity, the defining feature of the clippers was their speed. Although speed was certainly an important consideration in the design of the packets, to some extent it was sacrificed in favor of carrying capacity and sturdiness; these vessels were, after all, the workhorses of transatlantic trade, required to shuttle back and forth across the ocean whatever the conditions. For the clippers, however, the ability to sail at a fast "clip" was paramount, which dominated their design and gave them their name.

The emergence of the clippers was driven by two developments in the 1840s that greatly increased the demand for swiftness on the water: the growing popularity of tea in the US, and the discovery of gold in California.

Seventy years earlier tea had brewed up a storm in the political landscape of colonial America, and it now inspired a quieter change in the naval architecture of the independent United States. This time the locals were anxious to throw their tea into pots rather than harbors, and they wanted it to be as fresh as possible. Merchants therefore pressed for faster deliveries from China, causing shipbuilders to modify their designs to emphasize speed. Long before elaborate theories of marine engineering were available, they proceeded largely by trial and error. But over time a new class of remarkably fast vessels emerged. This was a gradual process, with no clear dividing line between the new class and the ships that preceded them. As Carl Cutler commented in his masterful work, *Greyhounds of the Sea*:

> One searches in vain for some heroic, outstanding figure as the "inventor" of the clipper and misses the thrill of being able to point to some beautiful vessel and say: "Here is the first true example." Model shaded

imperceptibly into model: new "improved rig" followed old "improved rig" until men felt it could serve no useful purpose to attempt to gain a further increase in speed. Somewhere between the first uncertain steps and the last glorious creation is the "first clipper."

Although Cutler was reluctant to identify any individual ship as the first of the clippers, he was happy to pinpoint one particular packet ship as the first step in their evolution. The *Roscius*, he argued, and to a lesser extent her sister ships in the Dramatic Line, had a major influence on the design of packet ships, and thus on the design of clippers; every liner built thereafter either copied or improved on the "new points of excellence" exemplified by the *Roscius*. Those points included an enormous area of canvas, with a main mast almost 160 feet high, and a main yard (the horizontal spar that carried the mainsail) 75 feet wide. By way of comparison, when the famous clipper ship *Flying Cloud* was built thirteen years later her mainmast and main yard were only a few feet bigger. The key difference separating the *Roscius* from the clippers was her hull, which had none of the elongated elegance of the later vessels. Thus Cutler describes her as "a blunt, chunky craft by modern standards." Nevertheless (he continues), she was "built to 'go' by past masters in the art of calculated recklessness, and 'go' she did." Asa Eldridge's experience on the *Roscius* would therefore have been highly relevant when he eventually commanded a clipper ship.

Other commentators have been more willing than Cutler to identify specific ships as the "first clipper." Two contenders often mentioned are the *Ann McKim* and the *Rainbow*, both of which were built for shipowners in Baltimore. If the *Anne McKim* was indeed a clipper then she clearly deserves to be called the first, since she was built in 1833, more than a decade before the *Rainbow* or any other candidate for that title.

Mention of Baltimore serves as a reminder that even before the *Ann McKim*, the phrase "Baltimore clipper" was in common use for a whole class of vessels that were rather different from those later called clippers. This earlier class had evolved from the fast-moving privateers that had taken on the British during the War of 1812, but its members were much smaller than the later generation of clipper ships. Strictly speaking, moreover, they were not actually ships but schooners—with two masts rather than three, and sails rigged parallel to the long axis of the vessel rather than across it.

While there may be no consensus on which ship was the first true clipper, there is general agreement on what qualified a ship to be so classified. The two crucial characteristics were those alluded to by Cutler in his critique of the *Roscius* mentioned above: "sharp lines" and a disproportionately large area of sail. "Sharpness" referred to the shape of the clipper's hull, which was narrower than previously typical for a vessel of its length and had a much more pointed bow than those of the packet ships. And to drive that hull through the water at extraordinary speed, the clipper was fitted with huge square sails arrayed on unusually tall masts, augmented by fore-and-aft sails mounted on the rear of each mast and on the bowsprit—all providing a vast area of canvas much greater than a traditional ship of similar size would carry.

By themselves, however, sharp lines and an abundance of canvas were not enough. In the eloquent words of Carl Cutler:

> ... there was a third essential, without which the other two were of little use. Her captain must be a "driver." The soul of the clipper was her master. Unless she were commanded by a "horse"—a thorough daredevil with a mania for speed, who left nothing undone to strengthen his rig and extend his spread of canvas, and then hung on until spars began to go and the head knees cracked, the finest ship that ever floated was a beautiful fabric and nothing more.

The first of the Eldridge brothers to test his mettle as a "horse" was Oliver, not Asa. In 1844, at the age of 26, Oliver assumed command of a new vessel called the *Coquette* that had been built for the China trade. Technically the *Coquette* was a barque, not a ship, because the rearmost of her three masts was rigged fore-and-aft rather than square. But according to Henry Kittredge in *Shipmasters of Cape Cod*, she belonged to a group of vessels "which, though not really clippers, were much sharper than the old models and have sometimes been listed in the clipper class." With Oliver Eldridge at the helm the *Coquette* was certainly fast. On her maiden voyage she set a new record of 89 days from Boston to Canton, and she followed this up with a number of swift passages between ports in Asia. Her reputation for speed even reached Liverpool, where Oliver had the gratifying experience of overhearing an English captain complain that he had "beaten everything in the China Seas except that damned Yankee, *Coquette*."

Although the *Coquette* is not generally considered to have been a clipper ship, Oliver's next vessel most certainly was—in spite of the fact that, like the *Coquette*, she was rigged as a barque. In July 1848 Oliver took command of the newly completed *Memnon* for a voyage that was routine for packet ships but which few clippers ever made: from New York to Liverpool and back. The *Memnon* may have been a clipper but Eldridge initially struggled to get her going, averaging only seventy-seven miles per day during the first six days. Towards the end of the voyage, however, she traveled 241 miles on a single day, and he confided to her log book that "I am now convinced the ship can sail."

The *Memnon* would go on to make history the following year, but without Oliver. When she arrived back in New York at the end of her maiden voyage the Dramatic Line had just been sold, and within two months Oliver had replaced his brother Asa as captain of the *Roscius*.

In former days the turnover at the Dramatic Line might have attracted significant attention among New York's mariners and merchants, but in the fall of 1848 they had a much more interesting topic to divert them. Startling news had recently arrived from California. Gold had been discovered! Reportedly, a few weeks' digging was all it took to make a fortune! Single nuggets weighing five ounces had been found! People were flocking to the gold fields by the thousands, making it imperative to get to California as quickly as possible and stake a claim. And the fastest way there was by sea.

Initially at least, this meant sailing around Cape Horn at the tip of South America. (Although subsidized mail steamers began service via Panama in late 1848, their capacity for passengers was limited.) The route around the Cape was long and dangerous: from New York, almost fifteen thousand miles to San Francisco. Nonetheless, the lure of gold was so strong that 1849 saw a huge increase in traffic. In the twelve months leading up to April 1, 1848, only four merchant vessels arrived in San Francisco from ports on the eastern seaboard. In 1849 an astonishing 775 did so. Together with vessels from other countries, they brought over 91,000 passengers in search of riches: the famous "49ers." Those passengers were not the only ones to race for the gold fields upon arrival; in many cases, officers and crews deserted *en masse*, leaving behind ships that never sailed again.

This frenzy created a demand for faster vessels than the traditional square-riggers, barques, brigs and schooners that had carried the 49ers to their destination. Clippers were the obvious answer, but were still relatively rare when the Gold Rush began. Only one of the ships that made its way to San Francisco in 1849 was a clipper: Oliver Eldridge's former charge the *Memnon*, now under the command of Captain George Gordon after Oliver's move to the *Roscius*. But with a new record time of 120 days from New

York, she perfectly illustrated the potential of her class. The stage was set for a massive boom in the building of new clippers.

The boom began in 1850, when thirteen new specimens took to the ocean. They were joined in the rush to California by several clippers that had previously been engaged in the China trade—notably the famous *Sea Witch*, reputedly the fastest ship in that trade. She quickly reinforced her reputation by sailing from New York to San Francisco in only ninety-seven days, a week faster than any of the new clippers. But even the slowest of these, the *Mandarin*, was over a month faster than most other vessels from the East Coast, taking 126 days compared with the overall average of 159.

After unloading in San Francisco, many of the clippers sailed on to China to pick up cargoes of tea and silks, then headed west to the US to complete a circumnavigation of the globe. The *Memnon*, for example, had followed this route after her initial voyage to San Francisco in 1849, arriving back in New York just three days short of a year after her departure.

By 1851, many California-bound passengers were choosing to travel on the steamship routes via Panama or Nicaragua, which could cut months off the overall journey time. The Panama route was now firmly established, while the shortcut across Nicaragua had recently been opened up by Vanderbilt. Far from slackening, however, the construction of new clippers accelerated. California's booming population needed many basic commodities that were not yet available locally, and which were difficult to transport by the over-land routes across Central America. With demand far outstripping supply, prices soared. Beef, pork and flour cost between $40 and $60 a barrel. Tea, coffee and sugar were $4 a pound. Spirits—ever popular with prospectors—commanded $10 to $40 a quart. A pick or shovel cost from $5 to $15. And so on. There was clearly money to be made by shipping these materials to San Francisco, even if it meant sailing around Cape Horn. Just as clearly, clippers were the vessels to get them there quickly, while prices were still astronomical.

The trend for the next few years was therefore to more and larger clippers. Whereas in 1850 there had been thirteen new clippers with an average size of about 1,100 tons, in 1853 there were fifty-one newcomers averaging over 1,400 tons. The size of the largest individual new example also increased substantially, from 1,535 tons in 1850 (the *Stag-Hound*) to 2,360 in 1853 (the aptly named *Queen of Clippers*). Indeed, the latter year also saw the construction of a monster clipper much bigger than either of these, the *Great Republic*, which was not included in the comparisons just made because she was not intended for the California trade. She will be described in more detail shortly.

Like many endeavors before and since, the construction of new clippers became a matter of competition between New York and Boston. Initially the New York shipyards took the lead, building eighteen clippers to the Boston yards' fifteen during the first two years of the boom, 1850 and 1851. But over the next two years the Massachusetts capital forged way ahead, completing forty-four to its rival's fifteen. Shipbuilders in other parts of the state also joined in the building frenzy. On Cape Cod, for example, eight new clippers emerged from the Shiverick shipyard in Dennis, just a few miles from Asa Eldridge's home in Yarmouth Port.

The most prolific individual builders were Donald McKay and Samuel Hall in East Boston, who each completed ten clippers between 1850 and 1853, and William Webb and Jacob Westervelt of New York, who produced nine and eight respectively over the same period.

The outstanding figure among all of these was Donald McKay, arguably the most famous builder not just of clippers but of any form of sailing ship. A Canadian who had trained in the New York shipyards of Brown & Bell and Isaac Webb, in 1841 he became a partner in a yard in Newburyport, thirty-five miles north of Boston. Four years later he was persuaded to open his own yard in East Boston by Enoch Train, for whom he had just completed the *Joshua Bates*—the first packet ship in Train's new White Diamond Line between Boston and Liverpool. By 1850 he had built five more packets for Train and almost a dozen ships for other owners. The *Stag-Hound*, completed in December of that year, was the first of his many clippers.

Four months later he launched the masterpiece that established him as the greatest of all shipbuilders, the *Flying Cloud*. At 1,783 tons and 225 feet long—almost the length of a Boeing 747 jumbo jet—she was his biggest ship yet. She completed her maiden voyage from New York to San Francisco in eighty-nine days and twenty-one hours, easily beating the record of ninety-six days that had been set just a few months earlier. On one particular day she covered 374 miles, further than any other ship—steamers included—had ever traveled in a day.

News of her accomplishment reached New York in early October, just as Asa Eldridge was preparing for the maiden voyage of the steamship *Pioneer*. He must have read with great interest the article in the *Evening Post* on October 6 under the banner headline "Another Triumph of American

Seamanship." The yacht *America* had recently trounced Britain's supposedly invincible yachts in the first running of what became the America's Cup, and the paper trumpeted the *Flying Cloud*'s new record as yet further evidence of American superiority at sea.

Meanwhile, the subject of this jingoistic pride was out on the ocean again and adding further to her reputation. Heading for Honolulu and China on her westward path home, she immediately repeated her feat of traveling 374 miles in a single day. Her passage to Hong Kong in thirty-five days was one of the fastest on record, just a day slower than the new mark set by another clipper sailing at the same time, the *Game Cock*. She eventually reached New York in early April 1852, completing her voyage around the world in just over ten months—nearly two months faster than the *Memnon* had in 1849-50.

Her arrival back in New York may have given Asa Eldridge pause for thought. Six months earlier, when he learned of her triumphant voyage to San Francisco, he would have been too preoccupied with his new steamer even to consider a return to sail. But much had changed in the interim. The *Pioneer* had been a disappointment on both legs of her maiden voyage to Liverpool, and had then been diverted to the California trade. While the long-term future clearly lay with steam power, the excitement generated by the *Flying Cloud* may have inspired him to dream about testing his mettle on a clipper. In five years on the Dramatic Line packets he had certainly shown he could drive a ship hard.

And the clippers were unquestionably driven hard, as was clear from the condition of the *Flying Cloud* when she arrived back in New York. The strain of constantly sailing at the limit had exacted a heavy toll. Her mainmast had been badly damaged even before she reached China, while her spars and rigging bore a patchwork of repairs improvised by the crew. So although she was less than a year old, she needed an almost complete refit.

Such damage became typical for clippers that circled the globe, adding to the already high cost of owning these vessels. Not only were they expensive to build, but their vast expanse of sail required larger crews to operate them. Whereas a typical packet ship might need a crew of thirty or forty men, a clipper could require up to three times that number. But so long as there were large profits to be made from selling basic commodities in San Francisco and Chinese luxury goods in New York, the clippers generated handsome financial returns for their owners.

For the transatlantic trade, however, the clippers were not really viable. The sleek shape that gave them their speed also limited their cargo capacity, and with freight rates lower on the Atlantic because of competition between numerous packet ships and steamers, the clippers could not generate enough income to offset their higher operating costs.

Any clipper that did make her way across the Atlantic was therefore guaranteed to attract attention. That was certainly the case for the *Typhoon*, which in March 1851 sailed from Portsmouth, New Hampshire to Liverpool in thirteen days and ten hours—the fastest crossing of the Atlantic that had ever been recorded by a sailing ship. In addition to being the first American clipper to visit Liverpool, at 1,611 tons and 225 feet she was also the largest merchant ship ever to do so. No surprise, then, that according to the *Liverpool Times* she attracted hundreds of admiring visitors.

In 1852 Donald McKay continued to raise the standard for new clippers with his *Sovereign of the Seas*, which at 2,421 tons was 35 percent larger than any other ship built that year. She was over 258 feet long—almost thirty feet longer than a Boeing 747—and required a crew of 105 men plus officers. (The lower photograph on the opposite page shows another object from the present day that provides a sense of the size of the clipper ships mentioned in this chapter. The object in question is the restored British tea clipper *Cutty Sark*, which is huge by comparison with the people and everyday items in the foreground of the photograph, but at 963 tons was much smaller than many of the American clippers under discussion here.)

Overseeing the *Sovereign*'s crew on her maiden voyage was Captain Lauchlan McKay, Donald's younger brother, who managed to reach San Francisco in 103 days despite severe damage to two of the ship's masts off the coast of Chile. From there he proceeded to Honolulu and, somewhat unusually, back around Cape Horn to New York. It was on this return journey that the big clipper really showed her speed, at one point covering 3,562 miles in eleven calendar days—which correcting for time differences due to longitude changes, translated to 330 miles every twenty-four hours. Her best distance in one such period was 424 miles, comfortably more than the record set by the *Flying Cloud*.

For her next voyage the *Sovereign* again followed a different route than most of the clipper ships, becoming one of the rare members of the class to sail from New York to Liverpool. This was not, however, with any intention that she should become a regular on that route; her owner had a different route in mind, namely the much longer passage between Liverpool and

Donald McKay.

The restored British clipper *Cutty Sark*, which despite her obviously considerable size was much smaller than many of McKay's and other American clippers.

The *Flying Cloud.*

A contemporary print depicting the *Red Jacket* surrounded by ice off
Cape Horn during her return to Liverpool from Australia in 1854—
her third record-breaking run that year.

Melbourne. Gold had recently been discovered in Australia, creating a strong demand for ships that could get there quickly. The crossing she made in June 1853 was therefore the only occasion on which the *Sovereign* sailed from New York to Liverpool. But she made it a memorable one, reaching her destination in just under fourteen days, which was a new record for any sailing ship traveling between these ports. For a good part of the crossing she outran one of Cunard's steamers.

By now the clipper-ship boom was reaching its peak. Fifty-one new examples were launched during 1853, compared with thirty-three the previous year. Although five of the new crop came from the yard of Donald McKay, only one was bigger than the *Sovereign of the Seas*, and she was not destined for California (despite early newspaper reports to the contrary). McKay had decided that he too would like to profit from the Australian gold rush, by building a leviathan clipper he would operate himself rather than sell to another owner. The *Great Republic* was an astonishing 4,555 tons and 335 feet long—almost double the tonnage of the *Sovereign* and longer than a football field—with four masts and four decks. She was the largest ship of any sort afloat. The city of Boston declared the day of her launch in October a public holiday, and over 30,000 people turned out for the event.

The following month she was towed down to New York to prepare for her maiden voyage to Liverpool, which was the home port for several regular services to Australia. Her departure was set for the end of December, but she never made it. On the night of December 26, 1853, disaster struck. Shortly after midnight a fire broke out in a bakery a block away from the South Street waterfront where she was moored. The flames quickly spread to nearby properties and raced through the neighborhood. Twenty different buildings were soon ablaze. High above the inferno, an incendiary plume of sparks and embers blew across South Street and rained down on the *Great Republic*. Although the crew had been stationed with buckets of water when the alarm was called, there was little they could do to prevent her giant sails from catching fire. With flames raging aloft, the captain decided to cut down the masts so as to save the hull. Initially his plan seemed to be succeeding: while the fallen masts did set the main deck alight, local firefighters had now arrived and were able to bring this new blaze under control. Below deck, however, the cargo had also caught fire and was burning uncontrollably, forcing the captain to scuttle the ship in a further attempt to save the hull. In the shallow water by the wharf she sank about ten feet before hitting bottom, and then took two days to burn down to the waterline.

Donald McKay was devastated. Some say he never recovered from the destruction of his masterpiece. She was not a total loss, however. Having settled his insurance claim, her underwriters sold her burned-out hull to a new owner who rebuilt her on a somewhat reduced scale. In her new incarnation she had only three decks, not four, and registered a mere 3,357 tons—which still made her the largest merchant ship afloat. She never did sail to Australia, but over the next decade made a number of voyages from her base in New York to Liverpool and to San Francisco.

McKay himself was finished with San Francisco. When he built the *Great Republic* for the long haul to Australia, he was responding not only to increased demand there but also to falling demand in California. After four years of frenzied activity the merchants of San Francisco were now reasonably well stocked with basic and luxury goods, and the rush to the gold mines was subsiding. In contrast, the Australian states of New South Wales and Victoria were experiencing much the same issues that California had faced several years earlier: a massive influx of gold-seekers and a shortage of key supplies. And so the 1,782-ton *Romance of the Sea*, completed a month after the *Great Republic*, was McKay's last California clipper. Beginning with the 2,083-ton *Lightning* in January 1854, all of his clippers for the next several years were built to sail to Australia.

McKay's judgment about the demand for California clippers proved to be correct. In 1854, the class saw only twenty new members—a precipitous drop from the previous year's fifty-one. In subsequent years the new examples numbered thirteen, then eight, then four. And in 1858, none at all were built. The boom was well and truly over. But as it faded into history, McKay could look back with great pride on his contributions. His ships had registered many of the best times from New York to San Francisco, including the one that remains on the record books as the fastest ever by a sailing ship on that route. In 1854, the *Flying Cloud* shaved thirteen hours off the record she had set on her maiden voyage three years earlier, and which no other ship had beaten in the interim. She arrived in San Francisco on April 20 just eighty-nine days and eight hours after leaving New York. Not for nothing is Donald McKay regarded as one of the world's greatest-ever shipbuilders.

BACK, THOUGH, to Asa Eldridge and his relationship to all of these events. As noted earlier, the exploits of the *Flying Cloud* on her maiden voyage in 1851-52 may have tempted him to try his hand at the helm of a clipper, particularly after his unsuccessful venture into steam with the *Pioneer*. Any thoughts of doing so were presumably put to one side, however, when Cornelius Vanderbilt asked him to take command of the *North Star* for her private cruise around Europe. That undertaking kept him busy until late September 1853, by which time the major news in the maritime community was the impending launch of the *Great Republic*. This took place shortly after Eldridge had arrived back in New York on the *North Star*, and he may well have been one of the 30,000-plus people who attended the launch. He and his wife now lived in Roxbury, the Boston suburb where she grew up, and he would surely have had a strong interest in seeing the world's largest sailing ship. Indeed, as a local shipmaster of considerable renown, he was quite possibly an invited guest for the festivities surrounding her launch.

One month later another Australia-bound clipper was launched from a New England shipyard, with much less fanfare but much more significance for Asa Eldridge. She had been built for the Boston firm of Seccomb & Taylor by George Thomas of Rockland, Maine. Although based in Boston, her owners had bypassed Donald McKay (who may have been too busy anyway) and chosen a rising young star to design their new ship. The son of a naval architect employed by the US Navy, Samuel Pook had apprenticed with his father and then struck out on his own as an independent ship designer—the first in the US to work for himself rather than as the employee of a shipbuilder. When he made this brave move in 1850 he was only twenty-three. Over the next couple of years he established a reputation for clippers that were both speedy and reasonably capacious. This combination was particularly appealing for the long haul to Australia, and in 1852 Seccomb & Taylor commissioned him to design a new clipper for that destination. Bypassing Boston again, they chose to have her built in Maine, where labor and lumber were both less expensive. Indeed, for that very reason Maine's shipyards were chosen more than any others for the construction of big ships during the 1850s.

The new clipper was the largest vessel ever constructed in Rockland, 2,305 tons and 260 feet long. Thousands turned out to see her launch and naming ceremony on November 2, 1853. Curiously, she was named after a famous Native American chief who had supported the British during the Revolutionary War. They had rewarded him with a highly embroidered coat, which chief Sagoyewatha was so fond of wearing that he became known instead as "Red Jacket." And so too did Pook's new clipper.

Contemporary accounts were effusive in their praise of the new ship, calling her the "handsomest of the large clippers put afloat by American builders." Her striking lines were matched by the luxury of her accommodations, which were finished in exotic rosewood, mahogany, zebrawood and black walnut, tastefully decorated with gilt.

Later that month the *Red Jacket* was towed down to New York by the steam tug *R.B. Forbes*. Under normal circumstances she might have been the subject of protracted interest in New York, but ten days later the same tug was back on the East River with another new clipper in tow: the *Great Republic*. From that point forward McKay's leviathan attracted all of the attention, with the *Red Jacket* virtually forgotten.

As a result, the appointment of a famous captain for her maiden voyage also went unnoticed. The purpose of this voyage was simply to deliver her to Liverpool for subsequent deployment on the route between that port and Melbourne. And the man chosen to deliver her was Asa Eldridge. Fresh from his triumph on the *North Star*, Eldridge could no longer resist the opportunity for one last test of his prowess under sail—the chance to show that he could drive a clipper as well as any man on the ocean.

First, though, there was work to be done. The immediate priority was to make sure the *Red Jacket* was ready. Like most ships of the period she had been launched without any masts or rigging installed; after hauling her down from Maine the *R.B. Forbes* would have dropped her off at an East River shipyard where these crucial components could be added. Given his long experience under sail, Asa Eldridge would have played an active role in supervising their installation.

Then there was a crew to be hired. Putting one together would not have been a simple task. Because so many vessels were now operating out of New York on the Atlantic and California routes, sailors with significant experience on square-riggers were in short supply. While Eldridge may once have had a loyal cohort of such men who had operated regularly under his command, almost four years had now passed since he last skippered a sailing ship, and so the sailors who knew him would have long since moved on. Adding to the challenge, the *Red Jacket*—like most clippers—needed a significantly bigger crew than the packets Eldridge had formerly commanded. The *Roscius* herself had required an unusually large crew because of the vast amount of canvas she carried, but her complement of forty-five men was still seventeen less than the number now needed for the *Red Jacket*. And the new clipper would be sailing in January, the very worst time of the year to recruit, when brutal winds and ice-coated rigging made the work of a sailor even more dangerous and less appealing than usual.

One other factor would also have had a major impact on the availability of suitable recruits: competition from the *Great Republic*. McKay's huge clipper was due to sail at the end of December, and because of her size would have needed an enormous crew. Initially this must have been yet one more obstacle to recruitment for the *Red Jacket*, but then came the terrible fire that consumed McKay's masterpiece. Tragic though this was, it meant that dozens of sailors were suddenly unemployed—and therefore available to fill any gaps still remaining in the *Red Jacket*'s roster.

With or without a boost from that source, by early January the *Red Jacket* had a full crew assembled. Eldridge was not particularly happy with them—he would later describe them as "indifferent" and "incompetent"— but at least he had enough men to take the new clipper across the Atlantic.

She made a slow start. After being cleared to sail on January 7, she did not actually leave New York until the morning of January 10. Perhaps Eldridge and his officers were busy training the mediocre crew. On her first day out the *Red Jacket* covered only 103 miles; had she continued at that pace it would have taken a month to reach Liverpool. Three of the next six days were not much better, so that by the end of the first week she had traveled only about 1,200 miles—little more than a third of the way across the Atlantic.

But then came a transformation. On every one of the next six days she sailed 300 miles or more; on the second of them she covered 413 miles, almost the record distance for a sailing ship in a single day. By the morning of January 23 she was closing in on her destination, with every chance of reaching it in the shortest time ever recorded under sail from New York.

Her rapid progress did not go unnoticed. A Liverpool-bound steamer was crossing the Atlantic not far ahead of her, and its crew must have realized that the majestic clipper coming up behind them might be headed for a new record. Arriving in Liverpool slightly before the *Red Jacket*, they alerted people to this possibility and to her imminent arrival. As the news spread along the waterfront, a crowd quickly gathered.

The spectators were not disappointed. From the moment the *Red Jacket* was close enough to discern, it was clear that she was still under full sail and moving at a fast clip. Ignoring the steam-tugs offering her the usual tow into port, she continued under canvas until the last possible moment. And then, on a barked command from Eldridge, her crew spilled the wind from her sails as he threw her into a sharp turn, deftly guiding her backwards into her berth. This audacious maneuver triggered thunderous applause from the crowd, one of whom wrote that "Not one master in a hundred would have dared to try it."

But there was more to the *Red Jacket's* arrival than this flourish. The steamer's crew had been correct in their surmise. The clipper had also just set a new record for the passage from New York to Liverpool by a sailing ship. Her time of thirteen days, one hour and twenty-five minutes was almost a day shorter than the mark set by McKay's *Sovereign of the Seas* the previous summer.

The significance of this accomplishment can be judged from the attention it received in *The Times* of London, arguably the world's most prestigious and influential newspaper in that era. *The Times'* initial report of the *Red Jacket's* crossing described her as "one of the handsomest vessels we ever beheld, possessing with the greatest symmetry of model immense strength and carrying capacity." This glowing assessment was followed by a detailed listing of her dimensions, concluding that she was "by some hundreds of tons the largest merchantman afloat." (The reporter had clearly forgotten about the *Sovereign of the Seas* despite her visit to Liverpool six months earlier; the previous record-holder was marginally bigger than her successor.) The report closed with a summary of the *Red Jacket's* log tabulating the miles she had covered on each day of the voyage from New York.

That inclusion led to a letter in the following day's paper casting doubt on the accuracy of the log. This missive came from a highly authoritative source—Lloyd's of London—but was signed only "A. W. J.". While the writer's identity may have been hidden, his incredulity was not. The letter opened by stating that the "extraordinary log of the Red Jacket... if correct, would prove her able to do what no steamship afloat has ever accomplished— to run 413 knots in 24 hours." Its mysterious author then questioned why the total mileage he calculated from the log of the *Red Jacket* was so much greater than the actual distance between New York and Liverpool "from wharf to wharf": 3,600 knots versus 3,084. Mail steamers, he argued, "habitually run within a few miles" of the latter figure. "Before we can credit the details of her log," he concluded," we must learn how, with fair winds, she ran over 500 knots of sea more than other vessels."

Since the log was the responsibility of the captain, this letter was effectively an attack on Asa Eldridge's integrity. As such, it drew a spirited defense of him from a fellow countryman. The next day's edition of *The Times* included a reply from "Young America," who objected to A. W. J.'s "very absurd conclusion" about the *Red Jacket's* voyage that "the log is (wilfully) incorrect, thereby throwing a slur upon the veracity of her commander." The anonymous correspondent, he continued, "seems to quite forget that a sailing ship rarely makes the same course as a steamer, but must go the shortest way the wind will permit." As for the plausibility of the *Red Jacket* covering 413 miles in twenty-four hours, Young America pointed out that several other sailing ships were already on record as having traveled further in a day—not least the *Sovereign of the Seas* on the same route the previous summer. The author closed by invoking *The Times*' "usual love of 'fair play to the Yankees'" to express no doubt that the paper would publish his letter. As indeed it did.

The final word in this correspondence came from Asa Eldridge himself. In a letter published by *The Times* on January 31 he provided a detailed response to his nameless critic. Since the letter in question is the only document found by the present author that is known to have been written by Eldridge, it is reproduced almost in full below:

TO THE EDITOR OF THE TIMES.

Sir, —Having seen an article in your paper of the 27th inst., signed "A. W. J.," respecting the log and passage of the ship Red Jacket, asking why, with a fair wind, she should have run 500 miles more than the steamers from the same port, I beg to say that Mr. "A. W. J." is labouring under a mistake, or has been misinformed, respecting the passage of the ship Red Jacket, as to winds, for I have not made any such statement, or conveyed any such idea to any one, as that I had fair winds all the way across the Atlantic. In reply, I will state that it was owing to adverse winds; and sometimes with a fair wind I was obliged to deviate from my true course, and keep the ship before the wind, for the gales were so terrific, and the sea running so high, I did not deem it prudent to run with both, or either, too much on the quarter; consequently, I ran more distance than I should if I had had pleasant gales and a fair wind all the way across the Atlantic....

To avoid any further mistake, I beg leave to refer you to an abstract log of my daily runs, setting forth the winds, courses, and distance sailed.—Left New York, Jan. 10, at 7 o'clock a.m.,—

Jan.	Lat.	Lon	Dis	Wind.		Course.		Remarks
11	40 33	71 45	103	S. by E.	..	E ½ N.	..	Rainy, unpleasant weather.
12	41 03	68 30	150	Ditto..	..	E. by S.	..	Rain, hail & snow.

13	42 19	62 41	265	S.S.E.	..	E. by N. ½ N.	Ditto.
14	44 25	58 20	232	S.E. by E.	..	N.E. by E.	..	Ditto.
15	46 35	54 15	210	Ditto..	..	N.E. ½ E.	..	Rain.
16	46 13	51 52	106	S.S.E.	..	E. by S.	..	Snowy & hailing.
17	45 55	49 03	119	Ditto..	..	E. ¾ S.	..	Ditto.
18	50 39	47 00	300	E. by S.	..	N. by E. ½ E.	Ditto.
19	51 58	35 55	417	W. by S. ½ S.,	E. by N.	..	Ditto, terrific gale, and high sea.
20	50 39	27 00	364	Ditto..	..	E. by S. ¼ S.	Ditto, and gale.
21	49 27	18 35	342	Ditto..	..	E. by S.	..	Ditto, fresh gales.
22	51 07	11 21	300	W.S.W.	..	E. by N. ½ N.	Snow, strong wind, & heavy squalls.
23	53 27	4 11	360	South..	..	Up Channel ..	Ditto, and squally, dirty weather.

I am, Sir, your obedient servant,

A. ELDRIDGE
Commander of the ship Red Jacket.

Liverpool, Jan. 28.

Interestingly, for eight of the thirteen days the *Red Jacket* was at sea, the daily mileages quoted by Eldridge in this letter are not identical to those cited in *The Times'* original article about his voyage. In all but one case the differences are small, but for January 14 the discrepancy was seventy-nine miles: 311 reported by *The Times*, as against 232 by Eldridge. One of the small discrepancies is also noteworthy, in that it increased the controversial figure for January 19 from 413 miles—already considered unlikely by "A. W. J."—to 417.

The reason for the differences between the two sets of figures is not clear. They may simply have resulted from errors in transcription. Whereas Eldridge's letter would have been written in his own hand and mailed directly to *The Times*, the information in the paper's original story would have been copied from the *Red Jacket's* log by the reporter, transmitted from Liverpool by a telegraph operator, and then received and written down by another operator in London; errors could have occurred at any of these steps.

Alternatively, aware of the intense scrutiny his log was receiving, Eldridge may have re-worked the calculations he had performed "on the fly" during the *Red Jacket's* voyage to give more precise answers. The entry in the log each day was based on his determination of the change in the ship's position—its latitude and longitude—compared with the previous day. This determination involved multiple inputs from chronometer, sextant and compass, and under the stormy conditions that clearly prevailed throughout most of the voyage, Eldridge may have felt it more important to devote his attention to handling his ship than to achieving complete precision in his calculations.

THESE NUANCES ASIDE, what is clear from Eldridge's letter is that the *Red Jacket*'s record crossing was accomplished under appalling conditions. Rain, snow, hail, gales, and high seas: every single day brought one or more of them. This makes Eldridge's achievement even more remarkable. The obstacles he faced were formidable. Four years had passed since he last commanded a sailing ship. The *Red Jacket* was completely new to him. She was also new to the crew—who in his assessment were mediocre. The Atlantic winter was at its worst. But Eldridge somehow managed to guide the *Red Jacket* from New York to Liverpool in a faster time than any other sailing ship has achieved before or since.

While "A. W. J" may not have been impressed, Liverpool certainly was. On February 15, three hundred of the port's most distinguished citizens came aboard the *Red Jacket* to admire her proportions and facilities and to attend a gala lunch. The event was described at length in the week's *Liverpool Mercury*, which opened its account by referring to the *Red Jacket* as "the magnificent new clipper ship... which recently made an extraordinarily rapid passage from New York to this port, during the prevalence of some severe gales..." After commenting favorably on the ship's spaciousness and accommodations, the *Mercury* provided a detailed account of the speeches given at the gala lunch. And since Asa Eldridge gave one of these, the report provides another rare example of communication that can be attributed directly to him. It also provides an even rarer insight into his thinking about his future.

Eldridge was responding to a toast from a Mr. William Fisher, who had commented on behalf of the guests that "as Englishmen, they were all delighted with seeing such a specimen of naval architecture." According to the *Mercury*:

> Captain ELDRIDGE responded in a suitable speech, in which, after remarking that he felt highly flattered by the compliment payed him in the toast which had been proposed, he said there was no man who liked to look upon a splendid specimen of naval architecture more than he did, and he thought the Red Jacket would bear the strictest examination. They had brought them something there of which they felt proud in America—(hear, hear)—and it would be gratifying to know that they all liked her as well in this country as they did on the other side of the

Atlantic. There were a great many ships built to cross and re-cross the Atlantic and traverse the different waters of the globe, but he had never seen any which, to his mind, could surpass the ship in which they were then assembled. (Hear, hear.) He did not speak from any selfish motives, because there was not a timber head of her which belonged to him in any way or shape. She belonged to a very humble citizen, but to a very noble and high-minded man, who had crossed the Atlantic with him (Captain Eldridge.). (Hear, hear.) He had partly made up his mind never to cross the Atlantic again, but when such a fine ship as the Red Jacket was offered to him, owned by such a noble and high-minded man as Mr. Taylor, he certainly could not refrain from once more coming to visit his friends on this side of the Atlantic, and showing them such a fine specimen of naval architecture, as they called it in the United States. They had got there something that would bear the examination, not only of the shipbuilders of Great Britain but of all nautical men. (Hear, hear.) After passing a high eulogium on Englishmen, whom he said he loved as part of himself, he said we were now getting to what were called war times; and if England and France could not beat Russia, he wanted them to call upon Brother Jonathan. (Cheers.) He would give them "England and America:" united together they could lick all the world. (Loud Cheers.)

As in his speech the previous year when the *North Star* visited South-ampton, Eldridge showed himself a diplomat who knew how to flatter and appeal to his audience. But while most of his remarks were of the superficial kind typical on such occasions, in this case one of them did reveal some of his private thoughts. The comment that "he had partly made up his mind never to cross the Atlantic again" suggested that he was thinking about retiring from the sea. If only he had done so, the sad events described in the next chapter might have been avoided.

In his own speech a little later, the *Red Jacket*'s owner provided an interesting anecdote about naming her. Mr. Taylor explained that he had originally selected a different name but refrained from using it out of deference to Donald McKay, who was planning to use exactly the same name for a clipper then under construction (but which McKay subse-quently called the *Great Republic*, not by the name Taylor had wanted). Otherwise the *Red Jacket* would have been the *King of Clippers*. Many in the audience might have thought this name very apt not just for Taylor's ship but for the man who had achieved such distinction on her maiden voyage.

Much as he admired the *Red Jacket*, Eldridge never sailed on her again. He had taken her across the Atlantic solely to deliver her to Liverpool for the Australian trade. The owner who accompanied him probably made the journey for the express purpose of selling her. Although Mr. Taylor may have been "noble and high-minded," as Eldridge described him, he was not above making a quick profit. A month after the gala lunch aboard the *Red Jacket* he sold her for $150,000, which was reportedly at least $50,000 more than she had cost to build. The buyers were Messrs. Pilkington & Wilson, who operated the White Star Line to Australia. Taylor was so pleased with this piece of business that he repeated many elements of it later the same year: he commissioned a second clipper for the Australian trade, named it the *Blue Jacket*, hired a Captain Eldridge to sail it to Liverpool (in this case Asa's younger brother, Oliver), and promptly sold it there.

The *Red Jacket* was a great success for the White Star Line. On both legs of her first roundtrip she set new records, 69½ days on the outbound leg to Melbourne and 73½ days on the return. The latter was achieved in spite of several days spent negotiating an ice field south of Cape Horn, an experience quickly immortalized in a print published by the firm of N. Currier (which mistakenly depicts the clipper under an American flag, although by the time of this voyage she was under British ownership). Including the stopover she made in Melbourne, the entire roundtrip was completed in five months and eleven days, a feat described by *The Times* as "the most extraordinary performance ever recorded." Her cargo on the return included one item that explained why fast transport to Australia was now so important: 44,943½ ounces of gold.

Although Asa Eldridge played no active role in the *Red Jacket*'s triumphant Australian voyage, he may deserve some of the credit for it. In October 1854, the British Association in Liverpool hosted a talk by Mr. J. Scott Russell on the subject of clipper ships and what made them so fast. And according to a local newspaper, "The Red Jacket came before us recommended not only by her very beautiful model, but by the fact, as well, that she had been built under the superintendence of one of the ablest seamen known to us—Captain Asa Eldridge—long known to others as well as ourselves in the trade between this port and the United States." Eldridge therefore appears to have collaborated closely with Samuel Pook on the design of the *Red Jacket*, and thus to have contributed to her performance in the hands of his successor.

His own record voyage at her helm was his last under sail, a fitting finale to more than twenty years as one of the very best sailing-ship captains on the planet. Even for his return to New York from Liverpool he chose a steamer, traveling as a passenger on the Collins Line's *Baltic*. And from this point forward, every voyage he made would be powered by steam.

7

MYSTERIOUS END

ANY THOUGHTS Asa Eldridge had of retiring from the sea did not last long. With his triumphant voyage on the *Red Jacket*, he had proved to himself and the world that clipper ships were just one more class of vessel he could sail as well as any man around. But as yet he could not make the same claim for transatlantic steamers, which had quickly become the most prestigious ships on the ocean. If he wanted to maintain his standing as one of the world's greatest mariners, he would need to prove himself an elite performer on these vessels as well. Retirement would have to wait.

Such may have been his thoughts as he made his way back to New York on the *Baltic*. His travel on that particular vessel may only have reinforced them. The *Baltic* and her commander, Captain Joseph Comstock, held the current record for the fastest westbound crossing of the Atlantic, which they had set three years earlier with the first-ever passage from Liverpool to New York in under ten days.

Eldridge would have welcomed the opportunity for long discussions with Captain Comstock. Few men could teach him more about operating under steam. Unlike the other three captains in the Collins Line fleet, who had all been long-term commanders of sailing packets, Comstock had spent almost his entire career on steamers. For many years he had been the popular skipper of the *Massachusetts*, which had shuttled between Rhode Island and New York. He then played a key role in establishing the Fall River Line of steamers operating between New York and Boston—overseeing construction and taking command of its flagship, the *Bay State*. And for last three and a half years he had commanded the *Baltic* for E.K. Collins. Crossing the Atlantic with Comstock on the fastest of all steamers, Eldridge would have been eager to absorb as much wisdom as he could from such a master.

For his part, Comstock may also have been keen to learn from Eldridge. Although headwinds and opposing currents had much less effect on steamers than on sailing ships, they could still add a day or two to any crossing; as a relative newcomer to the Atlantic, Comstock would still have been learning the best routes for avoiding these conditions, and would have appreciated the insights Eldridge could provide after more than two decades on the same ocean.

It is tempting to speculate that these insights helped Comstock to the crowning achievement of his career just a few months later. On July 7, 1854, he brought the *Baltic* into New York just 9 days, 16 hours and 52 minutes after leaving Liverpool. This not only broke the record he had set for the westbound crossing three years earlier, but also beat the fastest time in the opposite and easier direction—a crossing two years earlier by another Collins liner, the *Arctic*.

Eldridge, in the meantime, had not had the chance to benefit from Comstock's wisdom about steamships. There were still only eight American steamers operating on the Atlantic, and none needed a new master. The alternative, a British ship, would presumably have been out of the question.

Among American steamers the most appealing prospect would have been one of the Collins liners, which were firmly established as the fastest ships on the marquee route between New York and Liverpool. But in all four cases the original captain was still in place and performing well; each had at least one record crossing to his name.

The other four steamers were divided equally between the Ocean Steam Navigation Company (OSNC) and the New York & Havre Steam Navigation Company (NYHSNC). The OSNC, as noted in Chapter 5, was the company that had surprisingly won the first mail contract from the US government ahead of E. K. Collins. Its service ran between New York and Bremen in Germany, with a brief stop at Cowes/Southampton on the south coast of England. But even if a position had been available on this service, Eldridge might have been reluctant to accept it. The OSNC's steamers, the *Washington* and the *Hermann*, were slow and unreliable—hardly attributes that would help Eldridge establish himself as an elite steamship commander.

Those attributes were, in fact, responsible for the existence of the other company that might have offered an opportunity. The NYHSNC had been formed specifically to take over a second route that the OSNC had been awarded but failed to implement—largely because it was too busy trying to rectify the poor performance of the *Washington* and *Hermann* on its service to Bremen.

This second route was supposed to run from New York to Havre in France, again touching at Cowes. It had been awarded to the OSNC in 1845 along with the Bremen route, but almost four years later was still awaiting its first steamer. Although the OSNC was clearly in breach of its contract, the Postmaster General was sympathetic to the company's situation. In his annual report at the end of 1848 he noted two mitigating circumstances: that the OSNC's contract was much less generous than those subsequently granted to other steamship operators, and that unlike the latter, the OSNC had not received a substantial advance from the government to help fund construction of its steamers. His sympathy only went so far, however: in April of the following year he authorized the transfer of the Havre route to the newly incorporated NYHSNC. The new company also acquired a half-completed steamer called the *Franklin* that the OSNC had been building for the Havre service.

The route was now in capable hands. Whereas the OSNC had been formed by men with no prior experience of shipping, the NYHSNC's founders, Samuel Fox and Mortimer Livingston, had operated a line of sailing packets between New York and Havre for close to fifteen years. Moreover, in anticipation of the transaction with the OSNC they had won state approval for a corporate charter authorizing the NYHSNC to raise up to $1.5 million in capital—more than enough to complete the *Franklin* and to build a sister ship called the *Humboldt*.

In October 1850 the *Franklin* finally inaugurated the route to Havre. Early the following year she was joined by the *Humboldt*. Although both ships had been designed by the OSNC they incorporated various improvements to correct the worst flaws of the *Washington* and *Hermann*, and quickly proved themselves faster than these predecessors. On the return leg of her first voyage, for example, the *Franklin* significantly out-performed one of Cunard's steamers: despite strong headwinds all the way, her time from Cowes to New York was several hours less than the *Cambria*'s on the shorter run from Liverpool to Boston. And on her next eastbound run, in December 1850, the *Franklin* recorded the month's shortest crossing time to England, besting Collins' *Atlantic* by six hours and Cunard's *Niagara* by seventeen.

While the NYHSNC was rarely able to repeat this victory, its steamers did establish a solid reputation for speed. As one newspaper put it, they "ranked next to the Collins boats for speed in the accomplishment of their trips, and on several occasions they have come fully up to these vessels." Their performance made them a viable option not only for traffic to France but also for passengers and freight traveling to London and the South of England more generally.

The NYHSNC's first full year of operation, 1851, happened to coincide with Asa Eldridge's efforts to launch his own steamship line with the *Pioneer*. Although surely aware of the NYHSNC's debut, he would have been much too preoccupied with his own nascent enterprise to contemplate the possibility of working for the year's other newcomer.

Three years later, after his adventures on the *North Star* and *Red Jacket*, that possibility represented his best hope for command of a steamer. With the Collins Line having no vacancies and the OSNC no attraction, the NYHSNC was effectively his only option.

That depended of course on the availability of a position. And like the Collins Line, the NYHSNC had initially stayed faithful to its original captains, Wotton on the *Franklin* and Lines on the *Humboldt*. At the end of 1853, however, the *Humboldt* ran aground off the Canadian coast and was wrecked—fortunately, with no loss of life. Scrambling to find a replacement, the NYHSNC briefly leased a coastal steamer and then purchased the *Union*, which had been operating between New York and Panama. The announcement of this transaction came just days after Asa Eldridge arrived back in New York. But if he was hoping that the NYHSNC would now be looking for a new captain he was disappointed. Richard Adams, the long-time master of the *Union* for her previous owners, would be staying on in that role.

Three months later, however, another disaster for the NYHSNC provided Eldridge the opening he had been seeking. Just short of her destination on a return journey from France, the *Franklin* ran aground off the shore of Long Island. Again, no lives were lost but the ship was wrecked. And again, the NYHSNC had to scramble to find a replacement.

Fortunately for the company, a steamer called the *St. Louis* had just been completed in the New York shipyard of Jacob Westervelt, and her owner, the Pacific Mail Steamship Company, was willing to lease her to the NYHSNC—presumably for a hefty premium. And fortunately for Asa Eldridge, as a brand-new vessel the *St. Louis* had no established captain. In a hurry to maintain its schedule, the NYHSNC quickly chose him to fill the vacancy. He had finally achieved his goal. He was now the proud commander of a transatlantic steamer.

With Eldridge at the helm, the *St. Louis* steamed out of New York for her maiden voyage on August 1, 1854, less than two weeks after the wreck of the *Franklin*. Her preparation was so hurried that she carried no cargo, just eighty passengers and about $350,000 in *specie* (currency in the form of coins, which were used to offset imbalances in trade and which many ships transported). She reached Cowes (for Southampton) at 6 a.m. on August 13, eleven days and sixteen hours after leaving New York. For a maiden voyage this was a very respectable run, only four hours longer than the average crossing by a Cunard liner from New York to Liverpool. From Cowes Eldridge proceeded across the English Channel to Havre, a trip that typically took about half a day.

For her return journey two weeks later the *St. Louis* did have some cargo in the hold—350 tons of valuable French and Swiss merchandise—and twice the number of passengers. The transatlantic portion of the route, from Cowes to New York, was completed in twelve days and nine hours, exactly the same as the average time taken by Cunarders on their westbound runs.

This was a promising start for Eldridge. The maiden voyage of any steamer was often slow because of the need to "run in" her machinery, and yet he had taken the *St. Louis* across the Atlantic in times comparable to those of the long-established Cunarders. His potential to rise to the upper echelon of steamship commanders was clear.

The times he recorded on this voyage were notable for another reason. Earlier that year, in command of the *Red Jacket*, Eldridge had completed what is still the fastest crossing from New York to Liverpool ever made by a sailing ship; yet with a performance that was only average for a steamer, the *St. Louis* took rather less time than the *Red Jacket* to cross the Atlantic, even in the much tougher westbound direction. The challenge facing the sailing packets could hardly have been illustrated more starkly. They were now simply unable to compete for the most valuable passengers and cargoes.

Eldridge's next voyage was more eventful, issuing him a forceful reminder that the superior speed of steamships did not make them immune from the perils of ocean crossings. The outbound leg went smoothly enough, completed almost as quickly as on his first voyage. On the return leg, however, the *St. Louis* suffered significant damage during a storm and limped into New York more than eighteen days after leaving Cowes.

Harrowing though this must have been for Eldridge, the news awaiting when he arrived back in port would have made his difficulties on the *St. Louis* seem minor. The Collins liner *Arctic* had sunk with the loss of 350 people. About fifty miles off the coast of Canada on her way back from New York to Liverpool, she had collided with a small steamer hidden by fog. The bow of the smaller vessel had gouged a large hole in the *Arctic's* side below the waterline, too big for any temporary repair, and leaking too quickly for the pumps to keep up. Amid mounting chaos, and with the crew fighting passengers over lifeboats, the ship gradually filled with water. Finally, about four and half hours after the collision, she slipped beneath the waves.

The sinking of the *Arctic* was a massive blow not just to the Collins Line but to Edward Collins personally. His wife, two of his three children, and a brother- and sister-in-law were among those lost. It was also a huge shock to New York and the country as a whole; the loss of 350 lives in a single disaster was almost unprecedented.

Shock turned to outrage when survivors recounted the disgraceful behavior of the crew. Many crewmen had put their own safety first, taking the lifeboats for themselves at the expense of passengers. On a percentage basis, five times more crew members than passengers survived: 40 per cent of the former (61 out of 153) versus 8 per cent of the latter (only 23 of 281). More scandalous still, every single one of the 109 women and children on board was lost.

The public was appalled. As a letter to the *New York Daily Times* put it in the florid language of the day:

> The horror and lamentation occasioned by the catastrophe which over-whelmed the *Arctic* and precipitated so large a proportion of her passengers, and so small a one of her crew, to the bottom of the sea, is well nigh equaled by the indignation excited by the conduct of the survivors of the latter in abandoning the former to their fate.

The writer characterized most of the crew as "deserters," and went on to propose that "to prevent similar exhibitions of dastardly selfishness... deser-tion under such circumstances [should be] punishable in the same manner as military desertion in time of war"— in other words, by execution.

Presumably to the disappointment of this correspondent, no sanctions of any sort were imposed on those involved in the loss of the *Arctic*. A Grand Jury was convened to investigate the disaster but did not issue any indictments, only a series of recommendations that were primarily about lifeboat safety. Nonetheless, the reputation of the Collins Line had been damaged almost as fatally as the *Arctic* herself.

For Asa Eldridge, the shock of learning about the disaster came late. The *Arctic* had sunk on September 27, four days after Eldridge had departed for Europe on the *St. Louis*, and no word of the tragedy could have reached him until he returned to New York on November 11. Indeed, the city itself did not hear of the disaster until October 11, two weeks after it happened, when the first of the survivors arrived home from Canada.

Eldridge must have been deeply affected by the news. During his time on the *Roscius* as one of only four captains in the Dramatic Line he would have worked closely with E.K. Collins, and quite probably got to know his employer's family as well. What few accounts exist of Eldridge's personal qualities suggest that he was a gregarious and empathetic man, in which case the pain of Collins' personal loss would have been very apparent to him. Collins had retired to the seclusion of his Long Island estate to mourn his wife and children, and Eldridge may well have offered to help in any way he could with Collins' personal or business obligations.

This perhaps explains why Eldridge never commanded the *St. Louis* again. Her next scheduled departure from New York was canceled anyway, while the damage she had suffered on the way back from Havre with Eldridge was repaired. And when she did sail again in January 1855 her captain was James Wotton, who had been master of the *Franklin* before that ship was lost.

Collins was certainly in need of help. Even excluding the loss of his family, he had huge issues to contend with. The Collins Line was facing a drastic reduction in its payments from the government for carrying mail. The viability of the company depended heavily on this income, and the threatened reduction would be catastrophic.

The threat was not new. It dated back to 1852, when Collins had secured a hefty increase in the subsidy he had originally been granted. That amount had been $385,000 a year, for which he was required to make twenty roundtrip voyages between New York and Liverpool—one every fortnight for most of the year, and one a month during the four months of winter. This schedule was chosen to match that of the Cunard Line, but late in 1851, Cunard announced that it would continue to sail every fortnight during the winter. The US Postmaster General then asked Collins to do the same, which would increase his annual number of voyages to twenty-six.

Collins protested that the current subsidy was woefully inadequate even for the twenty voyages he was already required to make, and that he could not contemplate adding another six without a major increase in compensation.

To support his argument, Collins provided figures to Congressional supporters indicating that, on average, he lost $16,928.79 for every voyage he currently undertook; for a full year's quota of twenty roundtrips the total loss amounted to $338,574. Reacting to these figures, the Senate Finance Committee quickly added an amendment to a bill it was finalizing. The amendment proposed increasing the Collins Line's compensation from $19,250 for each of twenty voyages to $33,000 for each of twenty-six, taking the annual subsidy from $385,000 to $858,000 for the remaining eight years of the contract.

Congress as a whole was less easily persuaded than the Finance Com- mittee. The amendment was debated at length in both chambers—for over a month in the Senate and a further ten days in the House. Supporters contended that the Collins liners were vital for national prestige, valuable as auxiliary warships, and likely to repay their subsidy through increased mail revenues. Opponents disputed the latter two points on multiple grounds, but found the first harder to counter. The performance of the Collins Line was undoubtedly a source of national pride. Its contest with the Cunard Line was followed closely on both sides of the Atlantic, and the four record crossings it had already achieved gave deep satisfaction to the American public—not least because the British had been forced to acknowledge the superiority of the Collins liners, a welcome change from their usual tendency to crow over or patronize their former colony. Opposition to the increased subsidy might therefore seem unpatriotic. For that reason, foes were careful not to oppose the *principle* of funding Collins to lord it over the British, only the *cost*.

At its heart, though, the debate was more about conflicting regional interests than about the cost of patriotism. The South resented the large share of the profits from its cotton and tobacco that was taken by New York merchants, while the West had numerous infrastructure projects in need of funding; neither wanted to see any government subsidy to a private enterprise on the East Coast. One outburst from a Southern senator summarized their feelings: "My word for it, the people of this country away from the seaboard will look into the conduct of this Government paying extravagant sums of money for purposes of this sort."

Eventually, supporters of the increased subsidy recognized that some concession would be needed to secure its passage. And the concession they made became a ticking time-bomb for the Collins Line. When the bill was finally passed in July 1852 it included the requested increase in annual funding from $385,000 to $858,000, but also a crucial proviso: Congress would have the power to revoke the increase at any time after December 31, 1854 on six months' notice. From that date forward, the prospect of financial ruin would never be more than half a year away for the Collins Line.

The loss of the *Arctic* in September 1854 thus came at a particularly inopportune time, just a few months before Congress would first have the right to cut back the mail subsidy to its original level. Because the steamer and her cargo were well insured the impact of the loss was more operational than financial; the company still had an obligation to transport the mail across the Atlantic every fortnight but was now one ship short. The schedule could still be maintained with only three steamers, but at the cost of reduced downtime for the frequent repairs needed to keep these hard-driven vessels in service. And any slip in performance might give the Line's opponents in Congress the excuse they needed to revoke the additional subsidy.

As he struggled to keep the performance of his Line competitive, Collins received an unexpected boost from a conflict on the other side of the world. Indirectly, the Crimean War led to the temporary disappearance of his key competitor. Britain had entered the war against Russia six months earlier, and under the terms of its contracts with the Cunard Line, now commandeered eleven of the latter's steamers to serve as transports. Cunard was forced to suspend his service between New York and Liverpool, giving Collins a brief monopoly of the route. After the heavy skepticism voiced in Congress two years earlier about the utility of his own steamers to the Navy in time of war, Collins could have been forgiven a wry smile at this development.

Although it eased Collins' task in maintaining the dominance of his steamers, the suspension of Cunard's New York service did not provide him with much of a financial benefit. Under a clandestine agreement between the two Lines, all revenues were shared in a fixed ratio, irrespective of which company generated them. This pact had been signed soon after the *Atlantic* had inaugurated the Collins Line's service. It had been negotiated on the initiative of the Cunard Line, which was anxious to avoid a ruinous price war with its new competitor. In addition to fixing minimum prices for the carriage of passengers and cargo, the agreement specified how revenues were to be pooled and then shared between the two companies. Two-thirds of gross revenues were to go to the Cunard Line and one-third to the Collins Line, with each Line obliged to pay the other any excess revenues it recorded above its pre-agreed share.

Even though this arrangement was perfectly legal at the time, both companies kept it secret to avoid a huge scandal. The merest hint that these supposedly fierce competitors, both major beneficiaries of subsidies from their respective governments, might be operating a price-fixing cartel would have caused a furor.

The Collins Line certainly did not need to provide any more ammunition to its foes. As the deadline approached when Congress could first revoke the increase in the Line's subsidy, other companies were submitting competitive bids for the mail service that Collins provided to the government. The bidders included Asa Eldridge's former employer, Cornelius Vanderbilt, who was known for his ruthless pursuit of profit, and yet offered to provide the same service as Collins for $390,000—little more than the original subsidy.

In an attempt to remove the uncertainty now facing the Collins Line, in February 1855 one of his allies in Congress introduced a bill to repeal the government's right to terminate the increased subsidy—effectively guaranteeing the higher level of funding for the remainder of the Line's contract. The only commitment Collins would have to make in return was to build a new steamer to replace the lost *Arctic*, which he was planning to do anyway. But the move failed. The bill did win Congressional approval after several perilously close votes, but was then vetoed by President Pierce. The President cited various "insuperable" objections to the proposed repeal. To provide "a donation of such magnitude" and give it "the character of permanence" would, in his view, "establish a monopoly, in violation of the soundest principles of public policy, and of doubtful compatibility with the Constitution."

Given how close the votes had been for passage of the bill, Collins' supporters would not have been able to muster a sufficient majority to overturn the presidential veto, and made no effort to do so. Nor, however, did his opponents make any push for the statutory six months' notice to be given that would terminate the increased subsidy. With barely a murmur, the full amount of $858,000 was approved as an amendment to the annual appropriation bill for the Navy. The Collins Line was reasonably secure for at least another year.

Bolstered by this development, in May 1855 Collins went ahead and began construction of his new steamer. (Technically, this was not a replacement for

The steamship *Washington* of the OSNC, whose slowness contributed to the establishment of the NYHSNC.

The loss of the Collins liner *Arctic*, as depicted in a contemporary lithograph.

The Collins liner *Pacific*.

The *Persia*, the Cunard Line's first iron-hulled steamer and the largest ship in the world when she entered service in 1856.

the *Arctic* but the last of five ships his original contract had required him to build.) True to form, he did not let the uncertainty around his subsidy deter him from aggressive investment in the future. At 3,670 tons and 355 feet long, the *Adriatic* would be bigger than any other ship then in service, and was projected to cost $850,000—almost as much as the entire year's subsidy that had just been approved.

As summer turned to fall Collins made another revision to his fleet. This one was definitely a replacement, and involved a person rather than a vessel. Captain Ezra Nye, who had been in command of the *Pacific* since her maiden voyage in 1850, had decided to retire. And the man chosen to replace him was Asa Eldridge. After a gap of seven years, Asa would once again be working for E.K. Collins.

Unlike the *Pioneer* or the *St. Louis*, the *Pacific* would give Eldridge a real opportunity to prove himself one of the fastest men on the ocean under steam, just as he had been under sail. The *Pacific* had twice set new records on her route between New York and Liverpool, once in each direction: westbound in September 1850, and eastbound in May 1851. Her records had since been surpassed by other Collins Line steamers, the *Baltic* westbound and the *Arctic* eastbound, but she was still clearly one of the fastest ships on the Atlantic. Eldridge now had a stage on which to perform.

He started well. Leaving New York on the day before Thanksgiving, 1855, he took the *Pacific* to Liverpool in a mere ten days and seven hours. This was only fourteen hours more than the then current eastbound record, and an excellent time for a winter crossing. The *Pacific*'s passengers were certainly pleased. As the steamer neared landfall they drafted a glowing letter of appreciation to Eldridge that was subsequently published in Liverpool's main newspaper, the *Daily Post*. They wished him to regard this letter, so they advised him, "as a hearty, spontaneous and sincere address, emanating solely from the conviction that to your skill, as a seaman, we are indebted for our safe arrival; and to your urbanity, as a gentleman, for the really pleasant time which we have spent on board."

The return journey to New York was more challenging. The *Pacific* left Liverpool on December 15 and was expected in New York about twelve days later. The *New York Daily Times* even speculated that she would "take less time than the usual Winter run home," noting that she had made "a remarkably quick trip out." In the event she arrived a day later than expected, on December 28. But as on the outbound crossing, Eldridge had impressed his passengers to such an extent that they wrote him a testimonial letter that was published by a local newspaper in the port of arrival—in this case, by the *New York Herald*. In publishing the letter, the paper noted that "To those acquainted with Captain Eldridge it will come as no surprise, then, even on his first voyage as commander of the Pacific, that he should have so thoroughly won the regard of all those brought into contact with him." The letter itself complimented Eldridge for being "Always courteous and kindly, always mindful of our comfort and welfare, yet never neglectful of your higher duties as commander...".

The letter also explained why the *Pacific* had been a day late. As the following passage makes clear, the crossing had been rough:

> Through a tempestuous voyage and under trying circumstances, you have gained our respect and regard, as well as our implicit confidence in your skill....With sincere wishes that while encountering few such stormy seasons you may long continue at your present post...

Whatever future seasons might bring, that particular winter remained very stormy. Eldridge next steered the *Pacific* out of New York on January 5, 1856, just after noon. Four hours later she was hit by one of the most severe gales ever experienced on the Atlantic. In a report back to his superior in New York after the ship arrived in Liverpool, her Chief Engineer wrote:

> We arrived here at noon of the 17th, terminating a very rough eastern passage; the first 24 hours from New-York being the worst weather I ever saw. The remainder of the passage being against very heavy cross seas, ship pitching, and rolling[,] guards under water continually. The engines performed well, and are all right, so that you may expect us in New-York about the usual time.

That last prediction proved tragically optimistic. The *Pacific* steamed out of Liverpool again on January 23, and the "usual time" for her arrival back in New York would have been around February 4. She did not appear. When there was still no sign of her a week later, Collins chartered a steamer called the *Alabama* to go looking for her. The next day he persuaded the US Navy to send a screw steamer called the *Arctic* to join in the search; another ship had just reached New York with an alarming tale of being caught in an ice field, and the *Arctic* was the closest thing in that era to an icebreaker. But neither she nor the *Alabama* could find any trace of the *Pacific*.

By now the non-appearance of the steamer was big news on both sides of the Atlantic, with regular reports in both the US and British papers. As yet opinion was still hopeful. Five years earlier another Collins liner, the *Atlantic*, had been more than a month overdue before word reached New York that she had been forced back to Ireland after her engines failed. Indeed, a rumor briefly gained credence that the *Pacific* had put into the River Shannon and was safe.

Gradually, however, all hope faded. The North Atlantic was particularly brutal that winter. Dozens of ships were delayed for weeks at a time. Reports abounded of ice-fields and icebergs much further south than usual. Perhaps most telling, the Cunard Line's new steamer, the *Persia*, had left Liverpool three days after the *Pacific* and encountered "heavy fields of ice" that delayed her for thirty-six hours and damaged one of her paddle wheels. A week later, the Scottish steamer *Edinburgh* had passed through the same general area and spotted floating debris that clearly came from the cabin of a passenger ship: oak doors with white handles and windows with venetian blinds. Putting all of this together, in late March the New York *Courier and Inquirer* concluded that the *Pacific* had "unexpectedly encountered masses of ice" on or about January 28, and had sunk after colliding with one of them.

Others were not yet willing to give up completely. Somewhat belatedly, the Royal Navy sent two ships to scour the ocean for the missing steamer. Appropriately, one of the search vessels was named the *Desperate*. But she and the *Tartar* had no more luck than the American search vessels six weeks earlier.

Finally, reluctantly, the maritime community was forced to accept the inevitable conclusion. Whatever the reason, the *Pacific* was lost forever, together with forty-five passengers and her crew of 141. Chief among the latter, of course, was Captain Asa Eldridge. His life and lifelong career at sea were over.

TO THIS DAY, debate continues about the fate of the *Pacific*. For over 135 years the generally accepted view was the one offered by the *Courier and Inquirer* in March 1856: that she had collided with a mass of ice and then sunk. Overlaid on this general picture were question marks about the competence of the two most important men on the ship, Asa Eldridge and his Chief Engineer, Samuel Matthews. Even recently, a new account of the *Pacific's* loss stated that Eldridge "came from the crack clipper ship *Red Jacket*" and did not have "much prior experience in transatlantic steam."

The same account noted that "The *Pacific*'s chief engineer, who joined the crew just after Captain Eldridge, was also new to his job and machinery," and subsequently suggested this may have contributed to her disappearance.

Both men had rather more relevant experience than these remarks might suggest. The *Pacific* was actually the fourth steamer Eldridge had taken across the Atlantic. His stints on the *Pioneer* and the *St. Louis* were admittedly brief, but he had also spent four months steering Vanderbilt's *North Star* to, from and around Europe. Moreover, his first crossing in command of the *Pacific* had been considered "remarkably quick" by the *New York Daily Times*, demonstrating that he had more than mere competence at her helm.

Matthews was also no neophyte. Before joining Eldridge he had spent three and half years as First Assistant on the *Baltic*, whose engines and boilers were identical to those of the *Pacific*. He had also served as Chief Engineer on the steamer *Cherokee*, which operated between New York and—at various times—Chagres, New Orleans and Havana. And before that he had been a First Assistant Engineer in the US Navy. Few men in his position could have possessed such a broad knowledge of steam engines.

The doubts about Eldridge and Matthews can probably be traced to an unsavory communication from the *Pacific*'s previous commander, Captain Ezra Nye, even before her loss was considered certain. On March 8, 1856, the New York *Courier and Inquirer* published a letter from Nye whose stated purpose was to dispel rumors that he had quit the *Pacific* because she was unseaworthy. But after disposing of these rumors by stating that his only reason for quitting had been a wish to retire, he launched into some scandal-mongering of his own. Noting that the Collins Line had recently appointed Oliver Eldridge, Asa's younger brother, as captain of the *Atlantic*, Nye complained that he had wanted Oliver to succeed him on the *Pacific* but been overruled. He implied that this decision had contributed to the loss of his former ship, because it resulted in the resignation of many of the steamer's key officers. These officers, he claimed, would have been happy to serve under Oliver, having bonded with him when he traveled on the *Pacific* the previous year. And though careful to avoid direct criticism of Oliver's highly respected older brother, Nye did complain that Asa had not been obliged to buy out his shares in the *Pacific*, as Oliver would have done. His discussion of Matthews was less restrained. After praising his own Chief Engineer, he went on to say that "The man who filled his place, however competent he may have been, was totally unacquainted with the ship and engines, and it was his first voyage as Chief Engineer."

That last statement brought a sharp rebuttal from the Engineer-in-Chief of the Collins Line, who in a letter to the *New York Daily Times* laid out all of Matthews' prior experience, as recounted above.

Many observers reacted to Nye's letter with disgust. Thus the New York correspondent of the New Orleans *Daily Picayune* wrote that:

> The letter of Capt. Nye…is one of the most shameful acts (taken in connection with the general suspense that exists regarding the vessel) that he could possibly have been guilty of; and I have not conversed with a solitary individual who has not held the same opinion. His pretended reason for publishing the letter is, to answer the numerous applications that have been made to him as to why he left the ship. This, perhaps, was well enough; but after giving his reason, which he could have done in a dozen lines, he should have dropped his pen at once. But this, it appears, he was not disposed to do; but, in order to vent out a little personal spite against some of the company, he willfully writes, and causes to be published in a leading journal, a series of gross falsehoods…

Those falsehoods, the correspondent continued, included the claim that "nearly every person on the steamer left with him [Nye]." In fact, except for Eldridge and the new Chief Engineer, "In all other respects the hands on board the missing steamer remain as when under the command of Nye…"

Among some observers, however, Nye's indirect attack on Eldridge and disparaging remarks about Matthews were accepted uncritically, and even exaggerated. The *Brooklyn Daily Eagle*, for example, described Asa Eldridge as a "noble but impetuous man, with raw recruits in the engine-room," who had allowed the presence of "the new British monster, the *Persia*, behind, to goad him to a reckless running of his vessel." A paper in North Carolina incorrectly stated that "the captain of the Pacific was a new man, making his first cruise in the boat…" And so on. With stories such as these, the idea that rashness or incompetence on the part of Eldridge and Matthews had contributed to the loss of the *Pacific* became part of the historical record. Indeed, this view became so embedded in some quarters that a book published in 1962 confidently describes a meeting in which Eldridge told Collins he would take the *Pacific* "to the sea bed" if he could not "humble" the *Persia*. (The author seems to have ignored both the implausibility of such a statement being made by any captain, let alone when talking to his ship's owner, and the timing of the event to which Eldridge was supposedly reacting, a record-breaking crossing by the *Persia* that did not occur until two months after the *Pacific* disappeared.)

The false impression created by Nye's insinuations occurred in spite of a second letter he wrote that destroyed his own reputation—but ironically, may be much more relevant to understanding what happened to the *Pacific*. The second letter came just a few weeks after the first, in the fallout from that missive. In it, Nye acknowledged that on one occasion he had set out across the Atlantic even though he knew that the *Pacific*'s main engine shaft was cracked. He justified having done so by claiming that "to remain in Liverpool would have been most disastrous" for the finances of the Collins Line and the reputation of American shipping, and that he had been fully vindicated by the successful completion of the voyage.

Nye may have been persuaded by this logic but the press most certainly was not. From New York to Baltimore, from Boston to Chicago, the condemnation of his actions was universal; had that shaft broken halfway across the Atlantic, the ship and the lives of all on board might well have been lost. Several papers called Nye's behavior "criminal rashness." The *Chicago Times* went further, recommending not just a verdict but also the ultimate penalty. Captain Nye, it declared, "justly deserves hanging for his reckless disregard of the safety of the lives and property entrusted to his care."

Deplorable though its contents were, this letter does provide great insight into the pressures that Asa Eldridge would have faced as he steered the *Pacific* out of Liverpool in January 1856. The tenuous financial condition of the Collins Line that had led to Nye's flawed decision several years earlier had grown even more perilous. The annual appropriation for the Line's mail subsidy would soon be up for discussion again, and the prospects for a full renewal would certainly be better if the Collins Line could still claim superiority over the Cunard Line. But a new threat to that superiority was about to stalk Eldridge across the Atlantic. The *Persia*, Cunard's first iron-hulled steamer and the largest ship in the world, was due to leave Liverpool three days after the *Pacific* on her maiden voyage to New York. Eldridge would have been desperate to stay well ahead of her. He may therefore have been pushing the *Pacific* to her limits just as numerous ice floes began to appear unusually far south on the Atlantic. And if he plowed right into them as a result, the fate of the *Pacific* would have been sealed.

That of course was the charge laid against Eldridge by the *Brooklyn Daily Eagle* in its scathing article following Nye's first letter. Others, however, were less inclined to judge him. The *New York Herald* summed up the pre-vailing sentiment well:

> Whether living or dead we cast no word of reproach against Captain Asa Eldridge, commander of the Pacific. If, in a spirit of emulation, he exposed his ship and his life to hazard, he did only as they have done, who in his profession are everywhere regarded as patterns of prudence and ability. Captain Judkins, of the Persia, escaped narrowly. Captain Lines, of the Arago, struck heavily on ice. Captain Stone of the Arabia, was exposed to imminent peril from contact with ice; while Captain Comstock, of the Baltic, and Captain West, of the Atlantic, were in positions that caused them the gravest apprehension.

Implicit in this commentary was an acknowledgment that, irrespective of the conditions on the ocean, commerce had to go on. The Atlantic might churn, heave or freeze, but the men who braved its waters would take whatever risks were necessary to keep trade moving. All too often, a captain would lose his battle with the ocean, along with his life and the lives of others. But this was simply a toll that nations tolerated in order to do business with one another.

NEWS AND HUMAN NATURE being what they are, by the fall of 1856 the loss of the *Pacific* no longer commanded much attention. As the years and decades went by she was almost forgotten, warranting only an occasional mention in books about maritime history. The view remained that while cruising hard to stay ahead of the *Persia* she had collided with a mass of ice and sunk.

Then in 1992 came a new development. Divers working off the coast of North Wales, about sixty miles from Liverpool, found a wreck they identified as the *Pacific*. The wreck was in two large pieces about three miles apart on the sea floor, a bow section about 110 feet long and a stern section half as long again. Several factors pointed to these being the remains of the *Pacific*. The sunken ship was built of wood, and therefore unusually large for a vessel of that material. The profile of the bow section was that of a steamer rather than a sailing ship, and the combined dimensions of the two sections closely resembled those of the *Pacific*. Moreover, some of the cargo found on the seabed around the wreck matched items on the *Pacific*'s mani-fest when she left Liverpool—earthenware in the popular "Blue Willow" china pattern, and telegraph wire of a sort then being shipped to the US by a firm in Liverpool.

By themselves, these findings do not positively identify the wreck as the remains of the *Pacific*. The divers who discovered the wreck took steps to secure title to it, with the intention of exploring it as a historical site rather than as a source of profit from salvage. To date, however, no further reports about the wreck have appeared—none at least that can be found by online searching.

At this point, therefore, the fate of the *Pacific* is still an unresolved mystery. Even if the wreck off the Welsh coast is confirmed as her carcass, questions will remain about how she ended up there. What caused her to sink? A collision with another vessel seems unlikely, since none was reported missing. In which case, was her demise caused by an explosion? This might also explain why she split into two pieces found three miles apart. But if she were blown apart by an explosion, why was this not heard on the nearby coast? And why did no wreckage reach the shore? Or cargo? Or corpses? So many questions would remain without answers.

Absent further information about this wreck, the most definitive evidence about the fate of the *Pacific* may be the message recovered from a bottle that came ashore in the Hebrides in 1861. The message was scrawled in pencil across the two sides of a small sheet of paper, three inches by two, and difficult to decipher, but was eventually determined to read as follows:

On board the Pacific, from L'pool to N. York. Ship going down. (Great) confusion on board. Icebergs around us on every side. I know I cannot escape. I write the cause of our loss that friends may not live in suspense. The finder of this will please get it published. Wm. Graham.

After its discovery, the frail slip of paper was forwarded to the *Shipping and Mercantile Gazette* in London. The *Gazette* duly published the message, and then spent weeks investigating its authenticity. The release of hoax messages in bottles was not uncommon after maritime disasters, but after weeks of careful checking, the *Gazette* concluded that this particular example was genuine. The crew of the *Pacific* had indeed included a man whose last name was Graham, and although the manifest listed his first name as Robert, it was not uncommon for mistakes to be made during the hurried process of documenting the crew's names. Everything else the *Gazette* had learned was consistent with the message being an authentic record of the last moments of the *Pacific*. And so, too, of Asa Eldridge.

WHETHER THE *PACIFIC* exploded off the coast of Wales or struck an iceberg in the North Atlantic, sometime around the end of January 1856 Asa Eldridge met his end. By late May, the *New York Commercial Advertiser* felt there could no longer be any hope of his being alive, and published an anonymous but heartfelt obituary. This formed a fitting epitaph at the time, and will now serve as a fitting conclusion to this narrative of Eldridge's life:

> Four months ago this day, the steamer Pacific left Liverpool, and as nothing has been seen or heard of her since she was passed in the Channel on the following day, that she has been lost with all on board, there can now be but little doubt. [The reference to the *Pacific* having been passed in the English Channel relates to a report of such an encounter that was later discounted.]
>
> The loss of a steamer is a fearful thing, and sorrow to many loving hearts.
>
> The writer of this had many friends on board the Pacific, prominent among whom was her commander, Asa Eldridge, with whom he had been extremely intimate for many years.
>
> To those who knew Capt. Eldridge, it is unnecessary to speak of his many noble qualities, and the best evidence of his worth and the estimation in which he was held is the universal regret expressed at his fate by all classes with whom he was brought into contact, a regret constantly and continually shown on both sides of the Atlantic.
>
> Many tears will be shed for him by those who were indebted to him for their positions as mates, stewards and sailors; and many a shipmaster can bear evidence of the "good word fitly spoken" in their behalf.
>
> No matter how poor a man might be, if he was honest and capable, he was sure of having a friend in Asa Eldridge, and one who would stand by him in the hour of need. Bold and fearless, the only enemies he ever made was by openly and bluntly speaking the truth, he being incapable of doing a mean or dishonorable action, and he was famous for never cringing to wealth.
>
> This is not the place to speak of his qualifications as a seaman, or his sound judgment under difficulties. Those who have sailed with him know that he was equal to any emergency; and, if the truth could be known, it would be found that his well earned reputation was fully sustained at his death.
>
> These lines are written by one who appreciated his many noble qualities, and who deeply sympathises with his bereaved relatives and friends in their severe affliction.
>
> New York, May 23, 1856.

8

FORGOTTEN HEROES

IN AN ERA when messages cross the Atlantic in milliseconds and jumbo jets in an afternoon, it is easy to forget what a formidable barrier the ocean once was to communication and travel between the Old World and the New. Sending an e-mail or taking a flight are hardly heroic undertakings, but that is exactly what many transatlantic crossings were in the early days of the United States. Had it not been for the skill and courage of men like Asa Eldridge, the trade and immigration that shaped the country could never have happened. Every single voyage meant probable danger and possible disaster. But season after season, year after year, whatever the weather, these iron-willed men drove their ships and their crews to the limits of endurance, thereby ensuring a steady supply of profits and prospective citizens for the young nation.

Beyond these tangible rewards, America's merchant marine also boosted the country's morale with two key intangibles: pride and prestige. Britain had long been the world's maritime superpower, whose attitude towards the capabilities of its former colony was initially condescension. But thanks to the packet ships and their commanders, that attitude gradually changed into grudging acknowledgment, then open admiration. And the American press loved it. Each new flagship was greeted with lavish praise as a demonstration of the country's superior marine architecture; each new record or noteworthy voyage was dissected and eulogized.

The British response started a policy debate that continues to this day. Should public funds be used to support private industries of strategic importance? That was certainly the view taken by the British government in 1838. From its perspective the facility to move goods, people and information across the Atlantic was a key strategic capability that might prove crucial if there were ever another war with the US. (There had after all been two within living memory.) The virtual monopoly of transatlantic trade by American sailing packets was therefore a potential threat to national security. To create a British alternative the government chose to foster the development of transatlantic steamers—playing to the country's strengths as the leader in steam-engine technology, and nullifying the clear advantage held by the US in building sailing ships. And to achieve this goal it was willing to provide substantial funding to a private venture, ostensibly in payment for the transport of mail.

The American government was less convinced about supporting private industry in this way. More than five years went by after the inauguration of the Cunard Line before the US awarded its first transatlantic mail contract to the OSNC. Another year passed before a contract was awarded to the country's most dynamic shipowner, Edward Collins. And even after Collins had shown he could take on the Cunard Line and win, Congress put him on six months' notice that he could lose the support necessary to sustain his company. Under the constant pressure this created to outperform Cunard's ships, his captains took risks. The consequences were grim: two disasters with major loss of life, under circumstances suggesting that speed had taken priority over safety.

Following these disasters, the government's half-hearted support for the Collins Line quickly reverted to the bare minimum. In August 1856, in its first appropriations bill after the loss of the *Pacific*, Congress voted to terminate the extra compensation that had been granted in 1852. Although the termination did not take effect for six months, the government's payments were cut in half long before then by the Navy Secretary, as a penalty for late deliveries by the slow steamer chartered to replace the *Pacific*. A huge chunk of the Collins Line's income had disappeared.

Adding to these blows from the government, construction of the *Adriatic* was delayed by more than a year. She had been due to enter service in late 1856 but only did so in November of the following year. And as it turned out, her first voyage for the Collins Line was her last. Soon after she arrived back from Liverpool in late December news leaked out that she would not sail again until the spring; her running costs were very high, and the *Atlantic* and *Baltic* could fulfill the winter schedule without her. But worse was to come. As the departure date approached for the *Atlantic* in February 1858, Collins let it be known that she would not sail—either then or ever again on his behalf. His Line was finished. All that remained was for the *Baltic* to return from Liverpool, which she did on February 18. The Collins Line then ceased operations completely.

Congress was no more supportive of the other two transatlantic steamship lines than it was of the Collins Line. When the OSNC's mail contract for the Bremen route expired in 1857 it was not renewed. Nor was the NYHSNC's for the Havre route three years later. Both lines went out of business shortly after their contracts expired. Not a single US steamer then operated regularly across the Atlantic.

Samuel Cunard, in the meantime, continued to enjoy the support of the British government. Although there was significant debate when he pressed for an extension of his contracts in 1858, he eventually secured a continuation until the beginning of 1867. This was in spite of opposition from the country's Postmaster General, who was overruled by the Financial Secretary on the grounds that "national interests were involved"; one sixth of England's total trade was now with its former colony.

In that verdict lay the difference between the two countries. From the start, the US Congress had been ambivalent about the idea of supporting private enterprises, even in a sphere so important to the country as trade with Britain. While opposition to the mail contracts for transatlantic steam-ship companies was partly a product of regional jealousies, it also reflected an underlying philosophy that is still apparent in American politics today: that the government has no place in activities that can be conducted by private enterprise. The British, in contrast, were and are more receptive to government involvement in areas of strategic importance.

In the case of transatlantic steam this philosophy paid off. By subsidiz-ing the Cunard Line for as long as it did, the government helped to create a steamship industry that dominated Atlantic travel for much of the next century, and was then only displaced by airplanes. Meanwhile the US, having supported its steamship entrepreneurs for little more than a decade, was left with no real presence on the ocean.

One particular metric highlights the impact of the contrasting policies of the two governments: the record for the fastest westbound crossing of the Atlantic. Before the Collins Line began operations in 1850, the Cunard Line had held this record for seven of the previous ten years (the *Great Western* having held it for the other three). The Collins Line then needed only a few months to snatch the record, holding and improving on it several times between 1850 and 1856. But shortly after the *Pacific*'s disappearance, just as the US government began reducing its payments to Collins, the

Persia reclaimed the title for Cunard. Another 96 years would then pass before the *United States* took the record back for its namesake country. And in the interim, British steamers had held it for 79 of those 96 years.

To be fair to the Congressional leaders who established the US policy, Collins himself deserves a good portion of the blame for their decision to cut off support for transatlantic steamships. His aggressive approach to building the Collins Line resulted in substantially higher costs than were strictly necessary; had they been smaller, so might Congressional opposition have been.

From the outset, however, Collins was determined to follow the same "bigger, better, faster" strategy that had served him so well with the Dramatic Line of sailing packets. But in applying the same approach to his steamship line he made multiple miscalculations. While his steamers were indeed bigger and better than Cunard's, he had to borrow and spend much too much to build them. And while they were clearly also faster, he failed to anticipate how much their speed would cost when generated by coal-fired engines rather than the wind. Coal was expensive, and his ships burned a lot of it when running flat out to surpass the Cunarders. Moreover, the punishment inflicted on their machinery by constant hard running led to very high maintenance costs.

Compounding these problems, the cartel agreement Collins had signed with Cunard removed most of the benefit he could have gained by charging higher prices for his superior service. The agreement allocated two-thirds of their combined gross revenues to his competitor, no matter how much of those revenues the Collins Line generated. Any extra income from higher prices would therefore have gone mostly to Cunard. Collins' only other option to improve profitability was to reduce costs. But that could only be done by slowing down his steamers—which would have made his service much less attractive to customers, leading to a loss of revenues. Collins had thus boxed himself into a corner from which there was no escape. He had no feasible way to improve the profitability of his business, whose survival then depended on the generous government support he had been granted. But many in Congress were alienated by the extravagant designs that made his ships so expensive; his opponents derided his ships as "floating palaces" equipped with unnecessary luxuries at taxpayers' expense. The cutback in his subsidy that finished the Collins Line became inevitable. And having abandoned the standard-bearer for the country's transatlantic steamship industry, Congress saw no reason to continue supporting the lesser players.

Collins' missteps therefore contributed significantly to the policy decisions that ceded the Atlantic to Britain after decades of American dominance.

THE DEMISE of the Collins Line brought an end to its proprietor's long career in shipping. Like his country, Collins turned his attention away from the Atlantic and towards the interior. His business interests now lay underground rather than above water, as he pursued various mineral opportunities in the Great Lakes region. Although he enjoyed modest success from time to time—for example when coal and iron ore were discovered on a farm he had acquired in Ohio—he never again came close to the triumphs he had achieved on the ocean. He died in relative obscurity in 1878 with his wealth greatly diminished, but still substantial enough for his first wife's surviving son to file suit against his second wife over his will. Neither of them thought, however, to place a headstone on his grave in New York's Woodlawn Cemetery, and so he lacks even that commonplace memorial.

Two years after Collins died so did another famous figure from America's maritime heyday, Donald McKay. Overcoming his depression about the fire on the *Great Republic*, he had continued for several more years to build clippers for the Australia trade. The most notable of these was the *Lightning*, which made her maiden voyage from Boston to Liverpool in February 1854, just a month after Asa Eldridge's record-breaking voyage on the *Red Jacket*. Although her crossing was slightly slower overall, on her eleventh day out she covered 436 miles—nineteen more than the longest single-day run by the *Red Jacket*, and still the farthest ever traveled by a sailing ship in twenty-four hours.

In 1856, however, world events brought an abrupt halt to McKay's flourishing business. The end of the Crimean War caused demand for new ships to plummet, as vessels that had been requisitioned by the various combatants to serve as troop carriers were returned to civilian service, creating over-capacity in merchant shipping fleets around the world. In the four years leading up to the start of the American Civil War in 1861, McKay built only a single clipper. The War itself then killed any further demand for new sailing ships, although McKay did build one iron-hulled steamship for the US Navy. With the profits from that commission he bought a farm in Hamilton, north of Boston, and retired there, although he did build two more clippers in the late 1860s. The second of these, completed in 1869, was called the *Glory of the Seas*—an apt summary of McKay's contribution to US maritime history.

Indirectly, E. K. Collins also provided ships to the Yankee Navy during the Civil War. The two surviving members of his original quartet of steamers, the *Atlantic* and the *Baltic*, served as transports. After the collapse of the Collins Line they had been auctioned off and deployed between New York and Panama by their new owners, but were chartered on multiple occasions by the Union Navy during the War. And on some of those occasions, their captains were none other than Asa Eldridge's brothers—John and Oliver.

In Oliver's case, his wartime service was a return to a ship he knew well, the *Atlantic*. He had first assumed command of her in 1856, shortly after Asa and the *Pacific* went missing, and stayed with her until the Collins Line folded two years later. His familiarity with her, and her proven speed, presumably explain why they were chosen for a crucial assignment shortly after the War began. The *Atlantic* served as General Sherman's flagship for the expedition to capture Port Royal Sound in South Carolina, which was one of the first amphibious operations during the War. Oliver fully justified the faith shown in him, earning what the *New York Herald* called "encomiums… of the most gratifying character" from both Sherman and Rear Admiral Dupont for his skill in keeping the Union fleet of seventy-seven ships together.

Despite this success, his service thereafter on the *Atlantic* was limited. He took her back and forth between New York and Port Royal a couple of times in early 1862, but then turned his attention to civilian steamships. That summer he sailed a new example called the *Constitution* from New York to San Francisco around Cape Horn; the following summer he took another New York-built steamer, the *Golden City*, around the Horn to Panama, where she was placed in service to San Francisco. After one final contribution to the war effort, sailing the *Atlantic* between New York and Hilton Head in February 1864, he returned to the *Golden City* on the Pacific Coast. This time, however, he was a passenger, making a permanent move to San Francisco with his family. He had accepted a position there as general agent of the ship's owners, the Pacific Mail Steamship Company. This signaled the end of his career at sea but the start of a substantial career on land, which included positions as President of the California Drydock Company and of a life insurance firm, and service as a director of Wells Fargo and several utility companies. He died in 1902 aged 84, leaving just one married daughter.

Detail of the East River from an 1856 engraving of New York, with a Collins liner in the foreground—one of only two still surviving by that time. Note the South Street area to the left, crowded with sailing ships.

The *Adriatic*, last and largest of the Collins Line fleet, which made only one voyage before the Line collapsed. Note the gradual evolution in design away from sailing ships, with one more funnel and one fewer mast than the *Baltic* (overleaf).

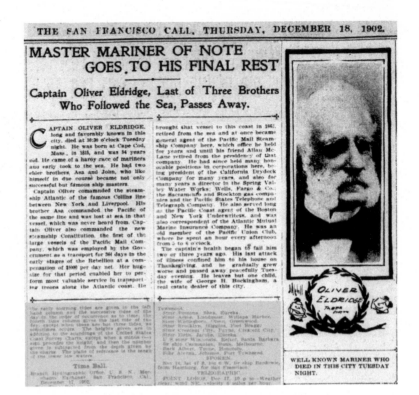

MASTER MARINER OF NOTE GOES TO HIS FINAL REST

Captain Oliver Eldridge, Last of Three Brothers Who Followed the Sea, Passes Away.

CAPTAIN OLIVER ELDRIDGE, long and favorably known in this city, died at 10:30 o'clock Tuesday night. He was born at Cape Cod, Mass., in 1818, and was 84 years old. He came of a hardy race of mariners and early took to the sea. He had two elder brothers, Asa and John, who like himself in due course became not only successful but famous ship masters.

Captain Oliver commanded the steamship Atlantic of the famous Collins line between New York and Liverpool. His brother Asa commanded the Pacific of the same line and was lost at sea in that vessel, which was never heard from. Captain Oliver also commanded the new steamship Constitution, the first of the large vessels of the Pacific Mail Company, which was employed by the Government as a transport for 361 days in the early stages of the Rebellion at a compensation of $1000 per day net. The huge size for that period enabled her to perform most valuable service in transporting troops along the Atlantic coast. He brought that vessel to this coast in 1867, retired from the sea and at once became general agent of the Pacific Mail Steamship Company, which office he held for years and until his friend Allan McLane retired from the presidency of that company. He had since held many honorable positions in corporations here, being president of the California Drydock Company for many years, and also for many years a director in the Spring Valley Water Works; Wells, Fargo & Co., the Sacramento and Stockton gas companies and the Pacific States Telephone and Telegraph Company. He also served long as the Pacific Coast agent of the Boston and New York Underwriters, and was also correspondent of the Atlantic Mutual Marine Insurance Company. He was an old member of the Pacific Union Club, where he spent an hour every afternoon from 3 to 6 o'clock.

The captain's health began to fail him two or three years ago. His last attack of illness confined him to his house on Thanksgiving, and he gradually grew worse and passed away peacefully Tuesday evening. He leaves but one child, the wife of George H. Buckingham, a real estate dealer of this city.

WELL-KNOWN MARINER WHO DIED IN THIS CITY TUESDAY NIGHT.

Oliver Eldridge's obituary reflected the high profile he achieved in San Francisco.

The *Baltic*, formerly of the Collins Line, which became John Eldridge's first steamship command in 1861, during the Civil War.

Unlike Oliver, John Eldridge had no experience on steamships prior to the Civil War. He was also sixty-three when the War broke out—twenty years older than Oliver—and had in fact been retired for nearly a decade. But he clearly did not regard his retirement as sacrosanct. He had already returned to action twice since giving up his long-term command of the packet ship *Liverpool* in 1851: once the following year, to fill in for Oliver on the *Roscius*, and a second time in 1854 to test his mettle on a clipper ship. In the latter case, his motivation to return may have been sibling rivalry. Asa's record crossing on the *Red Jacket* was making headlines at the time, and Oliver had already proved himself on a clipper when he took the *Memnon* on her maiden voyage several years earlier. John may therefore have wanted to show that he could still keep up with his younger brothers.

If so, he may have come to regret that impulse. His new adventure caused him rather more trouble than he had any reason to expect. The assignment he undertook was to sail a new clipper, the *Young Brander*, from Boston to Liverpool via New Orleans; the intermediate stop was presumably to pick up a cargo of cotton. John barely had time to get the feel of the ship before his troubles began. Just a few days out to sea the crew mutinied, forcing him to sail back to Boston and have them arrested. With a new crew on board he was able to reach New Orleans without further incident, but was then beaten almost to death by a gang of thugs who attacked him while he was out walking near his ship. Fortunately he was highly resilient, and five weeks later had recovered sufficiently to sail the *Young Brander* out of New Orleans, bound for Liverpool. The voyage took twenty-one days, an excellent time given the distance involved; at the average speed this represents, the crossing from New York to Liverpool would have taken about thirteen days and eight hours, not much slower than Asa's time on the *Red Jacket*. But in spite of this demonstration of her capabilities, the *Young Brander*'s presence in Liverpool failed to achieve what was almost certainly the main objective in sending her there, which was to sell or lease her for deployment in the Australia trade. So when no transaction had been concluded after a month in port, Eldridge sailed the clipper out of Liverpool and all the way back to Boston. And as far as he was concerned, that was enough. When the *Young Brander* left Boston a month later for a repeat voyage on the same route, he was not at the helm. Having proved he could still keep up with his brothers, he could now retire in peace. Or so he may have thought.

Seven years later, however, his peace went the way of his country's, as the Civil War began and he volunteered his services for the Union. But perhaps because of his age and lack of experience with steamships, his duties were limited. Although several sources imply a longer relationship between him and the *Baltic*, he appears to have commanded her just once, and even then for a relatively tame assignment: to evacuate the faculty of the US Naval Academy and their families from Annapolis to Newport, Rhode Island, in the second month of the War. Careful searching of online newspaper archives identifies only this single instance of a voyage by the *Baltic* with an Eldridge at the helm. She had participated in the relief of Fort Sumter a few weeks earlier but under the command of a Captain Fletcher, and for her voyages later that year she was skippered first by a Captain Alfred G. Grey and then by her old master from the Collins Line, Joseph Comstock.

While he may not have commanded the *Baltic* again, John did stay involved in the War effort. When the *Baltic* returned to New York in December 1861 from a mission to Fort Pickens, he appeared on the passenger list as a "government agent." And the following September, he rather than Oliver must have been the Eldridge who transported 870 sick and wounded soldiers from Alexandria to New York on the *Atlantic*, because Oliver was otherwise engaged taking the steamer *Constitution* to San Francisco. He then appeared at the helm of yet another former transatlantic steamer pressed into war service, but one that came originally from the NYHSNC rather than the Collins Line. In May 1863 he steamed out of New York on the *Fulton*, bound for New Orleans. How a transport ship from the North was able to make this voyage to the South in the middle of the War is a puzzle. But Eldridge was well known in New Orleans from his time with Collins' Louisiana Line, and seems to have been greeted warmly by his friends there; the *Daily Picayune* thanked him publicly for delivering newspapers from the North. It must have been a strange sensation for him to be in a place so familiar but now enemy territory.

Once the War was over John was able to resume his retirement, this time permanently. He returned to the house he owned in Yarmouth Port next door to his childhood home, and gained a reputation for his hospitality, the gourmet food he served, and the musical and literary gatherings he hosted. He died in 1874 at the age of seventy-five. His death made news as far away as California, where the *Los Angeles Daily Herald* noted speculation that the character Captain Truck in James Fenimore Cooper's *Homeward Bound* was modeled after him.

Looking back on the careers of John and Oliver, one particular distinction stands out. They were among the small and elite group of shipmasters to command all three of the nineteenth century's most important classes of vessel: transatlantic packets, clippers and ocean-going steamships. For John the trifecta included the packets *Webster*, *Liverpool* and *Roscius*, the clipper *Young Brander* and the steamships *Baltic* and *Fulton*. For Oliver the qualifying ships were the packets *Roscius* and *Garrick*, the clippers *Memnon*, *Blue Jacket* and *Titan*, and the steamships *Atlantic*, *Constitution* and *Golden City*. (The *Titan* was his first command after he left the Dramatic Line. On her maiden voyage in 1855 he sailed her from New York to Marseilles via Canada, and then transported over a thousand French infantrymen to the Black Sea for deployment in the Crimean War.)

There was of course a third Eldridge brother who achieved the same distinction. During his career Asa captained the packets *Roscius* and *Garrick*, the clipper *Red Jacket* and the steamships *Pioneer*, *North Star*, *St. Louis* and *Pacific*.

When the last of these vessels disappeared in 1856, so too did Asa Eldridge's bloodline. He and his wife Eliza had no children. But his name lived on for a while in an appropriate manner: on the clipper ship *Asa Eldridge*, which was built in the year he died and continued sailing into the 1870s. A bust of her namesake adorned the bow of the clipper, and a panel amidships bore an excellent portrait of him. During final preparations for her maiden voyage to San Francisco, the *New York Herald* observed that she "is named as a token of respect to the memory of the captain of the lost steamship Pacific, of whom it may be truly said that he was 'every inch a sailor and a gentleman.' He rose by his merits from the lowest to the highest grade of his profession, and was deservedly esteemed in every relation of life as a model man."

Sadly, the skill, courage and achievements of this model man have largely been forgotten. So too have those of his brothers, and of the hundreds of other American shipmasters who played a vital role in the early history of their country. The period following the War of 1812 was crucial in the development of the United States as a thriving new nation—not just independent of its former colonial master, but capable of competing with it. In the three decades that followed the war, America's sailing packets transformed transatlantic commerce and came to dominate it; they also transported legions of new immigrants to the US. In the half-decade that came next, clipper ships extended American leadership under sail, while the Collins liners established it under steam. All of this had a major impact on the shaping of the US, and yet few Americans today could name even a single one of the shipmasters who made it possible.

These men deserve much better. They should be celebrated alongside other valiant figures in American history. And few among them deserve that honor more than Captain Asa Eldridge, the lost hero of Cape Cod.

ACKNOWLEDGMENTS

MY THANKS to the Historical Society of Old Yarmouth for a variety of reasons: for agreeing to publish this book, for encouragement and support, for comments on the manuscript, for a digital copy of its daguerreotype of Asa Eldridge, and for permission to use this.

Among the many people on whom I inflicted early drafts of my manuscript for review, I would particularly like to thank James Jackson for his careful reading and constructive feedback. James taught French and Québec literature and history for twenty-five years at Trinity College in Dublin, and is the author of the recent award-winning book *The Riot that Never Was*. We knew each other fleetingly decades ago as schoolboys in Liverpool's Catholic junior seminary, and reconnected when he contacted me in 2013 to critique *Boys of the Cloth*, a book I had written about seminary life. He provided a similarly thoughtful assessment of the manuscript for this book and made many useful suggestions.

Given the major role played by online databases in my research, I would like to acknowledge those that were most useful. For historical newspapers, the key sources were Newspapers™ (newspapers.com), the California Digital Newspaper Collection (cdnc.ucr.edu) and the British Newspaper Archive (britishnewspaperarchive.co.uk). For genealogical information about the Eldridge family, Ancestry.com was important. And for digitized copies of old books, the collections of the HathiTrust Digital Library (hathitrust.org), the Internet Archive (archive.org), Google Books (books.google.com/books) and Wikisource (wikisource.com) were invaluable.

Many of the old books I initially found in digital form online were available in physical form at the Boston Athenaeum, whose staff were invariably helpful in locating the originals. For help with other items discovered online I am grateful to two museum curators: Elena Strong,

Curator of the National Museum of Bermuda (which incorporates the Bermuda Maritime Museum), who provided a copy of Edward Sloan's 1991 article about the wreck of the *Pacific*, which was published in the latter museum's Journal; and Olga Tsapina, Norris Foundation Curator of American Historical Manuscripts at the Huntington Library in San Marino, California, who advised me of the content of two of Oliver Eldridge's log books recently purchased by the Library.

Finally, I would like to thank my dear wife, Heather Campbell, for her understanding during the hundreds of hours I spent working on this book. Like Asa Eldridge and his fellow captains, the spouses of authors do not get the credit they deserve. So again, Heather: my heartfelt thanks!

NOTES

SOURCES ARE CITED for each significant topic within each chapter, in the order such topics arise. To distinguish between the names of sources and the names of ships, all of which are italicized, the latter are shown in **bold italics**.

For each topic, sources are cited in the following sequence: first, in alphabetical order by author, books or similar sources that are listed in the bibliography; second, in chronological order, articles or other items from newspapers; and third, specific Wikipedia entries or other internet sources not included in the bibliography.

Most items in the bibliography are referred to solely by the author's (or originator's) name, since in most cases this is sufficient by itself to identify them. In those instances where it is not, the date of publication is added in parentheses after the author's name to provide the necessary clarification.

All of the items cited from newspapers were initially identified in online databases, and can be found in those databases using the names and publication dates of the newspapers in question and the page numbers also included in the citations. In general, if the newspaper cited is American it will be found at newspapers.com, and if British at britishnewspaperarchive.co.uk. The main exceptions are *The Times* of London, which may be found at newspapers.com; the California newspapers, at cdnc.ucr.edu; the *Barnstable Patriot*, at sturgislibrary.org; and the various Asian journals from the 1830s, which may be found on Google Books.

The items cited from newspapers fall into three main categories: articles, advertisements and shipping reports. Items in the second and third categories are indicated by the suffixes "(Ad)" and "(SR)" respectively.

The following abbreviations are used for newspapers that appear more than once in the list: *BDE, Brooklyn Daily Eagle; BMP, Boston Morning Post;*

BP, Barnstable Patriot; BS, Baltimore Sun; DAC, Daily Alta California; DNL, Daily News (London); *DP, Daily Picayune* (New Orleans); *DPL, Daily Post* (Liverpool); *HA, Hampshire Advertiser; LM, Liverpool Mercury; MPL, Morning Post* (London); *NYB, New York (Daily) Tribune; NYEP,* New York *Evening Post; NYT, New York (Daily) Times; SDU, Sacramento Daily Union; TTL, The Times* (London).

PROLOGUE

- Red Jacket's arrival in Liverpool: Kittredge (1935), 194-5; Swift (1990), 12.
- "… a time that has never been bettered": That the *Red Jacket*'s maiden voyage remains the fastest crossing of the Atlantic by a sailing ship can be verified from the records listed in Cutler (1952), Sec. III, pp. 25-32.

1. EARLY YEARS ON CAPE COD

- Geological history of Cape Cod: http://pubs.usgs.gov/gip/capecod/glacial.html.
- "Bared and bended arm of Massachusetts": Thoreau, p. 2.
- Old King's Highway Historic District: http://www.townofbarnstable.us/ OldKingsHighway.
- Captains' Mile, including Eldridge and Hallet houses: http://www. yarmouthcapecod.com/captains-mile-walking-tour.
- Kittredge's esteem for Asa Eldridge: Kittredge (1968), 250-1.
- Eldridge and Hallet family trees: Reconstructed from data on Ancestry.com and the related "RootsWeb WorldConnect" project (wc.rootsweb.ancestry.com).
- Yarmouth's settlement and early history: Deyo, Ch. XVII; Swift (1884), Chs. III, VII-IX, XV, XVII; Historical Society of Old Yarmouth, http://www.hsoy.org/ history.htm.
- Stephen Hopkins on *Mayflower*: Wikipedia, "List of Mayflower passengers."
- History of Cape Cod more generally: Deyo; Kittredge (1968); Finch; Sheedy & Coogan.
- Boston/Massachusetts history: Baker; Boston History and Innovation Collaborative, Eras 1-3; Celebrate Boston; Morison, Chs. II-III; Writers' Program, Massachusetts, Chs. 1-II; Wikipedia entries for specific events and Acts of Parliament.
- Population growth in various communities: Deetz & Deetz; Morison, 20; Swift (1884), 281 ff.
- Massachusetts and coastal trade: Morison; Writers' Program, Massachusetts, Chs. 1-II.
- Events in US history: Taylor; Smithsonian Institute; Klose & Jones; WebChron; ushistory.org; Wikipedia entries for specific events or topics.

- Barnabas Eldridge: Deyo, 465; Swift (1884), 152, 160.
- Yarmouth's early declaration of independence: Swift (1884), 156.
- Decay of Cape Cod fleet during Revolutionary War: Kittredge (1935), 14-15.
- Salt production on Cape Cod: Cape Cod Saltworks; Gaines & York; Quinn.
- Continuing preference for transport by sea: Morison, 231.
- Yarmouth and coastal trade: Braginton-Smith & Oliver; Kittredge (1935), Ch. II; Mahoney.
- Ansel Hallet: Braginton-Smith & Oliver; Deyo, 115; Swift (1884), 210.
- Relationships between Hallets and Eldridges: reconstructed from Ancestry.com.
- John Eldridge Sr.: Deyo, 468, 476-7; Swift (1884), 181, 183-4; Braginton-Smith & Oliver. Evidence that his title was nautical: Cutler (1961), 67; *Philadelphia Public Ledger*, Oct 16, 1789, p. 3.
- Local and regional opposition to Embargo Act and War of 1812: Baker, Ch. XI; Swift, 1888, 181-5; Morison, Ch. XIII.
- Early start at sea for John (Jr.) and Asa Eldridge: Swift (1990); http://cihma.org/association-members/yarmouth.
- Races between Cape Cod packets: Mahoney, 32-8.
- Prestige of transatlantic packet-ship captains: Paine, 138-9.

2.   ADVENTURES IN THE FAR EAST

- Seaman's Protection Certificates: Dixon. Asa Eldridge's 1832 certificate was found on Ancestry.com.
- Newspaper databases: see introduction to these notes for more information.
- Asa Eldridge's early start at sea: Swift (1990); http://cihma.org/association-members/yarmouth.
- *America* under John Eldridge: *Oriental Magazine and Calcutta Review*, Vol. I, Jan 1823, 128 (SR) (note reference to "J." Eldridge); *NYEP*, Nov 1, 1823, p. 2 (SR); Apr 20, 1824, 2 (SR), and Apr 15, 1826, 2 (SR).
- John Eldridge then on *Ranger*: *NYEP*, Sep 16, 1826, p. 3 (Ad); Jul 17, 1830, 2 (SR), and Mar 17, 1831, 3 (Ad).
- Career of Josiah Richardson: Kittredge (1935), Ch. 5.
- *America*: ... under Asa Eldridge: *NYEP*, Oct 28, 1829, p. 3 (SR); Nov 19, 1829, 2 (SR); Jan 13, 1830, 2 (SR); Feb 12, 1830, 3 (Ad); Jun 17, 1830, 2 (SR); Jun 29, 1830, 2 (SR); Sep 13, 1830, 3 (SR); Apr 19, 1831, 2 (SR); May 5, 1831, 2 (SR); Dec 16, 1831, 3 (SR), and Jan 10, 1832, 2 (SR).
  ... under Robinson: *NYEP*, Mar 5, 1832. p. 2 (SR).
  ... under Cloutman: *NYEP*, Jan 8, 1833, p. 2 (SR).
  ... record voyage from Boston to Calcutta: Cutler (1930), 85, attributes this to "Captain Eldridge"; the *Calcutta Christian Observer*, Vol. II, records the captain

as "A." Eldridge in the issues of Aug 1833, p. 410 (SR) and Oct 1833, p. 515 (SR); Rev. J. O. Choules, who knew Asa Eldridge personally, refers to his "high nautical reputation as a commander in the India... trade" (Choules, 22).

- Operation of ships: Lever; Dana, 1841.
  ... hierarchy on board and career path: Albion, Ch. VI; Fairburn, Vol. IV, Ch. XXVIII; Maddocks, 89-100; Villiers.
  ... life at sea: Dana (1840); Melville.
  ... navigation and chronometer: Sobel; Wikipedia, "Celestial navigation," "Lunar distances" and "Marine chronometer."
- Trade with India and China: Cutler (1930), Ch. IX; Fairburn, Vol. II, Chs. XXI and XXVIII; Kittredge (1935), Ch. 7; Morison, Ch. XVII; Wikipedia, "India Wharf."
- Ice trade: Herold; Kistler *et al.*; Klein; Morison, 280-3; State Street Trust Company, 1918; Wikipedia, "Frederic Tudor"; *Pittsburgh Gazette*, May 24, 1833, p. 2; Jan 29, 1834, 2, and Mar 5, 1834, 2.
- Asa Eldridge's marriage to Eliza Hallet: Ancestry.com.
- Asa Eldridge's other commands in the Asia trade: ***Humboldt***: Eldridge, "Humboldt (Ship) logbook." *BMP*, Nov 16, 1836, p. 2 (SR); Feb 3, 1837, 2 (SR); Mar 3, 1837, 2 (SR), and Apr 24, 1837, 2 (SR); *Singapore Free Press*, Jun 29, 1837, 3 (SR). ***Steiglitze***: *Asiatic Journal and Monthly Register*, Vol. XIX, Feb, 1836, 148 (SR). ***Timore***: *Calcutta Monthly Journal and General Register of Occurrences*, Vol. 5, Jun, 1839, 109 (SR).

3. TO LIVERPOOL BY SAIL

- Liverpool's maritime history: Milne; Hugill; www.worldtravelguide.net/liverpool/history. Wealth in 19th century: Schumpeter; Platt.
- Golden triangle/slavery: International Slavery Museum; Wikipedia, "History of slavery."
- Industrial revolution: Wikipedia, "Industrial Revolution", "Spinning jenny", "Spinning mule" and "Cottonopolis."
  ... Liverpool and Manchester Railway: Grace's Guide.
- Cotton trade: Fairburn, Vol. II, Ch. X, 1128-31.
- Melville's voyage to Liverpool as a sailor: Gale, 383. His praise of Liverpool: Melville, Ch. XXIX ("Sailors love this Liverpool...") and Ch. XXXII (description of the docks).
- Asa Eldridge and the cotton triangle: ... first voyage on America: *NYEP*, Oct 28, 1829, p. 3 (SR); Nov 19, 1829, 2 (SR); Jan 13, 1830, 2 (SR), and Feb 12, 1830, 3 (Ad).
  ... later voyages on ***Colombo***: *MPL*, Mar 2, 1842 (SR); *LM*, Mar 13, 1842, p. 84 (Ad); *BMP*, May 19, 1842, 2 (SR); Oct 27, 1842, 2 (SR), and Apr 4, 1843,

2 (SR); *LM*, Jun 2, 1843, 183 (SR); *BMP*, Jun 6, 1843, 2 (SR); *NYEP*, Dec 12, 1843, 1 (SR); *DP*, Jan 24, 1844, 3 (SR), and Jul 14, 1844, 3 (SR).

- John Eldridge: ... on packet ship **Webster**: *LM*, Dec 30, 1842, p. 424 (Ad). ... on packet ship **Liverpool**: *NYEP*, Mar 28, 1843, p. 2; Jul 31, 1843, 3 (Ad); Nov 19, 1846, 4 (Ad); Aug 21, 1848, 1 (Ad), and Oct 26, 1848, 1 (SR). *BS*, Mar 9, 1849, 1.

- Asa Eldridge's first voyage on **Roscius**: *NYEP*, Oct 31, 1844, p. 1 (Ad).

- History of packet ships in general: Albion; Bowen, Ch. I; Bradlee, 1910; Cutler (1930), Ch. VI-VII, XI; Fairburn, Vol. II, Ch, X; Fox, Ch. 1; Lubbock (1925); Writers' Program, City of New York, 140-155.

- Announcement and early voyages of Black Ball Line: *NYEP*, Oct 27, 1817, p. 2 (Ad); Jan 6, 1818, 2 (SR); Jan 6, 1818, 2 (SR); Feb 5, 1818, 2 (SR); Feb 5, 1818, 2 (SR); Feb 23, 1818, 2 (SR); Feb 23, 1818, 2 (SR); Mar 5, 1818, 2 (SR), and Apr 13, 1818, 2 (SR).

- Newspaper stories illustrating age of news: *NYEP*, Dec 30, 1816, p. 2; Jan 9, 1817, 2; Jan 16, 1817, 2; Jan 2, 1818, 2; Jan 16, 1818, 2; Jan 21, 1818, 2; Jan 2, 1830, 2; Jan 8, 1830, 2; Jan 11, 1830, 2; Jan 18, 1830, 2; Jan 19, 1830, 2, and Jan 30, 1830, 2.

- Description of **Roscius** (reprinted from unspecified New York paper): *Chester Chronicle*, Nov 30, 1838.

- Dramatic Line/E. K. Collins: Albion; Bowen, Ch. I; Cutler (1930), Ch. IX; Fairburn, Vol. II. Ch. X; Fox, Ch. 1; Whitney.

- Flat floors of Dramatic liners: Bowen, 23; Cutler (1930), 95; Fox, 6. Resulting speed, as assessed by Commodore Hull: Cutler (1930), 97.

- Captains' pay: Albion, 154-5; Maddocks, 98; Kittredge (1935), 164.

- Rescue by **Roscius** under John Collins: *LM*, Dec 29, 1839, p. 410, and Jan 10, 1840, 14; *West Kent Guardian* Jan 25, 1840, 2.

- John Eldridge on **Yazoo**: *NYEP*, Oct 13, 1835, p. 3; *DP*, 25 Jan 1837, 4 (Ad); on **Huntsville**: *NYEP*, Jan 11, 1837, 3 (SR); *DP*, Feb 5, 1837, 3 (SR); *NYEP*, Nov 6, 1837, 3 (SR); *DP*, Feb 27, 1838, 2 (SR); *NYEP*, Aug 19, 1839, 3 (Ad); Feb 14, 1840, 3 (Ad), and Jun 9, 1841 (Ad).

- Oliver Eldridge on **Gaston**: *NYEP*, Jun 30, 1842, p. 3 (Ad); Dec 10, 1842, 3 (Ad); Jun 16, 1843, 1 (Ad), and Jan 3, 1844, 1 (Ad).

- **Roscius** under Asa Eldridge: *NYEP*, Oct 31, 1844, p. 1 (Ad); *MPL*, Jan 13, 1845, 8 (SR); *BS*, Mar 10, 1846, 1; *NYEP*, Mar 23, 1846, 1 (Ad), and Aug 19, 1846, 4 (Ad); *LM*, Oct 30, 1846, 528 (wreck of the **Cromwell**); *NYEP*, Nov 24, 1846, 4 (Ad); Dec 1, 1846, 3 (SR); Jan 5, 1847, 4 (Ad); Dec 7, 1847, 4 (Ad); Jul 8, 1848, 1 (Ad), and Oct 13, 1848, 3 (SR).

- Collins' sale of Dramatic Line: *DP*, Apr 3, 1845, p. 2; *BS*, Nov 18, 1845, 2; *NYEP*, Apr 5, 1847, 1; *BS*, Jul 22, 1847, 1; *NYEP*, Aug 19, 1848, 3, and Sep 7, 1848, 2.

- Collins' vision of steamers crossing the Atlantic in under ten days: Fairburn, Vol. II, 1333; Sheldon, 471.
- Asa Eldridge on *Garrick* after sale of Dramatic Line: *NYEP*, Feb 21, 1849, p. 1 (Ad); Feb 28, 1849, 3 (SR); May 31, 1849, 1 (Ad); Jan 12, 1850, 3; Apr 8, 1850, 4 (SR), and Apr 12, 1850, 3 (SR).
- Oliver Eldridge: ... on *Roscius*: *NYEP*, Nov 11, 1848, p. 1 (Ad); Mar 8, 1849, 3 (Ad); Jun 15, 1849, 3 (SR); Nov 21, 1849, 4 (Ad) and Feb 22, 1850, 4 (Ad); *NYB*, Oct 23, 1851, 3 (Ad).
  ... and on *Garrick*: *NYT*, Apr 3, 1852, p. 4 (SR); *LM*, Apr 9, 1852, 284 (Ad); *NYT*, Jun 17, 1852, 4 (SR).
- John Eldridge on *Roscius*: *NYEP*, Jun 29, 1849, p. 1 (Ad); *NYT*, Feb 28, 1852, 4 (SR); *LM*, Apr 9, 1852, 284 (Ad); *NYT*, May 24, 1852, 4 (SR).
- Cholera outbreak on *Liverpool*: *BS*, Mar 9, 1849, p. 1.
- Loss of *Roscius*: *NYT*, Sep 1, 1860, p. 8.

4. ADVENT OF STEAM

- Early transatlantic steamers: Armstrong, Ch. 1; Bowen, Ch. I-II; Bradlee; Fairburn, Vol. II, Ch. XI; Fox, Chs. 2-4; Tyler, Chs. I-IV; Wikipedia entries on individual vessels.
- Movements of early steamships: ... *NYEP*, Apr 18, 1838, p. 3; Apr 23, 1838, 2; Sep 27, 1838, 1; Oct 10, 1838, 2; Nov 23, 1838, 2; Jul 29, 1839, 2; May 8, 1841, 1; and May 22, 1843, 1 (Ad); *Pittsburgh Daily Gazette*, Oct 24, 1846, 2; *NYEP*, Nov 27, 1846, 3 (SR); *BS*, Feb 9, 1847, 1 (SR); *TTL*, Feb 22, 1847, 1.
  ... and of *Garrick* and *Sheridan* during same period: *NYEP*, May 12, 1838, p. 3, and Aug 17, 1839, 2.
- Parliamentary committee's view on American maritime superiority: Fairburn, Vol. II, 924, 1239. Solicitation by Admiralty for mail steamers: *TTL*, Nov 8, 1838, p. 2.
- Cunard Line:... inception and development: Armstrong, Chs. 1-2; Bowen, Ch. I-III; Fairburn, Vol. II, Ch. VII (943 ff., 1189 ff.), Ch. XI; Fox, Chs. 3, 5; Tyler, Chs.V-VI; *NYEP*, Aug 5, 1839, p. 2; Wikipedia, "Cunard Line."
  ... expansion to New York: *BS*, May 26, 1846, p. 2, and Oct 19, 1846, 2.
  ... financial reports: *DP*, Jul 18, 1846, p. 2, and Sep 22, 1847, 2.
- Passenger fare across Atlantic... on *Roscius*: *NYEP*, Jul 22, 1848, p. 1 (Ad); May 28, 1840, 1 (Ad); Jan 5, 1847, 4 (Ad); Mar 31, 1842, 1 (Ad); Jun 6, 1842, 3 (Ad); July 1, 1843, 1 (Ad) and Jan 15, 1844, 1 (Ad); *BS*, Mar 28, 1845, 4 (Ad); *NYEP*, Jul 8, 1848, 1 (Ad).
  ... and on Cunard Line: *BMP*, Sep 9, 1840, p. 3 (Ad); *NYEP*, Oct 20, 1848, 1 (Ad).
- Speed advantage of early steamers over packet ships in 1839: Bowen, 35.
- OSNC inception and development: Bowen, 51-3; Fairburn, Vol. II, 1333-5; Fox, Ch. 6; Tyler, 1935, Ch. IX-X; *NYEP*, Nov 22, 1845, p. 2; *Raleigh*

Register, Feb 27, 1846, 2; *BDE*, Apr 14, 1846, 2; *BS*, May 15, 1846, 2; *NYEP*, Apr 21, 1847, 3 (Ad); *DP*, Jul 14, 1847, 2.

- Collins Line: ... inception and development: Armstrong, Ch. 2; Bowen, Chs. 2-3; Fairburn, Vol. II, Ch. XI; Fox, Ch. 6; Tyler, Chs. IX, XII; Whitney; *NYEP*, Mar 5, 1847, p. 3, and Mar 6, 1847, 2; *Louisville Examiner*, Dec 25, 1847, 1; *Public Ledger* (Philadelphia), Oct 4, 1848, 1; *DP*, Jan 23, 1849, 2; *NYEP*, Feb 8, 1850, 4 (Ad); *Milwaukee Daily Sentinel*, Feb 12, 1850, 2; *BS*, Apr 18, 1850, 1; *BS*, Apr 24, 1850, 1; *NYEP*, Apr 27, 1850, 4 (SR); Wikipedia, "Collins Line." ... record voyages: Whitney; *DP*, Jul 30, 1850, p. 2; *DP*, Apr 20, 1851, 2, and Jun 11, 1851, 1. *NYEP*, Aug 16, 1851, 3.

- Impact of steamships on sailing packets, and boost for latter from immigrant trade: Albion, Ch. X; Fairburn, Vol. II, 1193 ff.

5. ASPIRING TYCOON

- Manifest for 1848 voyage of **Roscius** under Asa Eldridge: Immigrant Ships Transcribers Guild.

- Steerage conditions/incidence of disease: Fairburn, Vol. II, 1228-9; Maury, 6.

- *Pioneer*: ... early stories concerning: *LM*, Oct 11, 1850, p. 664; *NYB*, Feb 1, 1851; *LM*, Feb 18, 1851, 134; *NYB*, Apr 5, 1851, 5; *NYT*, Oct 9, 1851, 3 (Ad), and Oct 15, 1851, 1.

  ... philanthropic purpose: *Democratic State Register*, Mar 24, 1851, p. 2.

  ... maiden voyage to Liverpool: *NYEP*, Oct 18, 1851, p. 3 (SR); *The Standard* (London), Nov 7, 1851, 1; *LM*, Nov 11, 1851, 892; *Glasgow Herald*, Nov 24, 1851, 4 (SR); *TTL*, Nov 24, 1851, 5 (SR); *NYT*, Dec 15, 1851, 4 (SR).

  ... competitors' times: *TTL*, Nov 1, 1851, p. 6; *TTL*, Nov 8, 1851, 6 (SR); *NYT*, Dec 6, 1851, 4 (SR).

  ... diversion to Chagres route: *NYEP*, Dec 31, 1851, p. 3; *NYT*, Jan 23, 1852, 4 (SR); Jan 26, 1852, 2 (SR), and Feb 23, 1852, 2 (SR).

  ... ownership: Heyl, 347. *NYB*, Feb 1, 1851, p. 4; *The Standard* (London), Nov 7, 1851, 1.

  ... voyage around Cape Horn, subsequent wreck and rescue: *NYT*, Mar 18, 1852, p. 4 (SR); *NYT*, Jul 23, 1852, 1; *DAC*, Aug 21, 1852, 2; *DP*, Sep 13, 1852, 3.

  ... addition to Vanderbilt Pacific fleet: *NYT*, Feb 18, 1852, p. 4 (Ad); *NYT*, Mar 25, 1852, 4; *DP*, Apr 6, 1852, 4; *NYT*, May 27, 1852, 4 (Ad); *NYT*, Jul 9, 1852, 4.

  ... Asa Eldridge's travel and role in rescue: *Albany Evening* Journal, Apr 19, 1852, p. 3 (Ad); *NYB*, Apr 23, 1852, 8 (Ad); *NYT*, Jun 19, 1852, 4 (Ad); *NYT*, Jul 21, 1852, 4 (SR); *DAC*, Aug 19, 1852, 2; *DAC*, Aug 24, 1852, 2.

  ... salvage by Waterman: *DAC*, Mar 16, 1853, 2.

- Cruise of **North Star**: Choules, in particular 95-6, 110, 160, 352; Stiles, Ch. 9; *BDE*, Mar 5, 1853, p. 2; *DP*, Mar 19, 1853, 2; *BS*, May 21, 1853, 1; *NYT*, May 21, 1853, 8; *Sandusky Register*, May 23, 1853, 3; *NYT*, Jun 17, 1853, 3; *DP*, July 1, 1853, 1; *NYT*, Sep 24, 1853, 4.
- Rumor that Eldridge would take over **Baltic**: *Evening Star* (Washington), Nov 7, 1853, p. 1.

6. KING OF THE CLIPPERS

- Evolution of clippers: Clark, Ch. IV; Crothers; Cutler (1930) (the passages quoted are from pages 50 and 97-98, see also Chs. X, XIII-XVI); Fairburn, Vol. II, Ch. XIII and Vol III, Chs. XV & XVII; Knoblock; Paine, Ch. IX.
- Oliver Eldridge on **Coquette**: Cutler (1930), 113; Kittredge (1935), 162-163; *NYEP*, Jan 13, 1845, p. 3; *BS*, Feb 26, 1845, 1; *NYEP*, Oct 27, 1845, 3 (SR), and Aug 13, 1846, 3 (SR).
- California Gold Rush, boom in shipping traffic: Clark, Ch. VII, 100; Cutler (1930), Ch. XIV-XVIII; Fairburn, Vol. III, Ch. XVII.
- **Memnon**: … under Oliver Eldridge: *NYEP*, Jul 29, 1848, p. 3 (SR) and Sep 29, 1848, 3 (SR).
  … under Capt. Gordon: Clark, Ch. IX, 145-6; *NYEP*, Apr 9, 1849, p. 3 (SR), and Apr 9, 1850, 2 (SR).
- Prices in San Francisco during Gold Rush: Clark, 103; Fairburn, Vol III, 1904-5.
- Year-by-year review of new clippers and their builders; shift of destination from California to Australia: Clark, Chs. IX-XI, XIII-XIV, XVI-XVIII; Cutler (1930), Chs. XVI, XVIII, XXI-XXVII; Fairburn, Vol. II, Ch. XIII (especially 1534 ff.) and Vol. III, Ch. XV.
- Reviews of clippers in alphabetical order: Howe and Matthews.
- Donald McKay: Clark; Fairburn, Vol. II, Ch. XIII, especially 1516 ff.; Bruzelius; Wikipedia, "Donald McKay."
- Additional information about specific clippers beyond that found in general sources cited above: **Flying Cloud**: *NYEP*, Oct 6, 1851, p. 2; *NYT*, Apr 10, 1852, 4. **Typhoon**: *BS*, Apr 12, 1851, 4 (SR). **Sovereign of the Seas**: *NYT*, May 7, 1853; *DP*, May 19, 1853; *BS*, Jul 21, 1853; *BDE*, Sep 19, 1853. **Great Republic**: *BDE*, Oct 4, 1853, 3; *BS*, Oct 7, 1853, 4; *BDE*, Nov 4, 1853, 2; Nov 28, 1853, 3, and Dec 27, 1853, 2.
- Australian Gold Rush: See chapters in Clark, Cutler (1930) and Fairburn concerning shift of destinations, cited four bullet points above.
- **Red Jacket**: … Cutler (1930), 282-3; Clark, 270-2; Fairburn, Vol. II, 1286, and Vol. III, 1830-2; Howe and Matthews; Kittredge (1935), 194-5; Gratwick; Matthews; Penobscot Marine Museum; Swift (1990), 12; *Daily Whig and Courier* (Bangor, Maine), Nov 9, 1853, p. 2; *NYT*, Nov 18, 1853, 8, and Jan 10,

1854, 8 (SR); *TTL*, Jan 26, 1854, 5; *LM*, Jan 27, 1854, 10, and Feb 17, 1854, 12 (which includes account of speech by Asa Eldridge).

... letters to *The Times* about record voyage: Jan 27, 1854, p. 8; Jan 28, 1854, 8, and Jan 31, 1854, 8.

... subsequent sale and Australian voyage: *BS*, Mar 24, 1854, p. 1; *DP*, Apr 1, 1854, 5; *TTL*, Jul 15, 1854, 1 (Ad); *MPL*, Oct 11, 1854, 2; *TTL*, Oct 16, 1854, 6.

- *Blue Jacket*: *LM*, Oct 17, 1854, 6.
- Return of Asa Eldridge to New York on *Baltic*: *NYT*, Apr 5, 1854, 8.

7. MYSTERIOUS END

- Capt. Comstock's career: *BS*, Mar 31, 1847, p. 1; *NYEP*, May 12, 1847, 2; *NYT*, Aug 18, 1868, 4.
  ... record crossings on *Baltic*: *NYEP*, Aug 16, 1851, p. 3; *BS*, Jul 10, 1854, 1.
- Performance of *Washington* and *Hermann*: Tyler, 155; *DP*, Nov 15, 1847, p. 2 (SR), and Dec 30, 1847, 2; *BS*, Dec 8, 1848, 1; *NYEP*, Jun 18, 1851, 2 (SR).
- NYHSNC (prior to Asa Eldridge joining): Tyler, 178-9, 216-7; Fairburn, Vol. II, 1336; *NYEP*, Mar 21, 1849, p. 3, and Sep 15, 1850, 2 (Ad); *BS*, Nov 19, 1850, 1; *NYEP*, May 6, 1851, 4 (SR); *The Jeffersonian*, May 22, 1851, 2 (SR); *BDE*, Jun 25, 1851, 2 (SR); *TTL*, Nov 1, 1851, 6; *NYEP*, Nov 3, 1851, 2; *DP*, Dec 16, 1853, 6; *BS*, Jan 9, 1854, 4, and Apr 12, 1854, 4; *NYT*, Jul 1, 1854, 8 (SR); *BDE*, Jul 18, 1854, 2.
- *St. Louis*, under Asa Eldridge: *BDE*, Jul 22, 1854, p. 2, and Aug 1, 1854, 3 (SR); *DNL*, Aug 14, 1854, 2 (SR); *HA*, Sep 2, 1854, 6 (SR); *NYT*, Sep 13, 1854, 1 (SR); *BS*, Sep 25, 1854, 4 (SR); *TTL*, Oct 6, 1854, 6 (SR); *Alton Weekly Telegraph*, Oct 26, 1854, 3 (SR); *NYT*, Nov 13, 1854, 8 (SR), and Nov 13, 1854, 8 (SR); *BS*, Nov 14, 1854, 2 (SR), and Nov 20, 1854, 2.
  ... under Capt. Wotton: TTL, Jan 31, 1855, p. 12 (SR); NYB Mar 1, 1855, 3 (SR).
- Loss of the *Arctic*: Fox, 128-132; Whitney; *BDE*, Oct 11, 1854, 2; *NYT*, Oct 12, 1854, pp. 1-3; Oct 16, 1854, 1-2; Nov 29, 1854, 1, 4; Jan 22, 1855, 6, and Mar 10, 1855, 4.
- Congressional deliberations about funding for Collins Line: Fox, pp.125-8; Tyler, Ch. XIII-XIV; Whitney; *NYEP*, Feb 28, 1851, p. 2 and Mar 6, 1851, 2; *BS*, Mar 5, 1855, 1.
- Impact of Crimean War on Cunard Line: Fox, 132-3; Tyler, 217, 232-3.
- Secret agreement between Collins and Cunard Lines: Sloan (1998); Fox, 122-3, 133-4.
- Construction of *Adriatic*: Whitney; *DP*, Mar 15, 1855, p. 5; *BS*, Jun 2, 1855, p.1

- Asa Eldridge on the **Pacific**: ... first voyage: *DP*, Nov 24, 1855, p. 4 (Ad); *NYT*, Nov 28, 1855, 8 (SR); *MPL*, Dec 10, 1855, 6; *DPL*, Dec 10, 1855, 3; *NYT*, Dec 29, 1855, 1; *DPL*, Jan 18, 1856, 4.

  ... second voyage, outbound leg: *DPL*, Jan 18, 1856, p. 4; *NYT*, Mar 11, 1856, 4.

  ... return leg, departure: *Sheffield Daily Telegraph*, Jan 25, 1856 (SR).

  ... failure to arrive: Fox, 135-6; *BS*, Feb 11, 1856, p. 4; *NYT*, Feb 12, 1856, 4; *BS*, Feb 12, 1856, 2; *NYT*, Feb 12, 1856, 4; *BDE*, Feb 14, 1856, 2; *NYT*, Feb 20, 1856, 4; Feb 25, 1856, 8; Mar 3, 1856, 4, and Mar 6, 1856, 4; *LM*, Mar 19, 1856, 2.

  ... searches: *DP*, Feb 14, 1856, p. 2; *NYT*, Mar 21, 1856, 1; *HA*, Mar 29, 1856, 8; *Berrows Worcester Journal*, Apr 12, 1856, 7.

  ... discussions of fate: Fox, 136; *NYT*, Mar 17, 1856, p. 4; *BDE*, Mar 19, 1856, 2; *DNL*, Mar 20, 1856, 4; *TTL*, Mar 20, 1856, 11; *Lexington and Yadkin Flag*, Mar 21, 1856, 1; *DNL*, Apr 7, 1856, 5.

  ... first letter from Capt. Nye: *NYT*, Mar 3, 1856, p. 3, and Mar 11, 1856, 4; *DP*, Mar 19, 1856, 1, 3.

  ... supposed statement by Eldridge about "humbling" the **Persia**: Armstrong, 42.

  ... second letter from Capt. Nye: *NYT*, Apr 4, 1856, p. 4; *Boston Atlas*, Apr 5, 1856; *Chicago Times*, Apr 17, 1856.

  ... discovery of purported wreck: Fox, 136; Sloan (1993).

  ... message in bottle: *TTL*, Jul 24, 1861, p. 26.

- Obituary for Asa Eldridge: *DP*, May 31, 1856, Afternoon Edition, p. 1.

8. FORGOTTEN HEROES

- Contrast between British and American strategies: Armstrong, 46-7; Fairburn, Vol. II, 1548; Tyler, 378-9; *NYT*, Mar 20, 1864, pp. 4-5.
- Collins Line after loss of **Pacific**: Armstrong, 43-7; Fox, 137-9; Tyler, Ch. XV; *BS*, Nov 6, 1856, p. 4; *TTL*, Dec 9, 1856, 7; *BS*, Apr 9, 1857, 2; *DP*, Jul 22, 1857, 2; *NYT*, Nov 21, 1857, 4; *Richmond Despatch*, Nov 23, 1857, 2; *NYB*, Nov 24, 1857, 3 (SR); *BDE*, Dec 21, 1857, 2 (SR); *BS*, Jan 11, 1858, 4; *NYT*, Feb 11, 1858, 8; *Syracuse Daily Courier and Union*, Feb 11, 1858, 2; *BDE*, Feb 19, 1858, 2.
- Closedown of OSNC, NYHSNC: Tyler, 241-2, 293; *DP*, Jul 31, 1857, p. 1 and Jun 25, 1858, 6.
- List of record crossings by transatlantic steamships: Wikipedia, "Blue Riband."
- E. K. Collins after Collins Line: Whitney, 1857.
- Sale of Collins liners: Armstrong, 47-8; *New Bern Daily Progress*, Jul 21, 1859, p. 1; *NYT*, Oct 1, 1859, 8.

- McKay after **Great Republic**: Clark, Ch. XIX; *NYT*, Sep 22, 1880, p. 5; *Boston Weekly Globe*, Sep 29, 1880, 7.

- Oliver Eldridge: ... on **Atlantic**: *NYB*, Sep 18, 1856, p. 3 (Ad); *NYB*, Feb 27, 1858, 3 (Ad); *NYT*, Jan 24, 1862, 1; Mar 29, 1862, 1, and Feb 4, 1864, 8.

  ... on **Constitution** and **Golden City**: *DAC*, Sep 1, 1862, p. 4 (SR); *SDU*, Sep 1, 1862, 5 (SR); *Daily Milwaukee News*, Aug 14, 1863, 4 (SR); *DAC*, Nov 28, 1863, 1 (SR).

  ... career after retiring from sea: Kittredge (1935), 196-7; *SDU*, Dec 9, 1864, p. 4; *DAC*, Dec 12, 1864, 1; *San Francisco Chronicle*, Feb 18, 1865, 3; *San Francisco Call*, Dec 18, 1902, 10 (obituary).

- John Eldridge: ... on **Young Brander**: Kittredge (1935), 195; *BS*, Mar 1, 1854, p. 1; *Evening Star* (Washington), Mar 1, 1854, 3; *DP*, Mar 26, 1854, 3 (SR); *DP*, Apr 4, 1854, 1 (Ad); *DP*, Apr 11, 1854, 4; *MPL*, Jun 10, 1854, 7 (SR); *TTL*, Jul 19, 1854, 11 (SR); *NYT*, Aug 1, 1854, 1 (SR); *DP*, Oct 20, 1854, 3 (SR)

  ... on **Baltic**: Kittredge (1935), 195-6; *Davenport Daily Gazette*, May 6, 1861, p. 1; *National Republican* (Washington), May 11, 1861, 3; as passenger: *NYT*, Dec 27, 1861, 5.

  ... on **Atlantic**: *NYT*, Sep 6, 1862, p. 8 (SR).

  ... on **Fulton**: *DP*, May 23, 1863, p. 1.

  ... after retirement: *BP*, Feb 2, 1874, p. 2, and Feb 17, 1874, 2; *Los Angeles Daily Herald*, Mar 8, 1874, 1 (obituary).

- Civil War voyages by **Baltic** under other captains: *NYT*, Apr 19, 1861, p. 1; *Janesville Daily Gazette*, Nov 22, 1861, 2; *NYT*, Dec 27, 1861, 5; Jun 2, 1862, p.1, and Sep 4, 1862, 5; Sep 25, 1863, 5 (SR); Aug 1, 1864, 8 (SR).

- Oliver Eldridge on **Titan**: Kittredge (1935), 196; *BDE*, Apr 23, 1855, p. 3 (SR); *DP*, Sep 27, 1855, 2; *DP*, Nov 4, 1855, 3.

- Clipper ship **Asa Eldridge**: *BP*, Dec 23, 1856, p. 2; *Hawaiian Gazette*, Nov 11, 1868, 3; *DP*, Mar 4, 1873, 3.

Bibliography

Albion, Robert Greenhalgh. *Square Riggers on Schedule: The New York Sailing Packets to England, France and the Cotton Ports.* Princeton: Princeton University Press; London: Humphrey Milford; Oxford University Press, 1938.

Armstrong, Warren. *Atlantic Highway.* New York: The John Day Company, 1962.

Baker, William A. *A History of the Boston Marine Society, 1742-1981.* Boston, Massachusetts: Boston Marine Society, 1982.

Bartlett, W. H., Harding, J.D., Creswick, T. and others. *The Ports, Harbours, Watering Places and Picturesque Scenery of Great Britain.* Vol. II. London: Virtue and Co., 1840.

Blume, Kenneth J. *Historical Dictionary of the U.S. Maritime Industry.* Lanham, Toronto, Plymouth, UK: Scarecrow Press, 2012.

Boston History and Innovation Collaborative. "Innovate Boston! Shaping the Future from Our Past: Four Amazing Centuries of Innovation." 2006. http://bostonhistorycollaborative.com/index_era.htm.

Bowen, Frank C. *A Century of Atlantic Travel, 1830-1930.* Boston: Little, Brown and Company, 1930.

Bradlee, Francis B. C. "Old Transatlantic Steam Liners." *International Marine Engineering* 15 (Dec. 1910): 503-506.

Braginton-Smith, John, and Duncan Oliver. *Port on the Bay: Yarmouth's Maritime History on the "North Sea" 1638 to the present.* Yarmouth Port, MA: Historical Society of Old Yarmouth, 2001.

Bruzelius, Lars. "Ships built by Donald McKay." April 28, 1997. http://www.bruzelius.info/Nautica/Ships/D_McKay_Yard.html.

Cape Cod Saltworks. "History of Saltworks on Cape Cod." 2015. http://www.capecodsaltworks.com/index.php/about-cape-cod-saltworks/history-of-saltworks-on-cape-cod.

Celebrate Boston. "Massachusetts Bay Colony: A Brief History." 2015. http://www.celebrateboston.com/history/massachusetts.htm.

Chatterton, E. Keble. *Sailing Ships: The Story of Their Development from the Earliest Times to the Present Day.* Philadelphia: J. B. Lippincott; London: Sidgwick & Jackson, 1909.

—. *Steamships and their Story.* London, New York, Toronto and Melbourne: Cassell and Company, 1910.

Chenoweth, James. *Oddity Odyssey: A Journey Through New England's Colorful Past.* Lincoln, NE: Authors Choice Press (iUniverse), 2000.

Choules, John Overton. *The Cruise of the Steam Yacht North Star: A Narrative of the Excursion of Mr. Vanderbilt's Party.* Boston: Gould & Lincoln, 1854.

Clark, Arthur H. *The Clipper Ship Era: An Epitome of Famous American and British Clipper Ships, Their Owners, Builders, Commanders, and Crews.* New York and London: G. P. Putnam's Sons and The Knickerbocker Press, 1911.

Coogan, Jim. "A Message from the Sea." *The Barnstable Patriot,* Jun. 25, 2009.

Crothers, William L. *The American-Built Clipper Ship: Characteristics, Construction, and Details.* Camden, Maine: International Marine, 1996.

Cutler, Carl C. *Five Hundred Sailing Records of American Built Ships.* Mystic, Connecticut: The Marine Historical Association, 1952.

—. *Greyhounds of the Sea: The Story of the American Clipper Ship.* New York, London: G.P. Putnam's Sons, 1930.

—. *Queens of the Western Ocean.* Annapolis, MD: United States Naval Institute, 1961.

Dana, Richard Henry. *The Seaman's Friend, Containing a Practical Treatise on Seamanship.* London: Edward Moxon, 1841.

—. *Two Years Before the Mast: A Personal Narrative of Life at Sea.* New York: Harper & Brothers, 1840.

Deetz, Patricia Scott, and James Deetz. "Population of Plymouth Town, Colony & County, 1620-1690." 2000. http://www.histarch.illinois.edu/plymouth/townpop.html.

Deyo, Simeon L. (ed.). *History of Barnstable County.* New York: H.W. Blake & Co., 1890.

Dixon, Ruth Priest. "Genealogical Fallout from the War of 1812." *National Archives: Prologue Magazine, Vol. 24, No. 1 (Spring).* 1992. http://www.archives.gov/publications/prologue/1992/spring/seamans-protection.html.

Edward J. Renehan, Jr. *Commodore: The Life of Cornelius Vanderbilt.* Philadelphia: Basic Books (Perseus Books Group), 2007.

Eldridge, A. "Humboldt (Ship) logbook." 1836-1837. http://beta.worldcat.org/archivegrid/collection/data/797193602.

Fairburn, William Armstrong. *Merchant Sail.* Vols. II-IV. Center Lovell, ME: Fairburn Marine Educational Foundation, 1955.

Finch, Robert. *Cape Cod: Its Natural and Cultural History.* U.S. Department of the Interior, Washington, D.C.: National Park Service, 1993.

Flayhart, William H. *Disaster at Sea: Shipwrecks, Storms, and Collisions on the Atlantic.* New York: W.W. Norton & Company, 2003.

Fletcher, R. A. *Steam-Ships: The Story of Their Development to the Present Day.* London: Sidgwick & Jackson, 1910.

Fox, Stephen. *Transatlantic: Samuel Cunard, Isambard Brunel, and the Great Altantic Steamships.* New York: HarperCollins Publishers, 2003.

Gaines, Jennifer Stone and John York. "Saltworks." *Spritsail: A Journal of the History of Falmouth and Vicinity* 21, no. 1 (2007): 11-17.

Gale, Robert L. *A Herman Melville Encyclopedia.* Westport, CT: Greenwood Press, 1995.

Grace's Guide: British Industrial History. "Liverpool and Manchester Railway." 2015. http://www.gracesguide.co.uk/Liverpool_and_Manchester_Railway.

Gratwick, Harry. *Hidden History of Maine.* Charleston, SC: The History Press, 2010.

Herold, Marc W. "Ice in the Tropics: the Export of 'Crystal Blocks of Yankee Coldness' to India and Brazil." *Revista Espaço Acadêmico* 126 (2011): 162–177.

Heyl, Erik. *Early American Steamers.* Buffalo, N.Y., 1953.

Howe, Octavius T. and Matthews, Frederick C. *American Clipper Ships 1833-1858, Volume II: Malay-Young Mechanic.* Mineola, N.Y.: Dover Publications, 1986.

Hugill, Stan. *Sailortown.* London: Routledge & Kegan Paul Ltd., New York: E.P. Dutton & Co., 1967.

iBoston: Boston History and Architecture. "Population Trends in Boston 1640 - 1990." 2015. http://www.iboston.org/mcp.php?pid=popFig.

Immigrant Ships Transcribers Guild, Vol. 6. "Ship Roscius, Liverpool, England to New York." June 8, 1848. http://www.immigrantships.net/v6/1800v6/roscius18480608.html.

International Slavery Museum. "Liverpool and the slave trade." 2015. http://www.liverpoolmuseums.org.uk/ism/slavery/europe/liverpool.aspx.

Kistler, Linda H., Clairmont P. Carter, and Brackston Hinchey. "Planning and Control in the 19th Century Ice Trade." *Accounting Historians Journal* 11, no. 1 (1984).

Kittredge, Henry C. *Cape Cod: Its People and Their History, Second Edition, with a Post-Epilogue, 1930-1968 by John Hay.* Boston: Houghton Miflin Company, 1968.

—. *Shipmasters of Cape Cod.* Boston and New York: Houghton Mifflin Company, The Riverside Press Cambridge, 1935.

Klein, Christopher. "The Man Who Shipped New England Ice Around the World." August 29, 2012. www.history.com/news/the-man-who-shipped-new-england-ice-around-the-world.

Klose, Nelson, and Robert F. Jones. *United States History: To 1877.* New York: Barron's Educational Services, 1972.

Knoblock, Glenn A. *The American Clipper Ship, 1845-1920: A Comprehensive History, with a Listing of Builders and Their Ships.* Jefferson, NC: McFarland & Co., 2014.

Lever, Darcy. *The Young Sea Officer's Sheet Anchor, or A Key to the Leading of Rigging and to Practical Seamanship.* (Second Edition, J. Richardson, London, 1819). Republished in Mineola, New York: Dover Publications, 1998.

Lindert, Peter H, and Jeffrey G. Williamson. "VOX. America's Revolution: Economic disaster, development, and equality." July 15, 2011. http://www.voxeu.org/article/america-s-revolution-economic-disaster-development-and-equality.

Lipsey, Robert E. *U.S. Foreign Trade and the Balance of Payments, 1800-1913.* Cambridge, MA: National Bureau of Economic Research, Working Paper No. 4710, 1994.

Lubbock, Basil. *The Colonial Clippers.* Glasgow: James Brown & Son, 1921.

—. *The Western Ocean Packets.* Boston: Charles E. Lauriat, 1925.

Maddocks, Melvin and the Editors of Time-Life Books. *The Atlantic Crossing (The Seafarers).* Alexandria, Virginia: Time-Life Books, 1981.

Mahoney, Haynes R. *Yarmouth's Proud Packets.* Yarmouthport, MA: Historical Society of Old Yarmouth, 1986.

Matthews, F.C. "The Celebrated Clipper Ship Red Jacket." *Pacific Marine Review: The National Magazine of Shipping*, November 1922: 608-612.

Maury, Sarah Mytton. *An Englishwoman in America.* London: Thomas Richardson and Son, 1848.

McKay, Richard Cornelius. *South Street: A Maritime History of New York.* New York: Haskell House Publishers, 1934.

Melville, Herman. *Redburn: His First Voyage.* New York: Harper & Brothers, 1849.

Merrill, Tim, ed. *Nicaragua: A Country Study.* Washington, D.C.: U.S. Government Printing Office, 1993.

Milne, Graeme J. "Maritime Liverpool." In *Liverpool 800: Culture, Character & History*, edited by John Belchem, 257-309. Liverpool: Liverpool University Press, 2008.

Moby Dick on the Mersey. "Melville and Liverpool." 2015. http://mobydickonthemersey.org/melville-and-liverpool/.

Morison, Samuel Eliot. *The Maritime History of Massachusetts, 1783-1860.* Boston and New York: Houghton Mifflin Company, The Riverside Press Cambridge, 1921.

Neal, F. "Liverpool Shipping in the Early Nineteenth Century." In *Liverpool and Merseyside: Essays in the economic and social history of the port and its hinterland*, edited by J. R Harris, 147-181. Frank Cass & Co., 1969.

Paine, Ralph D. *The Old Merchant Marine: A Chronicle of American Ships and Sailors.* New Haven: Yale University Press, 1920.

Penobscot Marine Museum. "Collection Object: Ship Red Jacket." 2015.
http://www.penobscotmarinemuseum.org/pbho-1/collection/ship-red-jacket.
—. *Life at Sea: The Crew.* http://penobscotmarinemuseum.org/pbho-1/life-at-sea/crew.

Pilgrim Hall Museum. "Journey by Land: Footpaths, Cart Roads, Post Roads & Turnpikes." 2015. http://www.pilgrimhallmuseum.org/pdf/Journey_by_Land.pdf.

Platt, Edward. "The spirit of Scouse: A great port battling with the forces of recession." *New Statesman,* Jul. 19, 2012.

Quinn, William P. *The Saltworks of Historic Cape Cod: A Record of the Nineteenth Century Economic Boom in Barnstable County.* Orleans, MA: Parnassus Imprints, 1993.

Richards, Rhys. "Early American Trade with China 1784-1833." *Mains'l Haul: A Journal of Pacific Maritime History,* Spring 2003: 14-19.

Schumpeter (blog). "The View from Liverpool." Mar 17, 2012. http://www.economist.com/node/21550239.

Sheedy, Jack, and Jim Coogan. *Cape Cod Voyage: A Journey Through Cape Cod's History and Lore.* East Dennis, MA: Harvest Home Books, 2001.

Sheldon, George W. "Old Shipping Merchants of New York." *Harper's Magazine* 84 (1891-1892): 457-471.

Sloan, Edward W. "The Wreck of the Collins Liner Pacific - A Challenge for Maritime Historians and Nautical Archaeologists." *Bermuda Journal of Archaeology and Maritime History, Volume 5,* 1993: 84-91.

—. "The First (and Very Secret) International Steamship Cartel, 1850-1856." *Global markets: the internationalization of the sea transport industries since 1850.* Sevilla: Secretariado de Publicaciones de la Universidad de Sevilla, 1998. 41-48.

Smithsonian Institution. "On the Water, 2: Maritime Nation, 1800-1850." 2015. http://f.asp4.si.edu/onthewater/exhibition/2_1.html.

Sobel, Dava. *Longitude: The True Story of a Lone Genius Who Solved the Greatest Scientific Problem of His Time.* Paperback. New York: Bloomsbury, 2007.

Sprague, Francis William. *Barnstable and Yarmouth Sea Captains and Ship Owners.* Privately Printed, 1913.

State Street Trust Company. *Old Shipping Days in Boston.* Boston, 1918.

Stiles, T. J. *The First Tycoon: The Epic Life of Cornelius Vanderbilt.* New York: Alfred A. Knopf, 2009.

Swift, Charles F. *History of Old Yarmouth: Comprising the Present Towns of Yarmouth and Dennis.* Yarmouth Port: Charles F. Swift, 1884.

Swift, Theodore W. *Stories of Yarmouth Shipmasters.* Yarmouth Port, MA: Historical Society of Old Yarmouth, 1990.

Taylor, Jr., Quintard. "United States History: Timelines." 2015. http://faculty.washington.edu/qtaylor/a_us_history/us_timeline_index_page.htm.

The Maritime Heritage Project. "Ship Passengers, San Francisco: 1846-1899."
2015. http://www.maritimeheritage.org/index.htm.

The Ships List. "The Fleets: New York & Havre Steam Navigation Co." 2015.
http://www.theshipslist.com/ships/lines/ny&h.shtml.

Thoreau, Henry D. *Cape Cod.* Kindle. Cambridge: Thomas Y. Crowell & Co., The
University Press, 1908 (originally published 1865).

Tuel, Mr. "American Steam Marine: The Great Lines of Sea Steamers Connecting
American Ports, and the Old and the New World." *De Bow's Review and
Industrial Resources, Statistics, etc., Vol. 14,* 1853: 576-587.

Tyler, David Budlong. *Steam Conquers the Atlantic.* New York, London:
D. Appleton-Century Company, 1939.

University of Illinois. "Early American Trade with China." 2015.
http://teachingresources.atlas.illinois.edu/chinatrade/introduction04.html.

US Geological Survey. "Geologic History of Cape Cod, Massachusetts." 2015.
http://pubs.usgs.gov/gip/capecod/glacial.html.

ushistory.org. "The Intolerable Acts." 2015. http://www.ushistory.org/declaration/
related/intolerable.htm.

Victoria and Albert Museum. "Steam & Speed: The Power of Steam at Sea." 2015.
http://www.vam.ac.uk/content/articles/s/the-power-of-steam-at-sea/.

Villiers, Alan. *Square-Rigged Ships: An Introduction.* London: National Maritime
Museum, 2009.

Walton Advertising and Printing Company. *Ships and Shipping of Old New York.*
New York: Bank of the Manhattan Company, 1915.

WebChron: The Web Chronology Project. "United States of America Chronology:
The Navigation Acts 1650-1696." 2015. http://thenagain.info/WebChron/
USA/Navigation.html.

Whipple, A. B. C. and the Editors of Time-Life Books. *The Clipper Ships (The
Seafarers).* Alexandria, Virginia: Time-Life Books, 1980.

Whitney, Ralph. "The Unlucky Collins Line." *American Heritage,* February 1957:
Volume 8, Issue 2.

Writers' Program, Work Projects Administration, City of New York. *A Maritime
History of New York.* Garden City, New York: Doubleday, Doran and
Company, 1941.

Writers' Program, Work Projects Administration, Massachusetts. *Boston Looks
Seaward: The Story of the Port, 1630-1940.* Boston: Bruce Humphries Inc.,
1941.

ILLUSTRATION CREDITS

Many of the illustrations used herein are public-domain images downloaded from the website of the Library of Congress (http://www.loc.gov). Each such image is indicated by the abbreviation "LOC" followed by the relevant Reproduction or Catalog Number. Two other illustrations are images placed in the public domain by the Yale Center for British Art and downloaded from its website (http://britishart.yale.edu); each is identified by the abbreviation YCBA followed by its accession number. Several of the remaining illustrations are from books listed in the bibliography; in these cases, the images used are photographs taken or scans made by the author of the relevant pages in the original books, as cited below. Finally, images of classified ads and of Oliver Eldridge's obituary were clipped from the various databases of old newspapers described in the *Notes* section.

FRONTISPIECE

Asa Eldridge: daguerreotype from the collection of the Historical Society of Old Yarmouth; autograph copied from the photograph of Eldridge that faces page 10 of Choules (and is reproduced facing page 81 of this book).

1. EARLY YEARS ON CAPE COD

Schooner plaque on Ansel Hallet's house, plaque on Yarmouth Common, and remnants of wharf in Yarmouth Port: photographs by author. Plans and photograph of Chatham saltworks: LOC, Survey HABS MA-172, Enoch Harding Salt Works... West Chatham, Barnstable County, MA.

2. ADVENTURES IN THE FAR EAST

Map of Boston, 1814: excerpted from LOC, Cat. No. 2011589322. View of Boston, 1833: LOC, LC-DIG-pga-03408. Sail plan for full-rigged ship: Chatterton (1909), p. 279. Prime meridian at Greenwich: photograph by author.

3.   TO LIVERPOOL BY SAIL

Staten Island Quarantine: LOC, LC-DIG-pga-03535. Canning Dock and Custom House, Liverpool, 1840: from an engraving in the author's possession, originally from Bartlett *et al.* Packet ship *New York*: YCBA, Paul Mellon Collection, accession number B1981.25.105. Classified ad for *Colombo*: *Liverpool Mercury*, Mar 18, 1842, p. 84. Classified ad for *Roscius*: New York *Evening Post*, Oct 29, 1844, p. 1.

4.   ADVENT OF STEAM

The *British Queen*: YCBA, Paul Mellon Collection, accession number B1978.43.209. Samuel Cunard: Wikimedia Commons. Edward K. Collins: LOC, LC-USZ62-109875. The *Europa*: LOC, LC-DIG-pga-03635. The *Atlantic*: LOC, LC-DIG-pga-01191.

5.   ASPIRING TYCOON

Classified ad for the Pioneer Line: *New York Daily Times*, Oct 9, 1851, p. 3. San Francisco, 1850: LOC, LC-USZC4-3101. Classified ad for the *Illinois* and *Golden Gate*: *Albany Evening Journal*, Apr 19, 1852, p. 3. The *North Star*, Cornelius Vanderbilt and Asa Eldridge: Choules, respectively title page, frontispiece, and facing p. 10.

6.   KING OF THE CLIPPERS

Donald McKay: Clark, facing p. 256. The *Cutty Sark*: photograph by author. The *Flying Cloud*: Morison, facing p. 372. The *Red Jacket*: LOC, LC-DIG-pga-03627.

7.   MYSTERIOUS END

The *Washington*: LOC, LC-DIG-ds-00693. The loss of the *Arctic*: LOC, LC-USZ62-137402. The *Pacific*: LOC, LC-DIG-pga-03641. The *Persia*: Chatterton (1910), facing p. 130 (and referred to there as the *Scotia*; the two ships were identical, and the Cunard Line used the same image for both).

8.   FORGOTTEN HEROES

View of East River, New York: excerpted from LOC, LC-DIG-pga-03183. The *Adriatic*: LOC, LC-DIG-pga-00916. Oliver Eldridge's obituary: *San Francisco Call*, Dec 18, 1902, 10; layout re-formatted by author to fit in available space opposite page 133. The *Baltic*: LOC, LC-DIG-pga-03640.

INDEX

"A. W. J.", 100–102
"Young America", 100
49ers, 90
Adams, Capt. Richard, 110
Admiralty, the, 49, 57, 58, 59, 61, 63
Adriatic (steamship), 65, 117, 128
Alabama (steamship), 118
Albany, 39
Albion, Robert, 67
Alexandria, 134
Amazon (ship), 41
Ambros, Sir Edmund, 6
America (ship), 19–20, 27, 29, 31, 32, 35
America (steamship), 75
America (yacht), 93
American complacency, 59
Amity (ship), 37, 39
Ann (brig), 38
Ann McKim (clipper ship), 88
Annapolis, 134
Arabia (steamship), 123
Arago (Steamship), 123
Arctic (naval steamship), 118
Arctic (steamship), 65, 66, 108, 117
    loss of, 112–13, 115, 116, 117
Asa Eldridge (clipper ship), 135
Asa Eldridge (schooner), 74

Atlantic (steamship), 65, 66, 75, 115, 119, 123, 128, 132, 134, 135
Australia, 60, 95, 97, 105
    Gold Rush, 95, 96, 105
Avonmouth, 55
B&A Steamship Company, 53, 54, 55, 58, 60
Baltic (steamship), 65, 66, 75, 86, 106, 107, 108, 117, 120, 123, 128, 134, 135
Baltic Sea, 19
Baltimore, 41, 50, 88, 122
Baltimore clippers, 88
barque, 89, 90
Bass Hole, Yarmouth, 10
Bay State (steamship), 107
Beatles, The, 33
Betsey (sloop), 14
Biddle, Clement C, 17
Black Ball Line, 38, 39, 41
Black Sea, 135
Blackburn, 34
Blue Jacket (clipper ship), 105, 135
Bolton, 34
Boston, 27, 32, 41, 58, 107, 122, 131, 133
    clipper ships and, 89, 92, 95, 97
    cotton trade and, 34–36

Cunard Line and, 56, 58–59, 61, 63, 66, 109
early development of, 5–7
Eldridge family and, 10, 11–16
ship *America* and, 19–20
Tea Party, 7
trade with India, 30–31
trade with Yarmouth, 5, 6, 9, 10, 13
Bremen, 63, 64, 108, 109, 129
Brewster, 5, 13
brigs, 56, 90
Bristol, 6, 54, 55, 58, 60
Britannia (steamship), 59
British & American Steam Navigation Company. *See* B&A
British and North American Royal Mail Steamship Company. See Cunard Line
British Association, 105
British government, 43, 61, 63
and steamship policy, 56, 62, 127–30
British Queen (steamship), 46, 54, 55, 56, 59
Brooklyn Daily Eagle, 121, 122
Brown & Bell, 92
Brunel, Isambard Kingdom, 54, 60, 66, 74
Calcutta, 20, 27, 30, 31, 32
Caledonia (ship), 41
Calhoun (ship), 68
California, 27, 44
clipper ships and, 87, 90–92, 94, 96, 98
Gold Rush, 87, 90
Pioneer and, 75, 76–81
via Cape Horn, 90
via Nicaragua, 77
via Panama, 76
California Drydock Company, 132
Cambria (steamship), 109

Cape Cod, 3–16, 92, 136
Cape Horn, 77, 90, 94, 105, 132
Caribbean, 7, 8, 19, 31, 76, 77, 79
Chagres, 76, 77, 120
Challenge (clipper ship), 79
Charleston Courier, 40
Cherokee (steamship), 120
Chicago, 122
Chicago Times, 122
China, 15, 35, 47, 79
clipper ships and, 87, 89, 91, 93
cholera, 51, 72
Choules, Rev. J. C., 84, 85
chronometer, development of, 24
Civil War, American, 36, 131, 133
clipper ships, 20, 87–106, 135
building boom, 91
by Donald McKay, 92–96
evolution of, 87–89
size of crew, 93
Cloutman, Capt., 20
Collins Line, 52, 86, 106, 107, 108, 110, 120, 121, 122, 132, 135
and loss of *Arctic*, 112–13
cartel with Cunard Line, 115, 130
demise, 129
establishment of, 64–67
mail contract
award, 63
reduction, 128–31
renewal, 122
revision, 113–17
record passages, 66, 75, 117
Collins, Capt. John, 45–47, 48, 49
Collins, E. K., 42, 52, 68, 71, 72, 74, 75, 107, 108, 110, 116, 128, *See also* Collins Line
and Dramatic Line, 43–45, 49–50
and US Congress, 50, 63, 64, 113–17
last days, 131

loss of family, 112, 113
timing of move into steam, 53
Colombo (ship), 36
Comstock, Capt. Joseph, 107, 108, 123, 134
Congress, US
    Collins Line and, 63, 113–17
    steamships and, 62, 128–31
Constellation (ship), 41
Constitution (steamship), 132, 134, 135
Constitution, USS (warship), 45
Continental Congress, 8
Cook, Capt. James, 25
Cooper, James Fenimore, 134
Coquette (ship), 47, 89
Cork, 55, 58
Cotheal, H&D, 50
cotton trade, 34–36, 114
Courier (ship), 37, 38, 39
Courier and Inquirer (New York), 119, 120
Cowes, 63, 108, 109, 111
crew, life at sea, 27–29
Crimean War, 115, 131, 135
Cromwell (ship), 48
Cronstadt, 20
Cunard Line, 62, 65, 71, 75, 109, 113, 114, 115, 119, 122
    cartel with Collins Line, 115, 130
    expansion to New York, 63–65
    in government policy, 127–30
    initial success, 61
    origins, 56–59
Cunard, Samuel, 57, 61, 68, *See also* Cunard Line
Currier, N., 105
Cutler, Carl, 11, 87–89
Cutty Sark (clipper ship), 94
Daily Alta California, 80, 81
Daily Picayune, 83, 121, 134
Daily Post (Liverpool), 117

Dana, Richard Henry, 27-29
Denmark, 19, 85
Dennis, 92
Desperate (naval steamship), 119
Dominion of New England, 6
Dramatic Line, 43–52, 71, 73, 88, 135
    origins, 43–45
    sale by E. K. Collins, 49–50
Dupont, Rear Admiral, 132
Early American Steamers, 77
East India Company, 7
East River, 34, 38, 82, 98
Edinburgh (steamship), 119
Eldridge, Asa, 4, 28, 32, 33, 86, 92, 93, 116, 127, 135, 136
    and *America*, 19–20, 25, 27, 30, 31, 35
    and *Colombo*, 36
    and cotton trade, 36
    and *Garrick*, 51, 73, 135
    and *North Star*, 81–86, 110, 120, 135
    and *Pacific*, 132, 135
    and Philadelphia, 17–20
    and *Pioneer*, 69–77, 78–81, 92, 110, 120, 135
    and record voyage to Calcutta, 20, 27, 29
    and *Red Jacket*, 1–2, 96–106, 107, 110, 119, 131, 133, 135
    and *Roscius*, 37, 41, 42, 43, 47–49, 50, 61, 71, 73, 75, 88, 135
    and *St. Louis*, 110–13, 120, 135
    epitaph, 125
    family connections, 10–11
    marriage, 32
    misspelling of name, 32, 77
Eldridge, Barnabas, 8
Eldridge, Eliza (wife of Asa), 32, 85, 135
Eldridge, John, 3, 11

and *Atlantic*, 134
and *Baltic*, 134, 135
and Civil War, 133
and *Fulton*, 134, 135
and *Huntsville*, 47
and *Liverpool*, 36, 47, 48, 51, 72,
    135
and *Roscius*, 51, 52, 135
and *Webster*, 36, 135
and *Yazoo*, 47
and *Young Brander*, 133, 135
later years, 134
Eldridge, John, Sr., 3, 4, 10, 11–14
Eldridge, Oliver, 3, 11, 14
    and *Atlantic*, 120, 132, 135
    and *Blue Jacket*, 105, 135
    and Civil War, 132
    and *Constitution*, 132, 135
    and *Coquette*, 47, 89
    and *Garrick*, 51, 135
    and *Gaston*, 47
    and *Golden City*, 132, 135
    and *Memnon*, 89, 133, 135
    and *Roscius*, 51, 90, 135
    and *Titan*, 135
    later career, 132
Eldridge, William, 4
Embargo Act of 1807, 31
England, 4, 15, 23, 35, 54, 56, 57,
    58, 59, 60, 63, 67, 84, 85, 97,
    104, 108, 109, 110, 129
    Cape Cod history and, 4–9
English Channel, 84, 85, 111
Fairburn, William, 72
Fall River Line, 107
fare across Atlantic, 61, 62
Fletcher, Capt., 134
Flying Cloud (clipper ship), 44, 88,
    92, 93, 94, 96
fore-and-aft sails, xi, 22
Fort Pickens, 134
Fort Sumter, 134

Foster, James Jr., 52
Fox, Samuel, 109
France, 7, 12, 84, 85, 104, 109, 110
Franklin (steamship), 109, 110, 111,
    113
Fulton (steamship), 134, 135
Game Cock (clipper ship), 93
Garrick (ship), 44, 55, 73
    Asa Eldridge and, 51, 135
    Oliver Eldridge and, 51, 52, 135
Glasgow, 46, 59, 74
Glory of the Seas (clipper ship), 132
Gold Rush (Australia), 95, 96, 105
Gold Rush (California), 44, 75, 76,
    77, 90
Golden City (steamship), 132, 135
Golden Gate (steamship), 78, 80, 81
Gordon, Capt. George, 90
Graham, Wm., 124
Great Britain (steamship), 8, 60–61,
    66, 74
Great Famine, 67, 68
Great Lakes, 131
Great Republic (clipper ship), 91,
    95, 96, 97, 98, 99, 104, 131
Great Western (steamship), 42, 43,
    49, 53, 54–56, 57, 58, 59–61, 64,
    129
Great Western Railway, 54
Great Western Steam Ship Comp-
    any. *See* GWS
Great Yarmouth, 5
Greenwich, 23, 24
Grey, Capt. Alfred G., 134
Greyhounds of the Sea, 87
Guadeloupe, 11
GWS (steamship company), 54, 55,
    58, 60
Halifax and Quebec Steam Boat
    Company, 58
Halifax, Nova Scotia, 56, 57, 58
Hall, Samuel, 92

Hallet, Andrew, 4
Hallet, Betty, 3, 4, 10
Hallet, Capt. Ansel, 10–11, 14–15, 19, 52
Hallet, Capt. Charles, 52
Hallet, Edward, 11
Hallet, Lucy, 10
Hallet, née Eldridge, Anna, 10, 11
Hallett, Eliza (wife of Asa Eldridge), 32
Hamilton, 131
Harrison, John, 24
Harvard College, 27
Havana, 120
Havre, 39, 41, 75, 108, 109, 111, 113, 129
Hearst Castle, 78
Hebrides, 124
Helsingør, 19
Henry Clay (ship), 41, 68
Hermann (steamship), 108, 109
Heyl, Erik, 77
Hibernia (steamship), 64
Hilton Head, 132
Homeward Bound (novel), 134
Hong Kong, 93
Honolulu, 93, 94
Hopkins, Stephen, 4, 10
Hudson River, 39
Humboldt (ship), 32
Humboldt (steamship), 109, 110
Huntsville (ship), 47
ice trade with India, 30–32
Illinois (steamship), 80, 81
impressment, 12, 13, 17
Independence (ship), 41
India, 7, 15, 19, 20, 21, 32, 47, 58
    and ice trade, 30–32
    Boston trade with, 30–31
Industrial Revolution, 34
Intolerable Acts of 1774, 7
Ireland, 60, 67, 71, 119

Italy, 85
James Monroe (ship), 38
Jay Treaty, 30
Jefferson, President, 12
Johnson, Cave, 62, 63
Joshua Bates (ship), 92
Judkins, Capt., 123
Kendall, Larcum, 24
King George III, 24
King James II, 6
King William IV, 54
Kittredge, Henry, 3, 89
Kittridge, Capt., 76–79, 81
latitude, determination of, 23
Lever, Darcy, 21, 28
Lightning (clipper ship), 96, 131
Lines, Capt., 110, 123
Liverpool, 7, 19, 28, 32, 71, 92, 133
    Australia and, 96, 98, 105
    clipper ships and, 89, 90, 94–96
    cotton trade and, 36, 34–36
    Dramatic Line and, 42, 43–52, 55
    history of, 33–35
    Pioneer and, 73–77, 93
    Red Jacket and, 1–2, 98–106, 111
    rise of packet trade and, 37–43
    slave trade and, 33
    steamships and, 53, 54, 55–56, 59–69, 86, 107, 108, 109, 111, 112, 113, 115, 128
Liverpool & Manchester Railway, 34
Liverpool (ship), 36, 37, 47, 48, 51, 72, 133, 135
Liverpool (steamship), 55, 59
Liverpool Mercury, 46, 47, 73, 103
Liverpool Times, 94
Livingston, Mortimer, 109
Lloyd's of London, 100
London, 6, 23, 33, 47, 76, 83, 100, 102, 110, 124
    packets and, 39–41

steamships and, 53, 54, 55, 58, 74
Long Island, 110, 113
Longitude (book), 24
longitude, determination of, 23–25
Los Angeles Daily Herald, 134
Louisiana Line, 44, 47, 65, 134
lunar distances, 23, 25
Madden, Dr., 46
Madeira, 84, 85, 86
Maine, 6, 97, 98
Malta, 85
Manchester, 34
Marseilles, 135
Mary (schooner), 11
Massachusetts (steamship), 107
Massachusetts Bay Colony, 5, 6
McKay, Donald, 92–96, 97, 98, 99, 100, 104, 131
McKay, Lauchlan, 94
Melbourne, 95, 98, 105
Melville, Herman, 29
  and Liverpool, 33–35
  and *Redburn: His First Voyage*, 28
Memnon (clipper ship), 89, 90, 91, 93, 133, 135
Merchant Sail, 72
Mersey, River, 1
Messenger (sloop), 14
Mill Creek, Yarmouth Port, 10
Mill Pond, Yarmouth Port, 11
Moby-Dick, 28
Molasses Act of 1733, 7
Mortality onboard ship, 73
Mystic Seaport, 11
Navigation Acts, 5
navigation, methods, 23
New England, 3, 4, 30, 31
New Orleans, 13, 19, 35, 36, 44, 50, 120, 121, 133
New South Wales, 96

New York, 16, 28, 39, 41, 43, 68, 113, 115, 131, 132, 134, 135
  America and, 19–20
  Arctic disaster and, 113
  clipper ships and, 89–96
  comparison with Liverpool, 34
  cotton trade and, 34–36, 114
  Dramatic Line and, 43–52
  loss of *Pacific*, and, 117–23, 125
  North Star and, 82, 86, 97
  NYHSNC and, 108–11
  OSNC and, 108–9
  packet ships and, 37–43, 67, 71
  Pioneer and, 73–77, 79
  Red Jacket and, 1–2, 98–106, 111, 133
  South Street, 2, 38, 95
  St Louis and, 110–13
  steamships and, 53–56, 57, 58–61, 62–67, 68, 107, 108, 115
New York & Havre Steam Navigation Company. See NYHSNC
New York Commercial Advertiser, 125
New York Daily Times, 76, 112, 117, 120, 121
New York *Evening Post*, 18, 36, 37, 38, 40, 49, 51
New York Herald, 48, 72, 118, 123, 132, 135
New York Shipping List, 50
Newburyport, 92
Newport, Rhode Island, 134
Niagara (steamship), 109
Nicaragua, 77, 78, 79, 80, 81, 91
North Star (steam-yacht), 81–86, 97, 104, 110, 120, 135
North Wales, 123
Nye, Capt. Ezra, 117, 120–22
NYHSNC (steamship company), 108–11, 129
oakum, picking of, 29

Ocean Steam Navigation Company. *See* OSNC

Ohio, 131

Old Custom House Formula, xiii

Old King's Highway, 4
  Historic District, 3

OSNC (steamship company), 63, 64, 108–9, 109, 110, 128, 129

Pacific (ship), 38, 39, 40

Pacific (steamship), 65, 66, 117, 135
  loss of, 118–24, 132
  putative wreck, 123

Pacific II (ship), 41

Pacific Mail Steamship Company, 110, 132

packet ships
  captains' earnings, 45
  definition, 7
  effect on communication, 40–41
  growth in size, 41
  historical importance, 135
  impact of steamships on, 67–68, 111
  longevity of captains, 47
  size of crew, 93
  transatlantic, development of, 37–43

Paine, Ralph D., 16

Panama, 76, 77, 78, 80, 81, 90, 91, 110, 132

Parsons, Eben, 11

Persia (steamship), 119, 121, 122, 123, 130

Philadelphia, 17, 18, 19, 20, 41

Pierce, President, 116

Pilgrim (brig), 28, 29

Pilgrims, 4

Pilkington & Wilson, 105

Pioneer (steamship), 73–82, 86, 92, 93, 96, 110, 117, 120, 135

Plymouth Colony, 4, 5, 6

Pook, Samuel, 97, 105

Port Royal, 132

Portsmouth, New Hampshire, 94

Post Office Committee, US Senate, 65

Postmaster General, 109, 113, 129

President (steamship), 60, 61

Province of Massachusetts Bay, 6

Québec, 46, 48, 58

Queen of Clippers (clipper ship), 91

Queens of the Western Ocean, 11

R.B. Forbes (steam tug), 98

Rainbow (clipper ship), 88

Red Jacket (clipper ship), 1–2, 96–106, 107, 110, 119, 131, 133, 135

Red Star Line, 39, 41

Redburn: His First Voyage, 28, 33

Revenue Act of 1767, 7

Revolutionary War, 7, 8, 13, 17, 97

Rhode Island, 6, 107

Robinson, Capt., 20

Rockland, Maine, 97

ropes, on sailing ships, 22

Roscius (ship), 37, 41, 43, 44, 45, 49, 52, 53, 61, 68, 71, 73, 75, 90, 98, 113, 133
  as forerunner of clippers, 88, 89
  Asa Eldridge and, 47–49, 50, 135
  Capt. J. Collins and, 47
  John Eldridge and, 51, 52, 135
  loss in 1860, 52
  Oliver Eldridge and, 51, 135
  place in Dramatic Line, 43–45

Route 6A, 4, 11

Roxbury, 8, 32, 97

Royal Navy, 8, 13, 17, 21, 34, 45, 57, 62, 119

Royal Victoria (steamship). *See* British Queen *(steamship)*

Royal William (steamship), 58

Royal William II (steamship), 55

Russia, 19, 20, 85, 104, 115

Sagoyewatha, 97

sailing ships, operation of, 21–27

sailors, life at sea, 27–29

salt, Cape Cod, 8–9

salt, Caribbean, 7

San Francisco, 132, 134, 135

    clipper ships and, 90, 91, 92, 93, 94, 96

    Pioneer and, 76–81

    via Cape Horn, 90

    via Nicaragua, 77, 78, 79, 80

    via Panama, 76, 77, 90

Sarah Sands (steamship), 64

schooners, 26, 88, 90

Scotia (ship), 46

Scott, Capt. Wm., 38

screw propulsion, 73

Sea Bird (steamship), 78, 81

Seaman's Protection Certificate, 17, 19, 20

Sears, Capt. John, 8, 9

Seccomb & Taylor, 97

Secretary of the Navy, 64, 65, 128

Select Committee on Merchant Shipping (UK), 43

Senate Finance Committee, 114

Shakespeare (ship), 44

Shannon, River, 119

Sheridan (ship), 44, 50, 56

Sherman, General, 132

Shipping and Mercantile Gazette, 124

Shiverick shipyard, 92

Siddons (ship), 44, 45

Sirius (steamship), 55, 58, 59

slave trade, 33

Slave Trade Act of 1807, 34

Smith, Junius, 53

Sobel, Dava, 24, 25

South Carolina, 132

Southampton, 63, 64, 82, 83, 84, 104, 108, 111

Sovereign of the Seas (clipper ship), 94, 95, 100, 101

Spain, 7, 84, 85

Spofford & Tileston

    Dramatic Line and, 50, 51, 52, 64, 73

    Pioneer and, 72, 73, 74, 76, 77, 79

Square Riggers on Schedule, 67

square sails, xi, 21

St. George Steam Packet Company, 58

St. Louis (steamship), 110–13, 117, 120, 135

St. Simeon's Bay, 78

Stag-Hound (clipper ship), 91, 92

Steamships

    and US Congress, 62, 128–31

    as auxiliary warships, 62

    early failures, 61

    first transatlantic, 53–56

    impact on packets, 67

    limitations, 59

    performance, 59

steerage, 46, 67, 68, 71, 72, 73, 74

Steiglitz (ship), 32

Stone, Capt., 123

Strong, Caleb, 13

Sugar Act of 1764, 7

Swallowtail Line, 39, 41, 47, 51, 67

Tartar (naval steamship), 119

Taylor, Mr. (owner, *Red Jacket*), 105

Tea Act of 1773, 7

The Cruise of the Steam Yacht North Star, 85

The Seaman's Friend, 28

The Times (London), 100–102, 105

The Young Sea Officer's Sheet Anchor, 21

Thomas, George, 97

Thoreau, Henry David, 3

Tileston, Thomas, 74, 75, 79

Timore (ship), 32
Titan (clipper ship), 135
tonnage, xiii
Train, Enoch, 92
Transatlantic Steamship Company, 55, 60
Traveller (brig), 40
Treaty of Ghent (1814), 13
Treaty of Paris (1783), 8
Truro, 44
Tudor, Frederic, 30–32
Turkey, 85
Two Years Before the Mast, 27, 28
Tyler, President John, 62
Typhoon (clipper ship), 94
Union (steamship), 110
US Naval Academy, 134
Vanderbilt, Cornelius, 85, 91, 116, 120
  and cruise of *North Star*, 81–86, 97
  and Nicaragua route to California, 77–81
Varnam, Joseph B, 13
Victoria (Australia), 96

Wampanoag, 4
War of 1812, 13, 17, 31, 37, 45, 88, 135
Washington (steamship), 108, 109
Waterman, Capt. Robert, 79
Webb, Isaac, 92
Webb, William, 92
Webster (ship), 36, 135
Wells Fargo, 132
West Africa Squadron, 34
West Indies, 30, 33, 62
West, Capt., 123
Westervelt, Jacob, 92, 110
White Diamond Line, 92
White Star Line, 105
William of Orange, 6
Wotton, Capt. James, 110, 113
Yarmouth, 4, 5, 6, 8, 10, 11, 14, 15, 17, 44
Yarmouth Port, 3, 10, 11, 15, 92, 134
Yazoo (ship), 47
Young Brander (clipper ship), 133, 135

Lightning Source UK Ltd.
Milton Keynes UK
UKOW04f2136190717
305645UK00001B/175/P